social issues
through inquiry

social issues through inquiry:

coping in an age of crises

BYRON G. MASSIALAS
Florida State University

NANCY F. SPRAGUE
Falls Church Public Schools

JOSEPH B. HURST
University of Toledo

PRENTICE-HALL, INC., Englewood Cliffs, New Jersey

Library of Congress Cataloging in Publication Data

MASSIALAS, BYRON G
Social issues through inquiry, coping in an age of crises.

Includes bibliographical references and index.
1. Social sciences—Study and teaching.   2. Lesson planning.   I. Sprague, Nancy F., joint author.   II. Hurst, Joseph B., joint author.   III. Title.
H62.M2873   300'.7   74-28487
ISBN 0-13-815852-5

Printed in the United States of America

10   9   8   7   6   5   4   3   2   1

Prentice-Hall International, Inc., *London*

Prentice-Hall of Australia, Pty., Ltd., *Sydney*

Prentice-Hall of Canada, Ltd., *Toronto*

Prentice-Hall of India Private Limited, *New Delhi*

Prentice-Hall of Japan, Inc., *Toyko*

for all social inquirers of today and tomorrow

contents

3

inquiry into social values, feelings, and self:
new helpful approaches   *39*

4

the dialogue of social inquiry: classroom examples   *59*

5

selecting motivating springboards   *88*

6

social-inquiry teaching: some practical examples   *105*

7

evaluating social inquiry in the classroom   *133*

preface

What should young people learn? How should learning take place and under what conditions? How should what is learned in school be applied to everyday life? These are questions that continually confront us and are the source of much controversy among educators.

To answer these and related questions one is compelled to probe societal conditions in a worldwide context. *Dramatic change* in all social institutions is immediately observable, and this change occurs not only between generations but also within the same generation. How has this rapid change come about? Although there are many contributing factors, a combination of inventions and new technologies seems to be the key. As a result, our capability to harness the forces of nature has increased significantly a situation that has forced upon people new economic, social, and political arrangements.

The search for the proper arrangements within the new order, however, has generated conflict of far-reaching proportions. This has taken many forms, but it basically has centered on the direction and tempo of social change and the questions surrounding the many notions about what the good life is or should be. Much conflict among individuals, groups, and nations can be attributed to the general quest for a larger share of the world's resources. These conflicts and the apparent culture lag (advancements in technology not paralleled by advancements in human values) have caused violence and physical and psychological trauma for millions of people.

It troubles us that in an age when some farmers are being rewarded not to produce there is a global crisis in the production of cereals—resulting in starvation and in general undernourishment for millions of people in more than thirty-two developing countries. And this constitutes only one of the hundreds of worldwide problems developing out of disagreements over the distribution of resources.

The physical and social conditions that underlie the critical social problems are not going to change in the foreseeable future. What can and should change, however, are the way people look at the conditions and the means they develop to cope with the problems. This brings us to the learning process—how do people become sensitive to social problems, and how do they learn to handle social conflict? What is the responsibility of the school in this area?

We believe that the primary objective of the school is to provide the learning conditions and appropriate psychological climate in which to identify and reflectively probe the crucial issues of the time. Students must learn how to find the natural roots of the problem and what consequences its irresolution has or may have on the world society, country, community, family, as well as on the individuals themselves. The school is responsible for leadership in providing skills to enable youth to cope with a world in a state of continuous flux, and its attendant conflicts and crises. But skills in coping with conflict are not enough. The individual also needs to develop a determination to act—knowing about the problem is not sufficient. What is needed is responsible social action—action that will make the difference. To this end the individual assisted by the school creates a new humanism—a sympathetic frame of mind and an attitude of acceptance toward others.

This book relates the sustained experiences of a group of educators during a seven-year period, as they sought to identify the best possible school conditions under which each learner can become a critical prober of society's most pressing problems and can develop a predisposition to act. If an "inquiring, humanitarian activist" is the end result of the school experience then one of our prime goals will have been achieved.

Our work has gained significantly through collaboration with literally thousands of school children and youth. These young people have tried out many of the ideas discussed here; and they have shown us with their words and actions the genuine ways of learning, helping us to bring about a balance between theory and practice. For their contributions we are grateful.

Our appreciation also goes to colleagues who have shared with us their experiences over the years: Mary Friend Adams of the University of Cincinnati, Mary S. Murphy of Phoenix, Arizona, and Jo Ann Sweeney of the University of Texas.

Finally, mention should be made of the "Social Issues Project" at the University of Michigan and the "Criterion-Referenced Project" at Florida State University, the conduct of which gave us the opportunity to gain additional insight into social issues as inquiry.

B.G.M. / N.F.S. / J.B.H.

1

why teach social issues?

Education in any culture is always based upon the knowledge, beliefs, and values of that culture. The education system, both through formal and informal means, is deeply involved in the enculturation process whereby members of a society learn necessary elements of their culture. In enculturation shared knowledge, beliefs, and values are passed on to all members of society so that some degree of homogeneity and stability is maintained throughout the culture. In this way societies develop some measure of continuity among past, present, and future generations and, in a sense, survive.

For our purposes here we are concerned mainly with the formal means of education that relate directly to the role of the school and, within the school, to the role of social studies. It is the position of the authors that the present conditions of society make it imperative that its schools assume the role of creatively reconstructing the culture. The very nature of our pluralistic society, with its diversity and democratic ideals, demands that schools represent cultural variety, freedom of choice, and respect for human rights. The authors believe that it would be inconsistent with these principles to promote the interests and needs of any subcultures within our society at the cost of those of other subgroups. The school, therefore, should accept as its role the progressive or creative reconstruction of the culture. This means that the school must be carefully creative and discriminating in its selection and examination of beliefs, values, and knowledge, deliberately avoiding complete identification with any element or subgroup of the culture.

The nature of our society and its rapidly growing value conflicts

1

and problems suggest that the schools must prepare students for dealing with social controversy and cultural change in a systematic and creative way. Schools can no longer ignore the real world outside their walls and try to build a different social system within them, one in which conflict, controversy, and change do not exist. The prevailing conditions of our democratic society are such that the most important goal of American education is the rational examination of its culture—including beliefs, values, knowledge, institutions, human actions, social issues, and social problems. Obviously, within this role for the education system the role of social studies is important because so much of the content of social studies focuses on man and his culture and behavior. If the school is creatively reconstructing our pluralistic culture, it will have to consider the broad spectrum of cultural interests.

From among the many arguments and the different objectives for public education, citizenship education has emerged as the dominant goal of social studies education. The search for the meaning of good citizenship and the best instructional model to implement citizenship education has resulted in various definitions of citizenship and proposals for social studies curricula.

Any educational curricula, however, must be justified by an explicit and well grounded rationale. Such a rationale is best derived from and supported by five specific factors: (1) events in the real world, (2) an educational philosophy, (3) sound learning theory, (4) the nature of knowledge, and (5) educational research. Social studies education should be based upon such a rationale, and it should take much of the responsibility for educating students to be skilled in facing present and future social and personal problems. The authors view citizenship in our democracy as a continuous examination of American ideals and social institutions; they also view it as involving active participation in the American political system and the creative reconstruction of our culture. Active participation in citizenship is based upon inquiry. Citizens who reflect upon important issues facing themselves and their society often question policy recommendations, social institutions, and social action; they want reasons in support of specific positions and activities. Young people should become active inquirers in their society. They should learn to take social action that is warranted by democratic principles and that is responsible for insuring that the rights of others are respected and one's own rights are not abused. The role of the inquiring activist is in accordance with the creative reconstruction of culture because active citizens inquire into the nature of their society and act responsibly in trying to make necessary changes. This type of citizen has reached a high level of political efficacy, i.e., he understands well how the system operates and feels highly competent to change it. The approach to social studies education proposed in this book emphasizes open and reflective inquiry into public issues, or what shall be termed "social inquiry." Social inquiry, justified by the following rationale, provides several viable alternatives to educators for developing curricula and instruction aimed at creating an active, responsible citizenry in the future.

EDUCATION IN A DIVERSE SOCIETY

The conditions of our society present strong challenges to our educational system in its effort to transmit culture reflectively to young people. If a society is extremely cohesive, homogeneous, and stable, and if there is consensus about the goals of education, the job of educators remains relatively simple. Disagreements over the content and scope of education would probably develop, but for the most part the role of the schools would be clearly that of cultural dispenser. Few societies in the contemporary world, however, display great degrees of homogeneity and stability. On the contrary, in most societies today—and especially in the United States rapid change and cultural pluralism lead to many problems, issues, and crises.

> In the contemporary world the problems that attend cultural diversity and change—e.g., personal and social disintegration—are compounded. The plethora of cultural alternatives which have emerged from industrial and technological advances confront the young with a constant deluge of dilemmas and unforseeable consequences. It is on this basis that the assumption is made . . . that American society is pluralistic in such a thorough-going way that it now presents itself as a culture in crisis.[1]

The nature of our society and its growing number of subcultures and interest groups and expanding social alternatives create a cultural diversity or pluralism that generates continual conflict. One goal of education therefore, is for young people to learn to deal with cultural crises and the vast numbers of cultural alternatives and pressing conflicts and to do so in an atmosphere of reflection and tolerance. Students who learn to inquire into or reflectively examine social issues and participate in activities that attempt to solve social problems and resolve social controversy may be able to deal with our future cultural crises creatively and effectively.

The nature of our society also creates a dilemma for social studies

[1] Byron G. Massialas and C. Benjamin Cox, *Inquiry in Social Studies* (New York: McGraw-Hill, Inc., 1966), p. 4.

educators and for the social studies curriculum in public schools. As they select elements of our culture to include in the curriculum, educators in social studies cannot ignore the cultural diversity and conflicts in our society.

This book maintains that educators have three major alternatives in selecting ideas and topics for instruction in social studies. Educators can ignore cultural crises or believe that they do not really exist or argue they do not belong in their classrooms, but they cannot escape the responsibility for choosing something to be taught. One alternative is to select bland, noncontroversial issues and "facts" from the "great books" and from the social sciences that are beyond refute. In this way they can carefully put together a curriculum that they believe to be "absolute" or "correct." Even so, with the knowledge explosion in which we find ourselves today, this procedure is more impractical than appears at first glance. A second alternative is to present all the cultural alternatives and a number of social controversies in a neutral fashion, allowing the students to make up their minds about the material presented. This assumes that students are equipped, intuitively and psychologically, to make valid judgments and decisions about highly controversial issues where rational thought and open examination of conflicts are generally resisted. It also presents difficult choices to students without any attempt to solve important problems and without any instruction in how to resolve personal and public conflict. In this instance the teacher's role is very passive.

Another alternative is possible. Educators can develop social studies instruction by employing a method of inquiry—by establishing a curriculum based on a set of processes for examining social alternatives, identifying and stating problems and issues, testing out and grounding ideas and opinions about the resolution of conflict and exploring consequences of actions. Students are provided by their teacher with a supportive climate to examine their own values, and to make rational decisions. This course of instruction assumes that such learning will lead to an educated citizenry, one that can make important judgments and decisions through which our society may continue to function while still maintaining cultural pluralism and freedom. By employing a method of inquiry and value clarification as the core of social studies education, educators acknowledge that students skilled in the processes of thinking and evaluating can confront public controversies in the classroom, can develop creative solutions to urgent problems, and can take appropriate social action.

By focusing on what we define as social inquiry, educators, especially the teachers of social studies, can provide students with the opportunity to test their beliefs in an open, unthreatening atmosphere and to build their own set of defensible ideas and positions. This approach to instruction prevents their encountering the real world with untested beliefs that may be ridiculed and attacked by others. Social inquiry does not attempt to alter students' present beliefs or to leave them with no beliefs at all. It is a method that tries to provide students with the means to deal with personal and public problems. These problems require rational thinking, individual processes for developing and clarifying values, resolution of conflict, and effective decision making. The authors take the position that social studies teachers must help their students explore as many cultural alternatives as possible from our society's past and present. The teacher need not remain neutral; he may take a position and should defend it with the same vigor that he expects from his students, while being willing to accept that students' positions may conflict with and be as well founded as his own. At the same time, the content of the social studies should be drawn from the continuous flow of change, conflict, and controversy that has characterized our culture. In this way students can learn to cope with rapid change and to make the difficult personal and social decisions.

> Within this context of crises and necessary choice, education can no longer play the role of culture preserver, mediator, or innovator, but must make its important contribution within the area of intelligent choice and decision on the part of the individual. Education's major function is to create the conditions for the individual to inquire into beliefs, values, and social policies and to assess the consequences and implications of possible alternatives.[2]

Social inquiry offers a realistic approach to social studies instruction in a world marked by great cultural diversity and rapid technological and social change. The nature of our society and the world in which we live challenge our schools and social studies education. The complexity of our own society and the world creates vital, troublesome issues that our social studies educators must confront systematically.

SOCIETAL AND WORLD CONDITIONS

As we mentioned before, the world today is both an exciting and difficult place in which to live. War, violence, crime, pollution, inflation, mistrust, the struggle for civil rights, and for peace, are only a few of the challenges that face citizens. Space exploration, high-speed travel, expanding consumer choices, cultural exchange, and worldwide communication systems are also a part of our times. Turmoil, value conflicts, and personal decisions confront each American—and they will multiply in the future.

[2] Massialas and Cox, *Inquiry,* p. 7.

Of course, there has never been a time in which Americans have been free of important personal and social problems. Life in the United States has, in some measure, always involved a struggle for the realization of American ideals in real life. Every generation has had its critics who have demanded more of America's ideals—greater freedom, greater justice, greater equality, greater economic opportunity—for more people. These ideals are the foundation of a democratic society.

Today's—and tomorrow's—important personal and social problems, however, are for the most part rooted in the rapid acceleration of technological and social change. The tremendous explosion of cultural alternatives are in part the result of industrial and technological invention. Obviously a constant and ever accelerating rate of technological change is occurring in the world today. Nuclear submarines, space probes, weather satellites, computers, supersonic transports are only a few examples of the technological innovations introduced in the last three decades. The technologies of the modern world can only be explained by the processes used to develop them. Technology is not just the production of machines and tools; it is also the processes and knowledge of doing things.

The fantastic expansion of modern technology and of the human capability to produce new things and more things result from a cycle in which technology "feeds upon itself." This cycle includes discovery, development, application, diffusion, and further discovery. Not only does this cycle continue but it gathers momentum. Now that the dissemination of information has been developed to the point where scientific knowledge travels around the world faster than ever before, and now that technological progress has decreased the time needed to develop new ideas, the cycle of technological change repeats itself in shorter and shorter periods of time. An increased pace of invention, exploitation, and diffusion, has accelerated the whole cycle still further, says Alvin Toffler. New machines or techniques are more than a product, and serve as a source of fresh creative ideas.[3] Since this situation will probably continue, people in the future will have to learn to adapt to and cope more quickly with rapid technological and social changes.

According to Toffler, rapid change may be testing the limits of our adaptability and "copability" in the very near future. Indeed, we may be experiencing elements of "future shock" right now.

> We may define future shock as the distress, both physical and psychological, that arises from an overload of the human organism's physical adaptive systems and its decision-making processes. Put more simply, future shock is the human response to overstimulation.[4]

[3] Alvin Toffler, *Future Shock* (New York: Bantam Books, 1970), p. 28.
[4] Ibid., p. 326.

Understandably, different people will react to future shock in different ways. Reactions are likely to range from indifference and apathy to excitement and anticipation including: senseless violence and hostility, fear and anger, depression and anxiety. Toffler also points out that people may suffer from "decision overload," a condition in which they are deluged with new data and need to make several important decisions almost immediately. Some people may "freeze up decisionally." People in the state of future shock may also choose to ignore new data and refuse to make decisions. Therefore, Toffler reasons, people should be taught to deal with transience (everchanging environments and data), overchoice (a wide variety of alternatives), and diversity (wide differences in life-styles and beliefs).

Education for people of the future should, in Toffler's view, be radically changed from what it is today. It must involve a new "future orientation" that clearly distinguishes between data and skills.[5] The government, the church, the school, the mass media, and the family advise young people to stay in school, insisting that one's future is almost completely dependent upon education. The trouble is that, despite all this rhetoric and reasonable advice, our schools look back toward a dying system rather than forward to a new emerging society.[6] A future oriented school recognizes that knowledge and data—both so important in fueling the cycle of change—are expanding about as fast as they are becoming outdated. Therefore, schools of the future must include courses that focus on subjects that are not only related to the needs of the future but emphasize skills in three crucial areas: learning, relating, and choosing.[7]

The rapid expansion of knowledge and the increasing need for new data on which to base important decisions in the future will place a premium on the skills necessary for self-learning and for the manipulation of large amounts of information within short periods of time. Students, consequently, must be taught how to learn, unlearn, and relearn if they are to cope with future shock. The population explosion and the speed with which people are forced to move, change jobs, and interact with new people demand that schools today help students develop now skills in learning, in relating to and dealing with others who have different personalities, different beliefs, different life-styles and values. Finally, students need to develop skills related to choosing and making decisions that are vital to anyone trying to adapt and cope with tomorrow's changing world.

As overchoice deepens, the person who lacks a clear grasp of his

[5] Ibid., p. 411.
[6] Ibid., p. 399.
[7] Ibid., pp. 413-415.

own values . . . is progressively crippled. Yet the more crucial the
question of values becomes, the less willing our present schools are
to grapple with it. . . .

Students are seldom encouraged to analyze their own values.
. . . Millions pass through the education system without once having been forced to search out the contradictions in their own value
systems, to probe their own life goals deeply. . . .

Educators . . . must systematically organize formal and informal activities that help the student define, explicate and test his
values, whatever they are.[8]

The changes from our contemporary to our future culture and the
resulting problems for individuals and for society as a whole can also be
considered from the standpoint of conflict—between traditional and
emergent values. According to this position, a major shift is taking place
in our society away from traditional patterns of beliefs and values to new
beliefs and values that are emerging through the changes within our
culture. For example, the importance of such traditional values as thrift,
physical labor, competition, Puritan morality, patriotism, and nationalism
are now being questioned. New values, including cultural relativism,
diversity, social welfare, world cooperation, and improving the quality
of life are now coming to the fore.

The conflict among emergent and traditional values makes it more
difficult for people to arrive at creative, acceptable solutions to urgent
and profound conflicts and social issues. American society has become
riddled with sharp cleavages involving race, religion, ethnic groups, and
social welfare.[9] Our society is becoming more and more industrialized
and urbanized. Ensuing problems will, therefore, be more difficult to
solve because of the swiftness of change and our human limitations in
adapting and coping. Our lack of skills in resolving controversy and in
handling large amounts of changing data will be a tremendous handicap
in the future. It is the role of the educational system to provide such
skills, along with the meaningful elements of our culture, to young
people. It is the role of social studies education to offer students the
opportunity to develop behavioral skills, that will have relevance in the
future, that will help them analyze their own values and those of other
people, and that will enable them to explore a wide range of data-oriented
topics. Social inquiry is aimed toward this type of citizenship education.

---

[8] Ibid., pp. 416-418.
[9] Harold Sims, "Whitney Young's Open Society," *Annals of The American
Academy of Political and Social Science: America's Most Challenging Objectives* 396
(July, 1971): 72.

KNOWLEDGE
AND THE SOCIAL SCIENCES

Kenneth E. Boulding has stated that the world is going through a second "great transition" as a result of the rapid advances of technology. He argues that the transition is taking place not only in the fields of science and technology, and in the uses of energy, but in social institutions and in the personal lives of people. Social change, in turn, is leading to further change in technology. With this tremendous transition in scientific knowledge, Boulding sees a constant conflict existing between what he calls "folk" knowledge and scientific knowledge.[10] Folk knowledge, for the most part, is knowledge acquired from family, friends, and informal groups, not from formal schools and scientific experimentation.

Folk knowledge is often closely related to a person's own values and self-concept. When folk knowledge and one's image of the world are tied to an ideology or value-belief system, which is also closely bound to one's image of oneself, it is particularly difficult to change one's image of the world. In fact, under these circumstances, people may develop "filters" made up of their beliefs, values, and perceptions that block out all messages that contradict their image of the world and thus their image of themselves.

The interrelationship between knowledge and images, therefore, cannot be overemphasized. To Boulding, the whole process of the growth of knowledge involves images—along with inferences or expectations based on our images—and the messages we receive from our environment that influence our images. Says Boulding:

> The image is the actual content of a particular human mind—that is, it is the subjective content of knowledge. This is what man thinks the world is like. . . . Our image is subject to a constant input of messages from our immediate environment. These messages may either confirm our expectations or disappoint them. . . . I can deny the truth of the messages and say that it was a false message or illusion. I can deny the truth of the inference which gave rise to the expectation, and say that I should not have expected the message which failed to come. . . . I may change the image itself.[11]

According to Boulding, part of the tremendous success of the scientific community in creating knowledge can be attributed to its concern for

[10] Kenneth E. Boulding, *The Meaning of the Twentieth Century: The Great Transition* (New York: Harper & Row, 1964), p. 56.
[11] Ibid., p. 40.

truth that did not involve images of reality that were bound to the identity of the people who held them. That is, hypotheses being tested were generally dealt with in an atmosphere where people throughout the scientific community may even have been glad that their hypotheses were proven false. Despite many bitter personal controversies among scientists, says Boulding, "a considerable part of the success of the scientific community in advancing knowledge must be attributed to its value system in which an impersonal devotion to truth is regarded as the highest value to which both personal and national pride must be subordinated." [12]

The major difference between folk and scientific knowledge is that folk knowledge is not so concerned with truth. When folk images are often not supported by messages, people ignore or attack the messages and make excuses for the failure of their expectations rather than change their images of the real world. With scientific knowledge, theoretical or logical inferences are tested by observations (messages), which may or may not support the scientist's expectations. As more and more messages are collected, scientific knowledge is expanded because new inferences are developed, alterations in scientific images are made, better theories are generated, and new techniques to assemble needed data are created. While the folk image is static in nature, the scientific image is constantly being revised in the light of "deliberately acquired information and deliberately provoked disappointments." [13] It is required of education, therefore, that it develop scientific images in young people and not promote folk knowledge and static thinking. It should also provide opportunities for students to develop skills in making logical inferences, collecting data, and drawing reasoned conclusions.

The social studies field is able to provide scientific images from the social sciences and humanities through substantive concepts, or subject matter, and processes of social inquiry. One of the best ways in which to organize the content of social studies is to predicate the study program on key concepts and generalizations. Concepts have been defined in many different ways in the literature of psychology, philosophy, and education, but essentially they are abstractions derived from actual human experiences. They are cognitive categories or groupings into which otherwise unique and unrelated images (experiences) are classified together on the basis of their common characteristics or critical attributes. Generalizations are observed and stated relationships between two or more events or phenomena.

To understand himself, man tries to identify and test patterns and regularities, or general relationships, that explain human behavior and

[12] Ibid., p. 45.
[13] Ibid., p. 50.

social events. Just as the physical scientist attempts to discover valid relationships about natural phenomena that provide him with a greater ability to predict and explain events, so the social scientist is in the process of discovering and testing reliable relationships in human affairs. The major difference between physical relationships and human relationships is the degree of dependability and regularity of the relationships. Since it is maintained that physical relationships recur in highly predictable patterns, they are often referred to as laws. Social patterns, on the other hand, tend to be less predictable due to the "human element" and the complex nature of human affairs. A generalization may be descriptive, factual, historical, conditional, explanatory, definitional, value-oriented, present tense, or causal in nature—types of generalizations that are to be discussed in greater detail in this text. Throughout the process of social inquiry, generalizations from the social sciences, and from the humanities and physical sciences when relevant, are discovered and tested as possible hypotheses. During this process, students develop and test a wide variety of generalizations as they relate to specific social issues and problems under examination.

Several educators have identified important and useful concepts and generalizations for social studies instruction. One group at the University of Syracuse Social Studies Curriculum Center has identified three types of concepts that should direct the planning of social studies teaching and learning: substantive concepts, value concepts, and method concepts.[14] Substantive concepts are those drawn from the content of the social sciences. They are often described as making up the structure or framework of a particular discipline, and they include such ideas as scarcity, power, conflict, ecology, culture, population, citizen participation, social class, change, urbanization, and technology. Value concepts are related to ideals and beliefs, and to the scale of preferences of individuals and cultures. Justice, for example is a value concept; so are freedom, patriotism, loyalty, equality, legality, and morality. Concepts of method refer to processes and attitudes necessary for discovering and validating scientific knowledge. Observation, hypothesis, historical method, model building, objectivity, suspension of judgment, evidence, and reliability are all concepts related to method.

It is suggested here that teachers approach their own planning of teaching-learning activities with a conceptual framework in mind. Before collecting and designing materials for instruction, teachers should develop some sort of framework that organizes the subject matter to be taught into logically related topics that include substantive, value, and method con-

[14] Verna Faucett et al., *Social Science Concepts and The Classroom* (Syracuse, N.Y.: Social Studies Curriculum Center, 1968).

cepts. Verna Faucett and her colleagues suggest that (while planning instruction) social studies teachers examine questions similar to the following:

1. What are the major concepts to be explored?
2. What other concepts are needed to understand the major concepts?
3. Are there any other concepts that might be encountered during inquiry into this major topic?
4. What new concepts are being developed in closely related fields?
5. Will the students be able to link these concepts together to make meaningful and valid generalizations?
6. Have important value areas been examined?
7. Are students skilled in using concepts of method? [15]

With these and similar questions in mind during the planning of a social studies course, the teacher can begin to make rational and systematic decisions about materials, learning activities, and teaching strategies.

One set of educational materials, among new instructional materials based upon the conceptual approach to organizing the curriculum, is *World History Through Inquiry*.[16] The material is predicated upon the major substantive concepts of "political systems," "economic organization," "world order," "environment," "cultural exchange," and "social structure." These concepts serve as the general organizational framework for units of instruction. Each of these substantive concepts is related to other ideas. Economic organization, for instance, includes such subconcepts as scarcity, choice, market economy, planning economy, stages of economic development, and economic growth. Value-related concepts examined in the study unit on economic organization include poverty, wealth, competition, welfare, private property, and full employment. *World History Through Inquiry* is also based upon clearly stated and defined concepts of method: defining problems, forming hypotheses, exploring, evidencing, generalizing, maintaining objectivity, validating sources, and developing methods of historical analysis.

Each unit is also accompanied by descriptive and explanatory generalizations. The unit on economic organization encourages students to discover and test generalizations from economics and other disciplines. For example, a few suggested generalizations deal with traditional societies and technology:

---

[15] Ibid.
[16] Byron G. Massialas and Jack Zevin, *World History Through Inquiry* (Chicago: Rand McNally & Co., 1969, 1970).

1. If a society has a traditional economic system, then its members will tend to share products.

2. If people live in an economic system marked by a low level of technology, then needs and wants are practically the same.

3. As a society increases its level of technology, it may become more efficient at producing goods and services.

4. In a traditional economy, a person's occupation, status, and wealth will be largely determined by custom or long-standing social rules.[17]

SOCIAL PROBLEMS
AND ISSUES AS VEHICLES

All social studies curricula and instruction methods should help students discover, test, and use valid concepts and generalizations in their search to understand human behavior, human values, and human feelings. And one of the best ways in which to help them in this pursuit is to focus on social problems and issues. Problems are felt needs important to some person or group of people. Poverty, racial prejudice, crime, unplanned population change, peace, community health—all these are social problems. Personal problems may relate to one's work, family, leisure, or security, and often involve discrepancies or inconsistencies in one's information and image of reality.

Whereas problems refer to felt needs, issues involve competing interests and conflicts in values and beliefs. They are individual or group value controversies or value problems. The study of issues and problems involves the examination of many types of conflicts between, among, and within people.

Both problems and issues are powerful vehicles through which student exploration, discovery of scientific propositions, and development of scientific images of the real world can be facilitated. "The real significance of the social sciences," says Boulding, "is that they open up the possibilities of testing propositions about man and society which previously were thought to be open only to argument, persuasion, or coercion." [18] Social problems and issues as the content of social studies provide the means of replacing rhetoric and folk knowledge with "reality testing," with the in-depth exploration of socially significant subjects. All of this work lends to itself the advancement of scientific knowledge and the testing of personal beliefs and values. Shirley Engle places great emphasis on social problems and controversial issues simply because

[17] Massialas and Zevin, *Economic Organization, Teacher's Manual,* World History through Inquiry Series (Chicago: Rand McNally & Co., 1969, 1970), p. 9.
[18] Boulding, *Meaning,* p. 72.

they help students learn to make decisions and because they are connected with important and basic concepts from the social sciences.[19]

The problem-and-issue approach to the social studies, therefore, offers an opportunity for students to develop skills related to reflection and social science thinking. If students are encouraged to explore problems and issues openly in a classroom atmosphere characterized by systematic inquiry and value analysis rather than by folk knowledge and prejudice, they can then be taught to apply these skills to the creative solution of problems and controversies outside the classroom. Social problems and issues, then, serve as an excellent vehicle for the understanding and application of scientific knowledge (product) and for the development of cognitive and effective skills (process).

THE PEDAGOGICAL SIGNIFICANCE OF CONTROVERSIAL ISSUES

A great degree of conflict is characteristic of a number of cultures that have reached a relatively high level of technological advancement. Compared with many other cultures, that of America's seems to be excessively burdened with social and personal conflict. Maurice Hunt and Lawrence Metcalf see social conflict as oriented either outward or inward. "Students of present-day social conflict," they point out, "have identified two levels of conflict, *interpersonal* and *intrapersonal*." [20] Interpersonal conflict is exemplified by groups or individuals who have differences in beliefs and is often associated with controversial issues. Intrapersonal conflict involves a lack of self-understanding and a degree of confusion over values within a person. It also refers to the problems of self-identity and personal alienation.

Moral dilemmas and value conflicts are inherent in all areas of our culture. Some of these areas—religion, for example—have remained resistant to rational examination and are therefore riddled with folk knowledge, inconsistencies, conflicting beliefs, controversy, and irrational behavior. In them, people "ignore relevant messages" because there are many strongly held and untested beliefs, prejudices, uncertainties, and social taboos. Hunt and Metcalf call these areas "closed." They have identified many of them in our culture: power and the law; nationalism and patriotism; religion and morality; economics and business; race and

[19] Shirley H. Engle, "Thoughts in Regard to Revision," *Social Education* 27 (April, 1963): 182-184.
[20] Maurice P. Hunt and Lawrence E. Metcalf, *Teaching High School Social Studies* (New York: Harper & Row, 1968), p. 25.

minority-group relations; social class and customs; and sex, courtship, and marriage.[21]

If education is to develop a desire in our youth for scientific knowledge and a sense of social consciousness, through which they can analyze themselves and their culture from outside their own ethnocentrism, personal value systems, and identities, then teachers will have to encourage students to examine our culture's closed areas, and to begin rational exploration, dialogue, and action related to problems and issues in these areas. A large measure of education for free and responsible citizens who take an active part in their society, be it in the political, economic, or social realms, must release people from the restraints of narrow thinking, myopia, superstition, and folk knowledge. The careful and objective study of controversial issues and problems within the closed areas of American culture is an approach to social studies instruction that can only promote rational thinking, broad perspectives, and scientific knowledge.

Hunt and Metcalf point out that the closed areas have not been used to their best advantage in the implementation of social studies curriculum. They argue that: "The pedagogical significance of these closed areas is not well understood by most teachers of social studies. . . . Teachers rarely invade any closed area, even though every closed area can be opened by skillful, tactful, fair, and objective teachers." [22] Often teachers ignore the closed areas because scientific knowledge frequently conflicts with the beliefs and folk knowledge of students and parents. Teachers also ignore areas characterized by strong feelings and emotions so students and their parents do not get upset. For these reasons, among others, teachers fail to use the closed areas to their students' pedagogical advantage.

Content in social studies is more generally selected from those aspects of our society in which conflict is lacking and resistance to open inquiry runs deep. All too often outdated and bland issues and problems are studied rather than those that focus on real controversy and social problems. This approach ignores the many positive outcomes that can result from probing the issues and problems of the closed areas.

The first positive outcome is that of increased student interest, involvement, and motivation to act. Closed areas offer exciting topics for study. It is often the staleness of the content in social studies that leads to student boredom, poor attitude, apathy, and ineffective learning. The need for personal relevance and student motivation is a well-known and often-stated fact in educational literature. Educational theorists studying

[21] Ibid., Chapters 14 to 19.
[22] Ibid., p. 27.

motivation and "humanistic" learning emphasize that relevancy is made up of both cognitive and affective components. One of the arguments for inquiry, or discovery, learning is that it leads to greater student interest, involvement and motivation because it stimulates student curiosity, it "recharges" their interest in what is being studied. Research in the cognitive-dissonance theory also leads us to the conclusion that doubt and conflict related to one's beliefs create energy or motivation to re-examine one's beliefs and knowledge in order to eliminate or reduce any existing doubt, confusion, and inconsistency. People do want to be consistent. The basis of consistency theories, according to William McGuire, is that people adjust their beliefs, attitudes, and behaviors so that they can achieve a high degree of internal harmony within their belief system.[23] Consistency models are based upon the assumption that once individuals find themselves in a situation where an inconsistency in their beliefs, attitudes, and behavior is identified or created, a human drive toward cognitive consistency manifests itself.

Leon Festinger has developed a theory of cognitive dissonance based upon this very point. He argues that there is a "pressure to produce consonance among cognitions and to avoid dissonance."[24] A person is said to be in a state of dissonance when he holds, simultaneously, two cognitions that are inconsistent with each other. When the individual finds out that his beliefs, attitudes, values, and behavior are in conflict with one another, he will experience "psychological discomfort." This discomfort, in turn, serves to motivate the individual to reduce the dissonance and achieve consonance. The motivation toward cognitive consistency may manifest itself in such actions as rationalization, altering behavior, changing beliefs, and searching for new information.[25]

Hunt and Metcalf suggest that learning in social studies results from inquiry conducted to reduce cognitive dissonance in the closed areas of a culture. They contend that students develop higher levels of understanding through gaining increased levels of "insight" into problems and issues. It is important for learners to develop higher levels of insight. Thought may begin with doubt of a particular belief or element of knowledge. The thought may end with acceptance or rejection or modi-

[23] William J. McGuire, "The Nature of Attitudes and Attitude Change," in *Handbook of Social Psychology*, vol. 3, ed. Gardner Lindsey and Elliot Aronson (Reading, Mass.: Addison-Wesley Publishing Co., 1969), p. 142.

[24] Leon Festinger, *A Theory of Cognitive Dissonance* (Stanford: Stanford University Press, 1964), p. 9.

[25] Milton Baker, "Training Prospective Social Studies Teachers in Aspects of the Inquiry Method: The Effects of Different Modes on a Trainee's Attitudes, Intentions and Behaviors" (Ph. D. diss., University of Michigan, 1969), p. 38.

fication of the original belief or knowledge. During learning, new data are evaluated as additional facts are examined by the student. One's tested beliefs expand. One "knows more" because one has developed deeper factual and conceptual understanding.[26] Insight, as used here, can be defined as the discovery of possible solutions to problems. Inquiry into society's closed areas, then, serves three purposes—all of which result in greater cognitive motivation and involvement on the part of the student; it offers (1) interesting curricula content, (2) an opportunity for students to test their personal beliefs and insights, and (3) situations that can resolve doubt, inconsistency, and dissonance.

Inquiry into closed areas further adds a highly affective dimension to learning. Isaac Brown says that there should always be an "emotional" dimension to learning because emotions can involve students more deeply with the content and skills to be learned.[27] Hunt and Metcalf agree that when students "feel" a problem the most effective learning takes place.[28] Because controversial issues usually reflect strongly held beliefs, social inquiry will result in increased feeling, emotional involvement, and "valuing" on the part of the student.

The right kind of social studies programs in America's schools should produce free, responsible, and active citizens in the future. One approach to this goal is the development and *use* of rational processes that contribute to scientific thinking and knowledge. Social inquiry is also meant to lead to a more futuristic orientation because it (a) promotes the examination of one's values, (b) provides a testing ground for student ideas and beliefs, and (c) confronts students with real-life situations in which to apply thinking and valuing processes. It is high time for educators in social studies to understand the pedagogical significance of the closed areas of American society and to implement instruction focusing on social issues and problems. Social inquiry is the only defensible approach to the study of controversy in our democratic system. Any "bland" or prescriptive approach violates the principles of objectivity, relevance, and freedom of thought that must underlie all education. If citizens are to be both free and active in the future, and if they are to be able to cope with the future, then a social inquiry approach is necessary. If we continue to offer programs in social studies that ignore controversy, focus on isolated facts, honor learning by rote, and look toward the dying

[26] Hunt and Metcalf, *Teaching*, p. 56.
[27] Isaac Brown, *Human Teaching for Human Learning* (New York: The Viking Press, 1972).
[28] Hunt and Metcalf, *Teaching*, p. 51.

past, then our students will inevitably experience what Toffler calls "future shock."

SUMMARY

In this chapter we discussed several factors related to culture and society; the nature of education, knowledge, and social science; and educational planning and results of recent research. These factors were analyzed in terms of developing an explicit and well-grounded rationale for an inquiry-oriented curriculum in social studies supported by (1) actual events and predictions for the future, (2) a stated philosophy of education, (3) defensible learning theory, (4) the nature of knowledge, and (5) current research in education.

Contemporary society is marked by many problems, issues, and crises as a result of rapid social and technological change and expanding cultural pluralism. As the number of social alternatives, and the diversity of cultural values increase, and the knowledge explosion continues, individual citizens must cope with more and deeper interpersonal and intrapersonal conflicts.

Extensive changes in society and the need for an up-to-date educational system have not been accompanied, according to Toffler, by significant modifications in present school curricula. To cope with new problems, today's citizens and citizens of the future will need to develop skills in inquiry, value analysis, social interaction, and decision making, requiring a curriculum that emphasizes learning how to learn, relating to others, and choosing rationally.

Toffler's concept of a "future-oriented" curriculum emphasizes the need for social studies programs that refocus attention from rote learning of isolated facts, definitions and historical descriptions to a broader based curriculum. Such an expanded view of social studies includes concepts, generalizations, reflective thinking, decision making, value analysis, and active student participation. Social inquiry employs societal and personal problems and issues as stimuli and vehicles for learning in a psychologically open climate where students feel free to exchange and challenge each others' and their teacher's ideas and positions.

2

inquiry compared with other teaching styles

Social issues provide a natural springboard for inquiry in the classroom. A social issue is a recognizable aspect of a larger social problem in which real and meaningful alternatives are presented for critical analysis, decision, and possible action.[1] Generally, students feel that such issues are meaningful topics for their consideration. Given the opportunity, they will formulate hypotheses and take positions based on their own knowledge and values regarding possible explanations of or solutions to a controversy. The instructional problem for the teacher is not whether students will participate in the discussion on the issue, but whether their hypotheses and value positions are clarified, reflectively examined, and adequately grounded.

Teachers have a number of options before them. They may engage in exposition and thus limit the students' examination of the issue and the opportunity to explore for themselves the merits and ramifications of alternative solutions. Teachers may, on the other hand, opt to engage in the reflective examination of issues and try to create an open classroom climate that reinforces this approach. However, some teachers who have the most sincere intentions about inquiry instruction have difficulty implementing them consistently in the classroom. From our survey research, we find that many teachers support inquiry abstractly but rarely practice it in the classroom.

[1] John P. Lunstrum, "The Treatment of Controversial Issues in Social Studies Instruction," in *New Challenges in the Social Studies: Implications of Research for Teaching,* ed. B. G. Massialas and F. R. Smith (Belmont, Calif., Wadsworth Publishing Co., 1965), pp. 121-153.

One way to assist teachers with a basic propensity to inquiry teaching but who are not effectively implementing the method in the classroom is to show them in detail how the inquiry teacher performs and what the possible alternatives in the process are. The goal of this chapter is to clarify the components of inquiry teaching and to indicate the exact junctures where major instructional decisions on the inquiry process need to be made. The operations subsumed under important instructional decisions will also be spelled out and *actual* classroom dialogue will be used for illustrative purposes.

THREE STYLES
OF TEACHING

In much of the literature on teaching, teaching styles are classified as either teacher-centered or learner-centered. Most of those who write about teaching use some type of autocratic-democratic dichotomy to categorize classroom teacher behavior.[2] The autocratic teaching style is characterized by a resistance to change and tight control by the teacher of the dissemination of knowledge and of the pupils' classroom behavior. The democratic teaching style involves openness to the ideas of others and flexibility in classroom control on the part of the teacher. Studies of the democratic style are concerned primarily with the affective climate in the classroom and with the student-participatory aspects of learning. Researchers ask questions such as: Is the psychological atmosphere in the classroom open? Do students feel free to participate and interject their own ideas?

More recently, educators have stressed the cognitive nature of instructional styles. The central question has now become: What kind of thinking are students asked to do in the classroom? Donald Oliver and James Shaver have identified two basic teaching styles: "recitation" and "socratic."[3] In recitation teaching the teacher provides the information that students are expected to "know" through lectures or text materials. The student is expected to recall or supply the information when asked for it. Socratic teaching emphasizes the adversarial process by which students examine alternative points of view and use analytical concepts and strategies to arrive at a position.

One educator suggests that teaching styles may be placed on a continuum that has expository operations at one end and inquiry at

---

[2] Richard C. Anderson, "Learning in Discussions: A Résumé of the Authoritarian-Democratic Studies," *Harvard Educational Review* 29 (1959): 201.

[3] Donald Oliver and James Shaver, *Teaching Public Issues in the High School* (Boston: Houghton-Mifflin Co., 1966), pp. 176-177.

another.[4] Expository styles focus on telling, memorizing, and recalling information, whereas inquiry styles are based on students searching out and discovering knowledge for themselves.

In our research we have focused on the cognitive nature of classroom interaction. We have identified three distinct teaching styles: expository, opining, and inquiry. The opining teaching style has in the past often been confused with inquiry teaching. Opining, however, does not include a crucial element of the inquiry style: the clarifying and probing of hypotheses or positions.

1. Expository Teaching

In the expository style of teaching social issues, the teacher has investigated the issues and decided ahead of time what aspects of them are important for the class to know and remember. Teachers present the information that they consider important; they guide the class and reinforce the information that they feel students should learn. They point out why people disagree on an issue and explain possible solutions to the underlying problem. They may question students about what they have learned from class readings or lectures, and they may periodically ask them to summarize what has been covered. Also, the students may ask their teachers questions about what they have read, what has been said, or why one solution to a social issue is better than another. But basically, under the expository style of teaching, students are listeners, and they listen primarily to opinions of others. Our definition of expository teaching is similar to the teacher-directed recitation style discussed by Oliver and Shaver and the expository style discussed by Fenton. Thus, in expository teaching teachers are the authority on the issue; they know what information they want to cover, and students are expected to remember and recapitulate the essential features of the issue as presented to them. In a larger context the distinctions between inquiry teaching and expository teaching can be seen in Figures 2:1 and 2:2.[5]

2. Opinion Teaching

In opining discussions centering on social issues, students are encouraged to participate and add their own ideas. A psychological atmosphere of openness is created. The teacher usually presents the class with a springboard or problematic situation and asks students to give their opinions on the issue. Students identify and state problems, look for rela-

[4] Edwin Fenton, *The New Social Studies* (New York: Holt, Rinehart and Winston, Inc., 1967), p. 33.

[5] Adapted from Byron G. Massialas and C. Benjamin Cox, *Inquiry in Social Studies* (New York: McGraw-Hill Book Co., 1966), pp. 310-311.

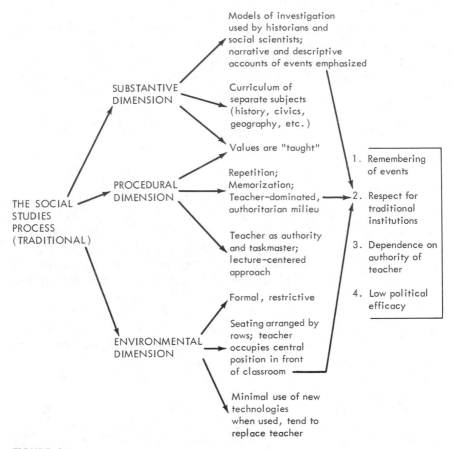

FIGURE 2:1
Traditional Teaching Model

tionships, and pose alternative hypotheses. The teacher concentrates on promoting discussion and interaction, and students feel free to give their opinions and experiences related to the social issue in question.

Teachers employing the opining style will invariably claim with confidence that they are indeed inquiry teachers. And on first glance, opining as a teaching style does appear to resemble the inquiry method. It is not as teacher-directed as the expository style, and students are exploring on their own. But opining is *not* inquiry. Opining lacks the underlying purposefulness and sense of direction that is central to reflective inquiry. Students take positions on issues in an open setting but do not clarify or probe alternative positions. Often, the teacher seems to be promoting discussion simply for its own sake, without any logic, order,

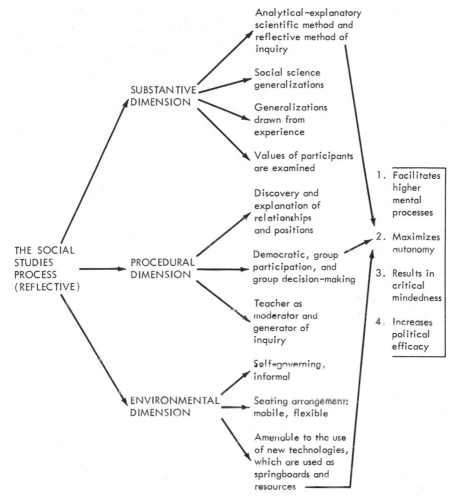

FIGURE 2:2
Inquiry Teaching Model

or end in view. Some students may agree that one position is desirable while others may favor another position, but there is little discussion on why one position is better than another or on the quality of the grounds upon which each position presumably rests.

There are two basic types of opining discussions: one is friendly in nature, the other is not. In the friendly discussion everybody expresses his own opinions and there is a mutual acceptance of all positions. The attitude seems to be: "You say what you think and I'll say what I think and we won't challenge each other." The discussion allows students to get their feelings into the open, though it tends to be a meandering, cathartic session rather than a focused intellectual probing of ideas or positions. The other type of opining discussion is combative in nature. Again, individuals express their opinions, but in this case students tend to have preconceived ideas related to the social issues at hand and are less tolerant of conflicting ideas. They are inclined to repeat arguments and stress their own position without really listening to or responding in a meaningful way to other positions. Sarcastic humor, emotion, and irrelevant arguments often prevail in this kind of discussion.

3. Inquiry Teaching

In inquiry teaching that deals with social issues, the classroom climate is psychologically open and there is a definite sense of purpose to the discussion. Either the teacher or the student presents the social issue in a problem context as a springboard. The goal of instruction is to clarify the issue and to offer different hypotheses or positions related to it, and then to resolve value conflicts that arise and to determine defensible solutions to them. The accepted solutions—presented either as hypotheses or positions—are sometimes followed by individual or group action. The teacher and students jointly explore aspects of the problem; rather than the teacher telling students about the problem, they investigate it together. The teacher's role is to create the conditions from which a problem may develop, to have materials and resources available that the students may tap to research the issue, and to encourage students through questions to identify issues, state hypotheses, and then clarify, probe, and resolve conflicting ideas and positions.

As students try to analyze the social controversy, they ponder the best ways in which to deal with it. Alternative hypotheses or positions are presented, and students are urged to gather information and assess their validity and desirability. They look at the value and factual dimensions of a position. After students gather information, they compare their findings, and decide how to proceed. Teachers are also participants—accepting the notion of defensible partiality [6]—but their primary role is to make certain that the class considers all possible alternatives and obtains sufficient evidence on which to make its decision. As the discussion progresses and the class comes to dead ends or points of conflict and does not know where to go next, teachers may draw upon their repertoire of experiences to suggest possible ways to overcome difficulties.

During the investigation of the social issue, it is possible that the class as a whole will not agree that one solution is better than another;

---

[6] Teachers are partial to the free examination of positions and their explicit grounding or justification. Ibid., pp. 153-178.

one group may hold different value bases than another. But even so, the various alternatives have been made explicit in terms of their logical implications and value assumptions, and the students have learned critical thinking skills that can be applied to other social issues in other contexts. One of the prime aims of inquiry is to provide students with a sense of efficacy, with the belief that they have the skills to look critically at their environment and to a large measure control their own destiny and influence the decisions affecting them.

THE FLOW
OF CLASS DISCUSSIONS

Most teaching styles, with the exception of straight expository lectures, depend on class discussions for their implementation. A discussion is a series of verbal statements and exchanges among members of a class. These statements include many different cognitive operations, such as exchanging information, making judgments, giving examples, clarifying values, and testing positions. Because the *overall* cognitive nature of the interaction is, at least in part, a reflection of the teaching style being used, it is essential that we understand how the teacher influences the type of thinking that is occurring. If we view a class discussion as composed of a series of cognitive interaction sequences, we will be able to see how discussions develop and how the teacher, at critical junctures, through questions, statements, and other cues, influences the nature of the exchange.

A cognitive interaction sequence is a verbal exchange of ideas, thoughts, and questions among individuals in a class. It is simply an episode in the discussion in which the participants are conveying related thoughts or ideas to one another. The cognitive sequences flow from and build upon one another. Some include hypothesizing. Some include clarifying the problem or defining terms. Others involve defending or supporting an idea or a position. Some phases of the discussion may be carefully guided by the teacher, while in others the students generate their own ideas or opinions. At almost any point a participant can interrupt a cognitive sequence and change the focus of the discussion.

Depending on their cognitive nature, interaction sequences may be viewed as expository, opining, or inquiry. Most discussions taken in *their entirety* contain bits of all three types of interaction sequences. An observer who walks into a classroom and listens for an entire period, however, usually finds that certain cognitive sequences predominate. From the flow of the discussion itself, it is possible to identify which of the three distinct teaching styles—expository, opining, or inquiry—is fostered in the classroom.

1. Expository Sequences

Expository sequences involve the sharing or summarizing of background information. Exposition generally encompasses the first two levels in Benjamin Bloom's cognitive taxonomy: knowledge and comprehension. Knowledge involves the recall of specifics and universals and emphasizes the process of remembering. Comprehension is a low level of understanding: the individual knows what is or was communicated and can summarize the material or idea without necessarily relating it to other material or seeing its fullest implications.[7] For example, a student who reads a *Time* article on the pollution of rivers by industrial waste and then summarizes the key points of the article for the class without tying what he has read to any other information on or ideas about pollution, is performing the cognitive operation of comprehension.

Most expository sequences are initiated by the teacher. In fact, in some sequences the only active participant is the teacher. When teachers lecture from notes, read from a book, show an informational film, or, explain material to the class, they are engaged in exposition. This type of instruction is really one-way transmission of information. The teacher is the authority who is conveying information to supposedly less-informed individuals. The students are expected to absorb the comments and material presented.

In other expository sequences, though, the students are more involved in the interaction. At the teacher's request, they may provide exposition by reading or summarizing a passage from a book or by repeating and paraphrasing remembered information. The following excerpt taken from a taped class dialogue is an example of an expository sequence in which both the teacher and students are sharing background information. The class is concerned with civil rights, and at this point the participants are discussing the history of the civil-rights movement.

Teacher: Amendments 13, 14, and 15 to the Constitution were designed to guarantee Negroes their rights as citizens of the United States. But in many places Negroes remained second-class citizens. In the 1950s, a movement began to obtain civil rights for the Negroes in the South. Polly, how did the civil-rights movement in the South begin?

Polly: Well, the movement started in the 1950s when a Negro woman wouldn't give up her seat on a bus to a white passenger. Martin Luther King led a boycott of the buses. Sit-ins were held in restaurants, pray-ins at churches, and wade-ins at beaches.

---

[7] Benjamin S. Bloom, ed., *Taxonomy of Education Objectives: Cognitive Domain* (London: Longmans, Green & Co., 1956), pp. 62-119.

Teacher: OK. What were they protesting? John?

John: Discrimination, not having rights.

Teacher: What kind of discrimination?

John: In housing, education, jobs. Being able to sit where they wanted in buses and restaurants.

At the beginning of this dialogue the teacher is providing background information. The teacher then asks a series of questions that elicit student exposition regarding the history of the civil-rights movement. The teacher has set the framework and is calling upon students to fill in the information that he, as the teacher, wishes to develop. The flow of input resulting in teacher-initiated exposition may be represented as in Figure 2:3.

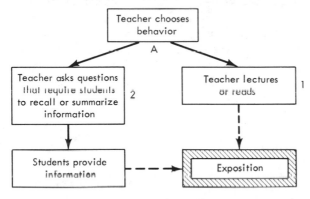

FIGURE 2:3
Teacher-Initiated Expository Sequences

At point A in the diagram the teacher chooses whether he will present the background information himself or whether he will ask students to recall and fill in the information. If the teacher lectures or reads (alternative 1), he has chosen to use, in Flanders' terms, direct influence.[8] The students do not have an opportunity to participate. In the dialogue the teacher briefly provides direct exposition when he states that "Amendments 13, 14, and 15 to the Constitution were designed to guarantee Negroes their rights as citizens of the United States. But in many places Negroes remained second-class citizens." The teacher has chosen an alternative that involves teacher exposition.

[8] Ned A. Flanders, "Teacher Influence in the Classroom" and Edmund Amidon and Ned Flanders, "Interaction Analysis as a Feedback System," in *Interaction Analysis: Theory, Research and Application,* ed. Edmund B. Amidon and John B. Hough (Reading, Mass.: Addison-Wesley Publishing Co., 1967), pp. 109, 125.

If the teacher selects alternative 2, as he did when he asked the question, "Polly, how did the civil-rights movement in the South begin?" he has chosen to use indirect influence.[9] Although the students now have an opportunity to participate, their participation is limited to finding out and presenting requested information. In responding with the requested information, a student may summarize what he has been told by the teacher or others, restate what he has read previously, or conduct some investigation to find the answer in other sources. In this example the student apparently already knew the information and responded that "the movement started in the 1950s when a Negro woman wouldn't give up her seat on a bus to a white passenger. . . ."

In both alternatives above the teacher initiated the expositions; yet it is also possible for students to initiate expository sequences. Students may desire new information or ask the teacher to explain material they do not understand. For example, a student may have seen a television news broadcast about air pollution and on her own initiative ask the teacher to state how automobiles contribute to air pollution. The flow of input resulting in student-initiated exposition may be diagrammed as in Figure 2:4.

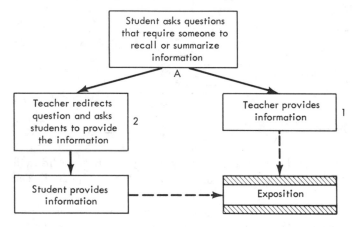

FIGURE 2:4
Student-Initiated Expository Sequences

The teacher may respond to the student's request by providing the information herself (alternative 1) or by asking another student to provide the necessary information (alternative 2). In our experience, though, we find that very few expository sequences are initiated by students. More often the teacher sets the framework of information that

[9] Ibid.

is to be presented in class. We also found that when an expository sequence is initiated by a student, teachers frequently choose to provide the information themselves rather than redirect the question to other students.[10]

2. Opining Sequences

Opining sequences differ from expository sequences in that the teacher and students do more than restate or summarize remembered information; instead, they are actively offering their *own* opinions, hypotheses, or positions. In opining sequences the speaker usually makes statements that include or imply phrases like "I believe," "I think," "I hold," "I feel," which are followed by the speaker's hypotheses, preferences, evaluations, or judgments regarding a given issue. Both the teacher and students participate in opining sequences. In the process of grappling with a problem, many positions or hypotheses may be posed. Some may deal directly with the problem, others may pertain to subissues brought up during the discussion. Teachers promote student position taking or hypothesizing by asking questions such as "What do you think?" "Do you have any suggestions?" "Any more ideas?" "Ruth, what is your reaction to Harold's ideas?" "How would you explain this incident?" "How do you explain the intent of this cartoonist?"

In the opining sequence below, class members are discussing compulsory education. They have been studying the public-school system in the United States and are debating whether or not compulsory education laws should be abolished.

Teacher: Do you think we should have compulsory education?

Sue: Yes, school is important. Everyone should have an education.

Teacher: George?

George: I think that is a bunch of garbage. We shouldn't have compulsory education. If people don't want to go to school, they shouldn't have to. I learn more outside of school, than I do in.

Sue: But you don't learn the right things outside of school.

George: Wanta bet? School is a waste.

John: You're a waste!

Class: Laughter.

George: If goody-goodies like you want to go to school, fine, but why force school on me. I don't want to go.

Carol: But school is important, George.

[10] See research findings in B. G. Massialas, Nancy F. Sprague, and Jo Ann Sweeney, *Structure and Process of Inquiry into Social Issues in Secondary Schools,* Vol. 2, (Ann Arbor: University of Michigan, 1970). Available in microfiche through the Educational Resources Information Center (ERIC).

The teacher touched off this brief sequence by asking if the students thought there should be compulsory education. The students then stated their positions on two issues: whether compulsory education should be abolished and whether school is worthwhile. Sue thinks there should be compulsory education. George does not. Sue thinks school is important; George disagrees. At this point in the discussion, the students have not defended their position and the teacher has not entered the discussion beyond asking the initial question.

On the affective level, opining sequences may be cathartic or combative. The above example involved combat. Sue and George have different views and are trying to convince each other of the rightness of their position without really providing explicit grounds for holding it. There is direct disagreement but no attempt to resolve the conflict between the parties on a logical or substantive level. In this type of opining sequence individuals may state subpositions related to the main position, as does George when he declares that "I learn more outside of school, than I do in," or they may resort to loaded language, personal attacks, or humor, as does John when he retorts, "You're a waste!"

Cathartic opining, as opposed to combative opining, consists of both exploring and sharing one's feelings and opinions regarding a social issue without comparing the grounds and assumptions of alternative hypotheses and positions. The following discussion by a class of ninth graders on the merits of drinking is an example of a cathartic opining sequence:

Sue: I personally don't like to drink and I don't like to go out with guys who do.

Joan: It doesn't bother me to go out with guys who drink. If you only have one or two, it's OK.

Dave: I think a person's feeling about drinking depends on his parents.

Teacher: Carol.

Carol: Liquor has a terrible smell.

Joan: It does when a person throws up.

Don: I remember when I got drunk once and threw up, what a bummer!

Carol: My parents let me drink in the house. They say they want me to have the experience when they are around. I don't drink at parties, though.

In this opining sequence a number of opposing views are expressed by several individuals with little or no conflict involved. Sue doesn't like to drink at all, Carol doesn't drink at parties, while Joan thinks a couple of drinks are fine. None of these students have given reasons for their opinions, nor have they or the teacher asked students to compare the merits of their positions. Dave has offered a possible hypothesis that could be tested by relevant data, but the point he raises is not pursued. Carol and Joan's opinions about the smell of liquor could be related to the issue of drinking, but seem somewhat extraneous at this point. The norm of this discussion, and many other cathartic opinion sequences seems to be, "I'll say what I believe, you say what you believe, but let's not really challenge the merits of each other's opinions."

3. Inquiry Sequences

Inquiry sequences differ from opining sequences in that the class participants probe, test, and compare their positions and hypotheses. They are actively involved in justifying hypotheses on substantive dimensions. Some of the operations that may occur in an inquiry sequence include:

1. Defining and categorizing concepts and distinguishing between ideas.
2. Clarifying values underlying positions.
3. Collecting and analyzing evidence.
4. Using evidence to validate or evaluate hypotheses or positions.
5. Exploring logical consequences of positions.
6. Generalizing.

In the following sequence, students are discussing alternatives to the property tax. At this juncture the class is trying to decide whether the property tax or the income tax is the more fair form of taxation.

Teacher: Don, which do you think is the fairer form of taxation?

Don: The income tax because how much tax you can afford to pay depends on your income. People can have a house but not be able to afford to pay taxes.

Carol: But what about those rich people who have big mansions. They should pay taxes. The property tax is the most fair.

Teacher: Why is the property tax more fair than the income tax? You said the property tax is most fair. Why?

Carol: Because I read that a lot of rich people get out of paying income tax. They have big houses though and have to pay property tax.

Teacher: Jack.

Jack: But Don is right. My grandfather is retired and doesn't have too much money. He said that he might have to sell his house because he can't pay the property taxes. It doesn't seem fair because he has lived in his house for 40 years or something like that.

Sue: Can he pay his income taxes?

Jack: I think so, at least he hasn't complained about them. Of couse he doesn't get too much money every month.

Carol: I still say the property tax is best. You might be right for your grandfather, but my father complains about his income tax. He wouldn't like it if he had to pay more income tax. Also with property tax, you don't have to buy a home. You can rent and not have to pay property tax.

Teacher: Don.

Don: But if a tax is fair everyone should pay taxes based on his ability to pay. Everyone has an income so everyone has to pay an income tax based on his income . . . well, except for the really poor. With property tax, not everyone has property so not everyone pays.

Carol: That's right. So property tax is more fair. You have a choice of buying a house or not.

Teacher: It seems to me that we have to decide what we mean by fair. Carol, what do you mean by a "fair" tax?

The students here are presenting their positions and attempting to defend them. Don thinks the income tax is fairer than the property tax. The reason he gives is that the amount of tax a person can afford to pay depends on his income. Carol disagrees. She thinks the income tax is less fair because rich people get out of paying their income tax. Jack supports Don's position by giving an example of his grandfather who has a small income and cannot afford to pay taxes on his house. Carol offers counter-evidence to refute Don. She states that the income tax is harder on her father than the property tax. Carol also introduces the idea that being able to choose to buy property makes the tax fairer. Don then tries to define what he means by "fair." He stresses that property taxes do not meet his definition. Besides calling on students, the teacher enters the interaction at two points—once when she asks Carol to support her position, again when she realizes that the students are using two different definitions of "fair" and asks Carol to clarify what she means by the term.

There are several ways in which the positions of students may be probed. Students may spontaneously support or clarify their own positions and challenge other students to do likewise. Or the teacher may ask questions that encourage students to define their terms or give reasons for their positions. Teacher probing often includes questions that begin, "Why do you think that. . . ?" "What do you mean by. . . ?" "Is there any evidence. . . ?" "What are your reasons. . . ?" It is more desirable for students to probe other students' positions rather than have the teacher intervene and request probing. When the students begin to ask each other for justifications, they have internalized an important aspect of the inquiry process.

4. Opining Sequences Compared with Inquiry Sequences

Figure 2:5 indicates how, during a discussion of social issues, teachers can use their classroom influence to promote either opining or inquiry sequences. At point A the teacher asks questions that encourage the students to give their opinions, hypotheses or positions relative to the problem at hand. For example, in the sequence dealing with education, the teacher asks, "Do you think we should have compulsory education?" Whereas in the sequence involving alternatives to the property tax the teacher asks, ". . . Which do you think would be the most fair?" In both questions, the teacher is not only using indirect influence, but is also opening up a wide range of possible responses on the part of the students. The teacher is encouraging the discussion to move toward the exploration and testing of alternatives.

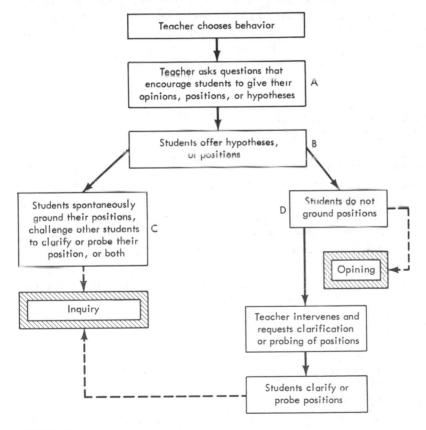

FIGURE 2:5

Opining and Inquiry Sequences

At point B in Figure 2:5 the students respond to the teacher's open-ended questions by offering their own opinions: "Yes, school is important. . . ." "I think that is a bunch of garbage. . . ." At this point students may also spontaneously support their positions and challenge their fellow students to do likewise; if they do so, they have arrived at point C, which is defined as an inquiry sequence because students are actually probing their positions. If the students do not spontaneously clarify or test their positions, or just continue hypothesizing and stating positions without defending them, the discussion has moved to point D. At this juncture, the teacher may choose to intervene and use influence to get students to ground or clarify their positions—a strategy employed twice by the teacher in the property tax versus income tax sequence. If the teacher does intervene, it is quite likely that the students will begin to probe their positions, thus again moving the sequence toward inquiry. If, on the other hand, the teacher does not intervene and the students do not ground their positions, the interaction is opining. The inquiry-opining diagram is, of course, oversimplified, but it does help one see how the teacher's behavior can influence and promote the development of opining or inquiry sequences.

USING DIALOGUE SEQUENCES
TO IDENTIFY TEACHING STYLES

As we mentioned earlier, few class discussions are composed of all expository, all opining, or all inquiry sequences. Most discussions have a mixture of all three sequences. To illustrate this point, let us consider the following dialogue taken from an actual high school class discussion. The class has read a summary of Malthus's *Essay on the Principle of Population* and is pondering the issue of population and its management:

Teacher:	What about this population? Can we do anything about decreasing the population growth rate?
Nancy:	We can control it.
Teacher:	How can we control it?
Nancy:	Well, there's birth control.
Teacher:	OK, planned parenthood, birth control. . . . Can you think of any other ways?
Judy:	Abortions.
Teacher:	What about abortions, do you think this is one of the ways to solve the problem?
Maggie:	No.
Teacher:	Why not?

Maggie: I think abortions are wrong. I don't think you should have it. And it depends, too, on what you call a life.

Teacher: Let's just say, if you are talking about abortion, you're talking about people being allowed to have an abortion any time. There are people in our country who feel that's the way it should go.

Maggie: It seems to me that now you have the pill and everything . . . someone could decide not to have a baby before they got to the point where they had to have an abortion.

Teacher: In other words, why wait until a child is conceived when you have so many other techniques to prevent birth from taking place to begin with.

Maggie: Yeah.

Sue: The other techniques wouldn't work under rape. Even though they have different techniques, conception could take place when you didn't want it to.

Maggie: Still you wouldn't want to kill the child. It is half-way yours, you know. I don't think there should be an abortion even with rape.

Teacher: At all? Under no circumstances?

Maggie: No, not under any circumstances.

Teacher: OK, Barb?

Barb: I agree with Maggie. The child can be raised with people who can't have children. Why would you have an abortion; kill the baby you're carrying when another person can give it a beautiful home?

Teacher: But is this realistic? There are many kids in orphanages, and places like that who aren't adopted now, Margaret.

Margaret: A lot could be eliminated if you didn't have to go through all that red tape to adopt a child. I think in California they're letting single people adopt babies. That could help.

Teacher: Don.

Don: But even if you let people who were raped have abortions, that still wouldn't do much to control the population. Not that many people are raped!

Nancy: Yeah, abortions wouldn't do much to control population. If a lot of people feel like Maggie then there wouldn't be many abortions. Birth control is better because not as many people are against birth control.

Teacher: Maggie.

Maggie: I can see how birth control is a positive check on the population, but how can Malthus say that famine, war, and disease is a positive check. They don't seem positive to me.

Teacher: Wait, you've got them mixed up. Malthus said that there were two types of control on the population. We have positive checks and preventive checks. Malthus called anything that increased the death rate a positive check . . .

Maggie: Why?

Teacher: The other one is a preventive check and anything that is con-
          cerned with lowering the birth rate is preventive. Famine, war,
          and disease are considered positive checks because they hold the
          population down. Carol?

Carol: What were Malthus's preventive checks?

Teacher: Birth control is one although Malthus really didn't believe in it
          because of his background in the clergy and religious beliefs. He
          thought postponement of marriage was one way, also you've got
          to remember when he lived, 1766-1834. Birth control pills didn't
          exist and people didn't live as long. He said that if you postpone
          marriage . . . let's say a woman is fertile from the time she is
          say thirteen, fourteen until she's about forty, forty-five. Now you
          can see the tremendous amount of years as far as being fertile are
          concerned. Malthus is saying that if you postpone marriage until
          she is about thirty or thirty-five then chances are she'll have a
          small family.

Robin: Wouldn't it be better to use preventive measures rather than rely
          on positive? I mean like firemen. You fight a fire or you have the
          preventive measures?

At the outset of this dialogue, the teacher asks students to suggest
factors which may make a difference in the population growth rate.
The teacher is posing a problem for the students to consider and is asking a question that may lead to an opining or inquiry sequence. Students
offer two ways in which to control population: birth control and abortion. No one provides a justification as to why birth control might work,
but the teacher does ask the students to take a position regarding whether
or not abortion is a suitable way to control population growth. In short,
the teacher is moving the discussion toward an inquiry sequence. Several students feel that abortions are wrong and argue that they do not
provide a good solution to population control.

In arguing that abortions are wrong the students are defending their
position that abortions are not an effective way in which to limit growth
by taking another value position. Often classes will, as does this one,
pursue the subsidiary value position and examine its merits before going
back to the main position. The arguments surrounding the subsidiary
position that abortions are wrong are somewhat limited because there is
minimal effort to clarify the values underlying this position; instead,
students stress alternatives to abortion. It should be pointed out that one
of the weakest forms of support for one's position is to take another
position, especially if the second position is ungrounded, as in the case
here. It would have been more desirable if students had been able to
present data indicating that voluntary abortions would not make a significant impact on the population growth rate.

Don brings the discussion back to the main hypothesis by stating that if abortions were only limited to rape, they wouldn't do much to control the population. Up to this point the students and teacher have engaged in a brief inquiry sequence. The students have been giving reasons for their view that abortion is not a good way to control population.

Certainly, the class could go further in the testing of their hypotheses, but Maggie then changes the focus of the interaction by asking the teacher to clarify Malthus's concept of positive population checks. In so doing, she has initiated a new sequence—an expository sequence. The teacher responds with the information the student requests and then another student, Carol, asks for examples of what Malthus considered preventive checks, thus maintaining the expository sequence.

After the teacher explains Malthus's idea of preventive checks, Robin offers a new position concerning population control: that preventive checks on population are better than positive checks. This student has started a new sequence, which again has the potential to be an opining or inquiry sequence.

Though most discussions contain elements of all three cognitive interaction sequences, an observer who walks into a social studies class room and listens to an entire discussion would usually find that certain patterns dominate the dialogue. It is usually possible to identify rather distinct teaching styles and to categorize the discussions as expository, opining, or inquiry. In our research we have developed and used the Michigan Social Issues Cognitive Category System to interpret classroom discourse.[11] Based on the analysis of time spent by the class on given cognitive operations, classes that allot a major portion of their time presenting, clarifying, and supporting hypotheses, positions, or opinions are characterized as *inquiry* classes. Classes that spend the majority of their time presenting hypotheses or positions but do not devote much time to probing or grounding these positions are characterized as *opining*. In classes where most of the time is devoted to exposition and very little is given to either presenting or probing hypotheses, the discussion is categorized as *expository*.

SUMMARY

The discussion of interaction sequences in this chapter has emphasized the importance of the teacher in initiating and supporting student inquiry. It has been argued that, on the one hand, the teacher limits student

[11] Massialas, Sprague, Sweeney, *Structure and Process of Inquiry*, Vol. 1.

discussion and inquiry by lecturing or asking questions that require essentially one, usually remembered, answer. On the other hand, the teacher promotes higher cognitive levels of student participation and inquiry by using indirect influence *and* by asking questions that encourage students to generate, probe, and test hypotheses and positions. Teachers in both opining and inquiry classes use indirect influence, but in the inquiry class, after a student presents a hypothesis, one of three cognitive events frequently occurs: (1) the student spontaneously grounds his hypothesis, (2) another student asks him to defend or clarify his position, or (3) the teacher requests that the position be probed further. In opining classes, these three cognitive events rarely occur after a student presents a hypothesis.

The teacher who is committed to inquiry needs to be conscious of the direction classroom discussion takes and be prepared to intervene at propitious points, asking for clarification of ideas or the grounds that support them. In turn, the teacher needs to be constantly on the alert to make instructional decisions that are compatible with inquiry teaching.

In the past, most of the research comparing the effects of types of teaching styles has grouped opining and inquiry classes together. No wonder most studies that compared styles of teaching—for instance, "lecture" versus "inquiry"—failed to show any significant differences. In our experience we found that when the inquiry teacher is carefully identified, the results are indeed significant. Future studies ought to explore further this line of analysis of the teaching act.

3

inquiry into social values, feelings, and self: new helpful approaches

HUMANISTIC INSTRUCTION

Education in general and social studies instruction in particular are entering another new era. The "new social studies" approaches of the sixties are now being challenged to provide more humanistic learning experiences for the students of the seventies. Just as the challenges to science education were the result of such world events as the successful sputnik launching, the new thrusts toward humanistic instruction are the result of world events defined as inhumane or dehumanizing: racism, poverty, environmental "ecocide," and war. Any positive view toward the new challenges to education assumes not only that man can change his world for the betterment of humanity but that man believes such a goal is imperative.

Learning is relevant, and humanistic when it has meaning for the individual. Social studies is relevant when students have feelings about what they are studying. George Isaac Brown suggests that human learning must include feelings and emotions because educators have known for a long time the importance of personal involvement in learning. If an "emotional dimension" is added to learning, increased involvement and positive changes in the learner's behavior will probably ensue.[1]

In *Human Teaching for Human Learning*, Brown defines the integration of affective and cognitive types of learning as "confluent educa-

[1] George Isaac Brown, *Human Teaching for Human Learning* (New York: The Viking Press, 1971), p. 16.

tion"; and this confluence results in what he calls "human learning." Human learning emphasizes affective education, which includes such elements as emotions, feelings, values, attitudes, and concepts of self. It has the characteristics of fostering rational thinking, valuing, feeling, discovering, creating, and active involvement. It is also characterized by a sense of immediacy and by such personal factors as acceptance and empathy. Humanistic learning causes changes in the learner because of the frequent intense interactions between the learner and the environment, an environment that is filled not only with other people and buildings and trees but with emotions and sounds and symbols and art and ideas. Learning can be ecstatic because the "actual moment of learning is delightful." It is personal, it is meaningful, and it is enjoyable.[2]

Nonhumanistic behavior is described as narrow, closed, impersonal, and ingenuine, all of which restrict student thinking and valuing. Humanistic teacher behavior, on the other hand, is open, flexible, stimulating, personal, and genuine. Typical nonhumanistic teacher behavior might include comments like these:

> That topic is too far away from our four discussion topics. Let's leave that for some other time.
> Everyone will read pages 77-90 and answer the "checking your memory questions" on page 91.
> Today we are going to discuss the three causes of the Civil War.

In contrast, a humanistic design for classroom activities would be exemplified by such behaviors as:

> Write down on a slip of paper some of the topics and unanswered questions you would like to study next.
> Let's brainstorm together and try to think of as many solutions to this problem as we can.
> What interested you most about our trip to the newspaper office?
> Who would like to volunteer for our public interview today?
> How did that story make you feel?

Direct, straightforward answers to students' questions are "humanistic" when they help students achieve a larger, more important goal, such as locating supportive evidence for hypotheses, outlining a policy recommendation, or creating an individual project. When teachers provide correct spellings, specific detailed facts, directions, feedback on obser-

2 George B. Leonard, *Education and Ecstasy* (New York: Dell Publishing Co., 1968).

vations, and information related to procedures and memory while students are working on complex tasks, they are facilitating student inquiry and valuing by freeing student energy for higher level problem solving.[3]

Indirect answers and questions, as humanistic teacher responses, are often used to encourage students to clarify, think about, and go beyond their own question or idea. Sometimes teachers should "count to ten" when they hear student questions in order to resist the impulse to give them all the answers and to think about a more stimulating response.[4] Many proponents of humanistic instruction suggest that teachers be less directive and less prescriptive in their interaction with students and more receptive, facilitating, positive, and genuine. Such teacher behavior increases humanistic behaviors in and out of the classroom.

SOCIAL INQUIRY:
A HUMANISTIC APPROACH TO LEARNING

In an inquiry-oriented social studies classroom, students and teachers alike are active participants in the search for an understanding of human behavior, human feelings, and human values. Together they seek answers to a variety of questions about the world around them. They not only explore ideas, values, and emotions, but think independently, evaluate, and feel. It is through the process of social inquiry that subject matter, thinking, valuing, and feeling "flow together into human learning."

To encourage and facilitate human learning, inquiry teachers should confront students with relevant and personally involving learning experiences. They should also establish a flexible pattern of questioning for both teacher and student. The questions themselves should elicit responses that will result in (1) clarification of ideas, values, and emotions; (2) formation of meaningful hypotheses and generalizations; (3) presentation of defensible value positions and judgments; (4) formulation of logical explanations and predictions; and (5) consideration of the four preceding results from the standpoint of the grounds that support them.

Teachers are well aware that the evidence for well composed and conducted lessons is more often found in the questions raised than in the answers given. A sample of a flexible pattern of questioning for social inquiry by the humanistic teacher is given below. It includes the following general categories of questions: informational, hypothesizing and defining, normative, feeling and value clarifying, and probing.

[3] Ibid., p. 37.
[4] Ibid., p. 38.

A Pattern of Questions
For Human Learning
Through Social Inquiry

Informational: What can you find out?

Who were some of the leaders of the American Revolution?
What factors cause people to migrate from place to place?
When did the Industrial Revolution begin to gain momentum?
How do African tribes celebrate their holidays?
Where are Americans moving today?
What is this song really about?

Hypothesizing and Defining: What do you think?

Why do people become violent?
When are people most likely to cooperate with one another? Why do you
    think so?
How are people from the two cultures different? How are they similar?
    Explain.
What does the idea "democracy" mean to you? Explain and give ex-
    amples.
Why are some people's incomes higher than others?
What have you learned about human beings today?
If that is true, what might happen in the future? Why?
What are the characteristics of all dictatorships?
What are some examples of prejudice in our lives?

Normative: What ought to be?

What should the president do? Why?
Which is the best plan? Why?
What would be right? Why?
How should people act? Why?
When do you believe the government should intervene? Why?
Is that a good way to do it? Why or why not?

Feeling and value clarifying: How do you feel and what do *you*
believe or value?

What do you feel like after doing something silly in front of other people?
    Why?

How would you feel during the trial if you were William Penn? Why
   would you feel that way?

What is your attitude toward someone like that? Why?

How might a prisoner have felt? Why do you think so?

When might people feel like that? Why?

How do you feel when that happens? Why?

What have you discovered about yourself?

What have you found out about other people?

How long have you believed this?

Have you considered any or all other alternatives?

Is that something you are proud of?

How have you acted on your beliefs?

Probing: What reasons can you give?

(See all the "whys" and the "explains" after each question above).

Why do you think that is true?

Can you give examples of that idea?

What would happen if everyone acted or believed that way?

Have you ever had that happen to you or to someone you know?

Who supports what you say? Can you think of reasons for or against
   Johnny's proposal?

What are the consequences that might come from that policy?

What criteria did you use to judge that decision?

How can you prove that?

What makes you think so?

Informational questions encourage orientation toward the specific
and general data, ideas, opinions, judgments, positions and emotions contained in the learning materials and activities, be they case studies, films,
text readings, simulations, role plays, or other learning encounters. They
are often aimed at identifying and defining problems and issues. The
hypothesizing and defining questions ask students to define important
concepts, state hypotheses, make meaningful comparisons, analyze data,
explain, predict, and draw logical conclusions. Normative questions are
aimed at getting students to offer value positions and judgments about
human behavior and social institutions; normative questions are intended
to encourage students to take a stand on important problems and issues.
Feeling and value-clarifying questions are designed to have students explore their personal feelings, emotions, and beliefs as well as empathize
with those of other people. Students should always be asked to share their
feelings if they want to but never be forced to "open up" in front of the

entire class. Some educators suggest that much of the "value clarification" in the classroom can be done with students individually.[5]

Probing questions are the most important for effective inquiry. They encourage students to clarify, support, and justify with evidence their ideas, hypotheses, value positions, judgments, predictions, and conclusions. Probing questions ask students to "dig a little deeper" into subject matter, social science procedures, experiences, ideas, values, and emotions that are relevant to the problem under examination. In this way, probing questions lead to meaningful learning. Without them, classroom inquiries become exercises in letting off steam or "shooting the bull."

Social inquiry is humanistic because it leads to confluent education. Inquiry teaching stimulates and facilitates the natural flowing together of subject matter, thinking, valuing, feeling, creativity, and active personal involvement.

Other New Approaches

There are new approaches to values and social issues that offer teachers any number of alternatives in providing instruction to students about values. In implementing social inquiry in the classroom, the teacher may be forced to use different techniques to initiate and sustain student interest. Often one technique may not appeal to all students or may not fit into the teaching situation or the teacher's own style. Two of these new techniques are value analysis and value clarification. Both are discussed below. The first focuses upon inquiry into value concepts and the testing of "generalizable and repetitive concepts" (generalizations and value statements) with "unique and nonrepetitive" concepts (facts or data).[6] There is a systematic analysis of value concepts and policy decisions.[7] There is also an attempt in this approach to generate doubt in students as they are "caught" in situations emanating from problematic areas of our culture where there are value conflicts. The second approach stresses the use of free and open discussion which leads to examining and clarifying beliefs and values held by members of a group.[8]

VALUE ANALYSIS

Student inquiry often uncovers value-laden concepts and what might be called "cue concepts." Value concepts include such ideas as "equality,"

[5] Louis E. Raths, Merrill Harmin, and Sidney B. Simon, *Values and Teaching* (Columbus, Ohio: Charles E. Merrill Publishing Co., 1966).

[6] John T. Mallan and Richard Hersh, *No G.O.D.s in the Classroom: Inquiry into Inquiry* (Philadelphia: W. B. Saunders Co., 1972).

[7] Maurice P. Hunt and Lawrence E. Metcalf, *Teaching High School Social Studies* (New York: Harper & Row, 1968).

[8] Raths et al., *Values and Teaching*.

"good citizen," "peace," "justice" and "individualism." Cue concepts, according to John Mallan and Richard Hersh, refer to ideas or groups of things. Terms like "democracy," "citizen," "government," and "scarcity" are cue concepts. Both value and cue concepts do not tell us very much, and they are not in a form that can be easily tested. But they involve data and ideas and relationships that can be tested and supported by evidence. In the words of Mallan and Hersh:

> The term democracy implies a host of data and relationships. But the data and the organization are not explicit. We have to view the term simply as a "cue" concept—it cues us into other concepts but, in and of itself, it denotes no explicit data or organizatio̶ of relationships. In its existing form, the term does not lend itself to testing through any evidence. We would have to go beyond the term before we could get a concept to teach.[9]

This "going beyond" a cue or value concept implies that both student and teacher have to discover and state generalizations, which when subjected to data or evidence can be tentatively accepted, rejected or modified. For example, if democracy is the cue concept being explored in a class inquiry, the teacher might ask questions that would elicit generalizations leading to the definition of the concept "democratic governments." Sample questions that would prompt a definition of the concept of democracy might include:

> What do all the democracies we have studied have in common?
> What is the relationship between political power, government, and the people in any democracy?
> What are constitutional democracies?
> Where is the source of power in constitutional democracies?

In response to these questions students might offer any number of defining or descriptive generalizations about the characteristics of democracies. For instance, they might hypothesize:

> Democratic governments are based upon the principle that political power arises from, and only from, the consent of the governed.
> Democracies are governments of, by, and for the people.
> Constitutional democracies are founded on both written and unwritten rules and established rights for their citizens.
> Democratic governments generally favor laws that apply equally to all citizens.

[9] Mallan and Hersh, *No G.O.D.s in Classroom,* pp. 156-157.

The teacher should also ask questions that would probe students and lead to explicit statements of their criteria for making value judgments. The simple question, "What do you mean by a good citizen?" opens up the process of social inquiry sparked by such an initial student remark as "He was a good citizen." Student responses should then be encouraged to state generalizations or, in this case, "value criteria" for what is meant by the value concept, "good citizen." Value criteria are standards by which priorities are measured. They are generally used to appraise the worth of something, whereas defining generalizations refer to the characteristics of a specific class of phenomena.

Student responses to the question, "what do you mean by a good citizen?" would naturally take many forms, depending upon the value criteria they and other people use to judge citizens. For instance, the value criteria below were taken from a seventh-grade class inquiry into citizen participation:

> Good citizens are active in political affairs.
>
> Good citizens keep up with current happenings.
>
> Good citizens obey laws or try legally to change laws they think are unfair.
>
> Good citizens do not infringe upon the legal rights of others.
>
> Good citizens think about the qualifications of leaders they select to run their government.
>
> Good citizens stand up against things that are wrong or unfair.

Not only should students be encouraged to state value criteria, they should also be encouraged to offer value positions (what should or ought to be) and make recommendations on policy (courses of action). By asking "normative questions" similar to the three that follow, the teacher can also stimulate students into making value judgments and taking positions and recommending policies.

> How should local governments try to develop good citizens? Why do you think so?
>
> Do you think excluding groups of people who are not "good citizens" from voting should be continued? Explain.
>
> If you were a political leader, what recommendations would you make to Congress about voting laws and campaign rules? Why?

Finally, just because class inquiry is dealing with value concepts, the teacher need not ignore social science generalizations—what Mallan and Hersh refer to as "generalizable and repeatable concepts." For instance, teachers might ask students to state testable hypotheses—hypotheses, in other words, that are explanatory, predictive, conditional, or "if-then" in nature. Such questions could include:

How are decisions usually made in a representative political system?

Why might education be an important element of democracies?

Why might people in democratic political systems be able to make individual decisions in many areas of society?

These questions are intended to initiate student hypothesizing so essential in establishing testable relationships about value concepts and phenomena. Here are three possible hypotheses:

If a society has a representative form of government, then major political decisions are usually based upon the will of the majority.

If a political system is democratic, then it will demand a high degree of political awareness and active participation on the part of its citizens.

Political systems in which each individual citizen plays an important and active part and is given a high degree of freedom are generally characteristic of cultures that also allow a high degree of freedom in all aspects of life.

In practical terms, the teacher takes advantage of the students' interest during the inquiry process into values in order to encourage them to: (1) define major concepts; (2) state value criteria, especially their own, for making judgments; (3) take value positions and make policy recommendations; (4) make generalizations from related concepts; and (5) collect, analyze, and apply relevant and valid evidence. Throughout class inquiry, which may last several weeks, both teacher and students are analyzing the meaning of value concepts and are stating various relationships between man and his world that are then subject to testing against evidence.

In planning their courses, social studies teachers should collect, adapt, and create materials and learning activities that will promote social inquiry, that will result in students developing values of their own and acting upon them inside and outside the classroom. As we mentioned before, the processes of valuing include examining alternatives, identifying the consequences of holding certain values, choosing values freely, stating value positions in public, acting consistently with expressed values, identifying interpersonal and intrapersonal conflicts, being open and honest with oneself, and grounding values with defensible evidence.

The selection below, adapted from *The Congressional Record,* is a good example of how a simple story can be used to stimulate student inquiry about and into values. The story can serve as a springboard for students to inquire not only into the values of other people but into their own values and those of their classmates, community, and society. The questions following the story demonstrate some of the types of queries teachers can pose during student discussions; small group or individual research, data collection, and analysis activities; and other teacher-student interactions. These questions, which are designed to promote valuing processes through value analysis, are broken down into defining, value-criteria, normative, feeling, and hypothesizing and defining categories.

I WALKED IN HIS MOCCASINS
by Laura B. Jones

This story was written by a woman who worked with people in Alaska. She was a teacher and leader of other teachers for 15 years. The story was written in 1952. Do you think it still means something today?

Some people make fun of others without understanding them. Some laugh at people without feeling. Some tease others without being kind. Some people judge others only by what they look like. The Eskimos say that these people should "for two moons walk in my moccasins."

For two moons, I walked in his moccasins. Happily, tiredly, and sadly I walked. I walked along the far away trails and the old paths. Wearing the Eskimo's moccasins, I learned many things.

I learned that all men are the same. It is the same things that make all men sad. Some men have dry eyes and are quiet. Others have tears and moans. The death of a loved one can be told by tom-toms, the smoke of a fire, or a sad group walking along the street. All men feel sadness.

It is the same things that make men happy. Some men laugh, some men chuckle, and others just smile. A mother is happy when her baby takes his first step. You can see it in her face. A father is proud when his son shows courage. These feelings are the same in all countries.

Far out on the trail one day, I met a man. He offered me five beaver skins for my knife. I told him "no." He answered, "Here on the trail your cheap knife is worth very much. Back in town, it is worth only two dollars."

Then I saw that the true value of anything comes from what man needs. I saw, too, that sometimes man does not get what he needs. Then men can be violent towards one another.

I was once alone and lost in a storm on the tundra. A boy found me and led me to safety. He spoke no English. I found out the true meaning of education. A man is not stupid just because he does not know what I know. A man is stupid only when he does not know what he needs to know.

I learned that no man alone knows beauty. No man alone has happiness. The Red man's sky is just as blue. The yellow man's sun is just as warm. The Black man's stars are just as bright. The white man's grass is just as green. Beauty is for all men. Happiness at the end of a long day is not given to only some colors or to some races.

There was a time that the moccasins I wore kept me from going places. A sign on a door told me "no." I learned that there are men who do not believe that all men are equal. There are men who only talk about the rights of other men. I saw that all men are the same. Most men are good. Some make up stories about how people are not equal to each other.

I learned too, that sometimes men are blind and foolish. They sing of peace on earth. They pray for peace. But they look for peace with bombs and war. This kind of peace does not stay.

We want peace forever. We want peace made of good will among men. It is seeing that men are the same that makes good will. Understanding why men look and act different leads to peace.

Yes, for two moons I walked in his moccasins. Wearing them, I learned many things.[10]

Value-Oriented Questions

Defining Questions:

1. What does the statement, "walk in his moccasins," really mean?
2. What is "peace"?
3. How would you define "education"?
4. What are the characteristics of actions that are prejudicial?
5. Can you give any examples of actions that are prejudicial?

Value-Criteria Questions:

1. What makes someone a "kind" person? Explain.
2. In what ways are all people equal? Why?
3. Are most men good? What makes any person a "good" person? Explain and give examples.
4. How do people judge the worth of others?
5. What is a foolish person? Why do you think so?
6. What makes something beautiful? Why?

Normative Questions:

1. Should all people be at peace? Why or why not?
2. Should we all try to walk in other people's shoes? Explain. How could we best walk in another person's shoes?
3. How might prejudice and hate be ended? Why do you think so?
4. If you were in a situation where people were showing prejudice toward others, what ought you to do? Explain.

[10] Laura B. Jones, *Congressional Record—Senate* Vol. 118, No. 84, pp. S8361-S8362.

Feeling Questions:

1. How does this story make you feel? Why?
2. How do you feel when someone shows prejudice against you?
3. How do you feel when you realize that you have shown prejudice against someone? Why?

Hypothesizing and Defining Questions:

1. What is this story really about?
2. Does anything seem to be wrong? Why do you think so?
3. Would people really learn from "walking in other people's moccasins"? Explain.
4. Why might people tease and make fun of others? Can you cite some examples?
5. Why are some people prejudiced against other people?
6. Why do some people believe that everyone is created equal? Why do others believe that everyone is not created equal?
7. How might man ever achieve world peace?
8. What other information might we obtain from this story?
9. What have we learned about people and prejudice today?
10. What would you like to study next?

Sample Activities

Social inquiry is more than just inductive discussion in which problems are defined, hypotheses stated, and values clarified. Once the initial activities have stimulated student interest, thinking, and valuing, the real work begins. Data must be collected and carefully analyzed so that scholarly grounding, probing, challenging, and testing follow hypothesizing and position taking. Subsequent lessons must confront students with activities where they apply new ideas, to better predict, explain, and describe human behavior in more complex situations.

After a class discussion of Laura Jones's story, student thinking and valuing might be further stimulated by various activities, some examples of which are listed below. Many of the preceding questions might be asked or reexamined during student participation in these activities.

Reading case studies involving prejudice and discrimination against blacks, migrants, Jews, women, the aged, Protestants in Ireland, and other minority groups around the world.

Examining federal laws that pertain to discriminatory practices against minority groups (Supreme Court decisions, immigration laws, for example).

Role-playing situations and data presentation skits depicting situations where discrimination is practiced openly.

Analyzing personal accounts of prejudice.

Responding to a number of value clarification exercises related to equality.

Researching individually one specific example of prejudice.

Analyzing open-ended pictures related to inter-culture dating and marriage.

Analyzing charts and graphs comparing income of blacks and whites and of males and females in the same jobs.

Writing essays or creative stories.

Listening to historical and popular songs related to prejudice.

Studying current and historical literature related to women's rights.

Discovery or guided discovery is an important method that teachers should bear in mind when organizing materials, activities, and questions. Giving a few cues, instead of all the answers, leads to student motivation, involvement, thinking, and valuing. That is, rather than tell students all the answers and then have them locate these answers again in textbooks, documents, games, charts, and other materials, teachers should purposefully put students in situations where they are "in the dark," where they do not have all the facts or all the answers. Only in this way can students develop and practice inquiry and valuing skills while discovering important concepts, generalizations, and solutions.

Many teachers use charts, tables, and graphs in their classrooms, and many are placed in social studies textbooks. Generally, these materials are clearly titled and carefully described so that students do not "miss the point." The teacher employing the discovery principle, however, realizes the need for students to become involved (cognitively or emotionally or both) with the data in the chart, table, graph, or other source material. Therefore, rather than give the students a long introduction which might tell them the historical background, significance, and the exact meaning of the data, the discovery-oriented teacher presents the data as though they were a cue and then asks for student ideas about their meaning and significance. The chart below was developed by a student teacher introducing the topic of population:

Year	Population	Food Supply
1800	1,000,000	1,000,000
1825	2,000,000	2,000,000
1850	4,000,000	3,000,000
1875	8,000,000	4,000,000
1900	16,000,000	5,000,000
1925	32,000,000	6,000,000
1950	64,000,000	7,000,000
1975	128,000,000	8,000,000
2000	256,000,000	9,000,000

Can you see the impulse of some teachers to use this table as a visual aid to accompany a lecture rather than as a tool for discovery? The student teacher showed the chart to her students and asked:

What is this chart about?

If it is true, what does it say about our future? Why do you think so?

Do you think the chart may be true? Why or why not?

What should people do, if it is true? Why?

What recommendations would you make to our government and other governments around the world? Why?

How does this information make you feel? Why?

What other information do we need?

Where can we get it?

What related ideas and topics would you like to study now? Why?

These and similar questions can be used in a number of patterns to initiate and sustain social inquiry in the classroom. Much of the success of inquiry teaching, and the use of the discovery principle, is contingent upon the teacher having clear, identified goals for a study unit, a commitment to exploring alternatives, skill in posing questions, motivating materials and activities, and a sixth sense for gauging the mood and direction of students.

Teachers must also try to develop skills in posing a variety of questions, even though they themselves may not have all the answers. Open-ended, or divergent, questions are often posed during inquiry not only because they result in many possible alternative answers but because they "open up" student thinking, valuing, and exploration. The difference between the two sets of questions below is obvious, especially when we anticipate the possible student responses to each set:

Divergent	Narrow
How might people feel in similar instances?	How did the boy feel in the story?
Why do people like one another?	Why did the boy say he liked Ann?
Why do people dislike one another?	Who disliked the old man?
How do you feel about what happened?	When did they start to like him?
What would you have done?	

Sometimes questions are posed that have a small range of alternatives so that student attention is focused upon a particular problem, issue, or topic. For example, a teacher may want to ask a question about the particular feelings or values of a specific group of people: "How do you think the Quakers felt about the trial?" "What recommendations did the Populists make?" In combination with divergent questions, more focused, or convergent, questions lead to a greater in-depth analysis of feelings, emotions, values, policy statements, judgments, and value criteria. The teacher can, therefore, use both divergent and convergent questions to generate alternatives for exploration.

VALUE CLARIFICATION

One of the most popular new approaches to social issues and affective education is value clarification. It is an approach based upon the work of Louis Raths and his associates,[11] who in turn extended the work of John Dewey. Unlike other approaches to the teaching of values, value clarification is not concerned with the final product—the content of peoples' values—but with the valuing process, with the procedures through which values are acquired, held, and acted upon.

The need for such an approach to values in the schools is rooted in the complex world in which students live, where there is widespread confusion over values, a multitude of influences, and a great necessity for making rational responsible choices. The proponents of value clarification take the position that children are ultimately free to choose what ever values and advice they want to follow.

Raths and his colleagues point to the many elements of contemporary life and world affairs that make it increasingly difficult for children—and adults, too, for that matter—to acquire a consistent, clear set of personal values. They identify such factors as broken homes, the tremendous potency of mass communication, technological innovations, rapid social change, the decline in influence of religious traditions, shocking world events, and the values held by extremists of society as being correlated with value confusion and inconsistency.[12] In such a chaotic world, many adults moralize about what values children should hold, simply because there are so many different opinions and living examples to follow. There are also adults who believe that children need some assistance in building their own value system just as they are aided in building their own ideas and thinking processes through an inquiry approach. According to Simon, Home, and Kirschenbaum, students need an approach to values that will help them cope with and resolve some of the difficult problems and situations with which they are faced:

[11] Raths et al., *Values and Teaching.*
[12] Ibid., p. 15.

How is the young person to sort out all the pros and cons and achieve his own values? When it comes time to choose an occupation or a spouse, or a candidate, or to decide how far to go in the back seat of a car on a Saturday night date, how does the young person choose his own course of action from among the many models and many moralizing lectures with which he has been bombarded? Where does he learn whether he wants to stick to the old moral and ethical standards or try new ones? How does he develop his own sense of identity? How does he learn to relate to people whose values differ from his own? [13]

Value clarification or valuing, according to Raths and his associates, consists of seven processes under the three general actions of prizing, choosing, and acting on one's values. They outline the processes as follow:

A. Prizing one's values and actions
  1. Prizing and cherishing.
  2. Publicly affirming, when appropriate.
B. Choosing one's beliefs and actions
  3. Choosing from alternatives.
  4. Choosing after consideration of consequences.
  5. Choosing freely.
C. Acting on one's values
  6. Acting.
  7. Acting with a pattern, acting consistently, repeating one's actions.[14]

The value-clarification approach does not try to inculcate any particular set of values. Rather, its purpose is to encourage student application of the seven processes of valuing listed above; in other words, it involves students in the use of cognitive and affective processes to develop ideas and values of their own. Similar to the process of inquiry, value clarification confronts students with real-life issues and asks them to think, to identify philosophical arguments, and to draw their own conclusions. One might view it as an inquiry into one's own values when confronted with the real value conflicts that daily life—or the classroom—offers. During lessons aimed at value-clarification the student is continually urged to look inside himself and ask: "What do I believe?" "Where do my values come from?" "Why do I hold them?" "Do I talk and act in a manner consistent with my values?" "What are the implications and consequences of holding and acting on these values?" The role of the teacher in value clarification, as in social inquiry, is that of planner, of introducer, of questioner and sustainer, and of investigator.

[13] Sidney B. Simon, Leland W. Home, and Howard Kirschenbaum, *Values Clarification* (New York: Hart Publishing Co., 1972), p. 18.
[14] Adapted from Raths et al., *Values and Teaching*, p. 30.

Simon and his colleagues have defined the goal of the teacher during value clarification as that of helper. The teacher assists students in the use of the seven processes of valuing in their own lives and in applying the processes to the beliefs they already hold and to those they are still considering.[15] Teachers committed to value clarification in their classrooms have three alternatives in planning their learning activities. They can set aside specific times for valuing exercises; they can combine value clarification with whatever topic from the standard curriculum is under consideration; or they can combine the valuing processes with the reflective processes of inquiry where students search for solutions to problems and for relevant data to support their ideas and hypotheses. In this way, students can be involved in a search for knowledge and a search for their own values at the same time. Reflective thinking and value clarification can best be stimulated through problems, issues, and questions related to such areas as politics, race, friendship, the law, family, religion, and economics—areas of our culture where discrepancies in data and opinion exist right along with confusion and conflict over values. However, teachers who choose to include value clarification as one element of their objectives must assume tremendous responsibility and demonstrate professional discretion. Large group "valuing" sessions are extremely difficult to lead effectively and value clarification takes time and careful planning and execution. Too often value clarification activities are used as time-filling exercises rather than as a systematic, concerted effort throughout the school year or entire school curriculum.

In an inquiry into the topic of religious persecution and migration, for example, students would most likely explore data, concepts, and generalizations related to prejudice, social pressure, conflict, intolerance, freedom, violence, travel barriers, transportation, and religious beliefs. Simultaneously, they could be clarifying their own values by taking value positions, examining the consequences of religious persecution and hatred, and carefully analyzing the bases of their own beliefs and actions. The teacher acts as questioner during inquiry—"Why might the Quakers have moved?" "Does this happen often? Explain." "Why do people feel that way?" "What were some of the Quakers' beliefs?" "Why did they hold them?" The teacher can also serve as value clarifier by interjecting clarifying questions along the lines suggested by Raths, Harmin, and Simon.[16] Such questions avoid making any positive or negative judgments on students' remarks that directly reflect their values; they are

[15] Simon et al., *Values Clarification*, p. 20.

[16] Raths et al., *Values and Teaching*, pp. 260-261. In *Values and Teaching* and *Values Clarification* there is a wealth of practical suggestions for value-clarification activities in the classroom. Most of the suggestions are useful for all grades and all subjects and are similar to the design of inquiry materials discussed here in Chapter 5.

open-ended, nonjudgmental, and related to the seven valuing processes outlined above. Here are a few examples:

> Do you really want to? How long have you thought so?
> Were you free to decide?
> What alternatives did you consider?
> What may happen if you don't?
> Have you ever really thought about it?
> What have you done about it?
> Just how important is that?
> How often do you do it?
> Should everyone act that way?
> Do you act that way often?
> Are there any other ways to do it?
> Would you recommend that to other people?
> Are you proud of that?
> Who else have you told about this?
> What would happen if everyone believed (acted) this way?

There are many techniques for clarifying student values, and almost all of them confront students with real or contrived situations where values can be identified and clarified. According to Raths, Harmin, and Simon, the teacher can systematically use a number of techniques to engage students in all of the seven value clarifying processes.[17] Teachers should also keep in mind that in many classes students are asked to state their values but are not probed for reasons and for the consequences of their beliefs and actions. If this occurs, little value clarification is taking place and students may develop casual or combative approaches to valuing.

Throughout value clarification, the teacher poses nonthreatening and nondirective questions asking students to consider their own values:

1. Were they chosen freely?
2. Were they chosen from alternatives?
3. Were they chosen after careful consideration of the consequences of the alternatives?
4. Are they prized and cherished?
5. Are they publicly affirmed in appropriate situations?
6. Are they acted upon?
7. Are they acted upon consistently?

[17] Raths et al., *Values and Teaching*, Chapters 6 and 7.

Value clarification does not attempt to instill any particular set of values but aims to encourage and assist students in using the seven processes of valuing in solving their personal value problems. Teachers will find that most of their value-clarifying responses can be in notes to students on essays or projects, brief one-to-one dialogues before or after class, or in other personal interactions with individuals or small groups of students.

Research on Value Clarification

What little research there is related to the use of value clarification in actual classrooms seems to have positive results. According to Simon, Home, and Kirschenbaum, there is a small amount of empirical research indicating that students exposed to this approach have become less apathetic, less flighty, less conforming as well as less contentious. They also claim that value clarification has led to better success in school for under-achieving students.[18]

Lawrence Gagnon, in examining the results of questions designed to help students clarify their values, employed techniques in one group that involved questions aimed at other outcomes than value clarification. In a second group he used questions that helped students clarify their own ideas and values. He found that students in the group in which a high incidence of clarifying questions were posed participated to a significantly greater degree in discussions and scored higher on a written critical-thinking test than those in the classroom where few clarifying questions were asked.[19]

In an earlier study by James Raths, 100 students in four grades of an elementary school were evaluated by teachers in the following dimensions:

Attitudes toward learning.
Perseverance.
Active participation.
Raising of questions and alternatives.
Initiation and self-direction.

Four teachers then conducted a program throughout the year that emphasized elements of value clarification. At the end of the year, a final rating showed that 88 out of 100 students made gains on all of the rating dimensions.[20]

[18] Simon et al., *Values Clarification*, p. 20.
[19] Lawrence Gagnon, "An Analysis of an Experimental Methodology for Teaching, Thinking and Clarifying Values" (Ph.D. diss., Wayne State University, 1965).
[20] James Raths, "Clarifying Children's Values," *The National Elementary Principal* 42 (November, 1962): 35-39.

SUMMARY

Social studies education can be viewed in many ways: learning about social science knowledge, using social science knowledge, learning about thinking processes, using thinking processes, learning about values, learning to value, learning about decision making and making decisions. Social inquiry stresses the use of thinking and valuing processes to discover and use social science knowledge as it relates to public and personal problems and social issues. Social inquiry also focuses on the study of values as they relate to people and their problems as well as on the development of the student's own values and ideas and the processes through which they are acquired, questioned, and grounded. Finally, social inquiry attempts to build a free and open atmosphere where students can think, use their knowledge, discuss public controversy, and make decisions instead of just studying *about* issues and social science.

Throughout the conduct of social inquiry, teachers deal with concepts, generalizations, beliefs and values, positions and judgments, opinions, controversy and evidence (and the search for and validation of evidence). The approaches in this chapter provide teachers with alternatives for planning and carrying out classroom activities directed at value problems, public issues, and personal value conflicts.

4

the dialogue of social inquiry: classroom examples

Inquiry into social issues begins with a springboard related to a social issue. The springboard should establish a problematic situation that interests the students and provokes them to go deeper into the social issue for themelves. The students examine the issue by clarifying its dimensions, generating hypotheses or positions, and then testing their hypotheses or positions in relation to values, logic, and factual evidence.

Social issues may be introduced to a class as discovery episodes, analytical episodes or prescriptive episodes. In discovery episodes the students figure out for themselves that certain social issues have existed or do exist. In analytical episodes they try to establish the causes of and reasons for a particular social issue or problem. Prescriptive episodes are the most value-laden in that they focus on desirable courses of action to resolve a social issue. A summary of these types of inquiry episodes, which will be discussed in this chapter, may be found in Figure 4:1. Note that the figure makes a distinction between historical and current social issues.

Often teachers think of social issues as only current conflicts, but in actuality the springboard may deal with a historical as well as a current issue. Many historical questions are important, yet remain unresolved. Questions such as, "Why did the stock market crash?" or "Should the United States have dropped the atomic bomb on Hiroshima and Nagasaki?" are still debated by scholars, and answers to these questions have implications for today's society. If history and great literature are placed in a social-issue context, students are encouraged not only to think as

	DISCOVERY	ANALYTICAL	PRESCRIPTIVE
HISTORICAL	WHAT WAS "How were American Indians treated in U.S. History?"	WHAT CAUSED WHAT WAS "Why were Indians treated certain ways by the U.S. Government?"	WHAT SHOULD HAVE BEEN OR SHOULD HAVE BEEN DONE "How should the U.S. Government have treated the American Indians?"
CURRENT	WHAT IS "What are the effects of pollution?"	WHAT CAUSE WHAT IS "What causes pollution?"	WHAT SHOULD BE OR SHOULD BE DONE "What should be done about pollution?"

FIGURE 4:1
Types of Inquiry Episodes for Social Issues

historians and literary scholars but also to participate in decision making on social policy.

The remainder of this chapter presents examples of discovery, analytical, and prescriptive episodes that took place in three different classes. Certainly there is some unavoidable overlap among these main categories but we tried to identify tendencies in the episodes and to group them accordingly. The class discussions were tape-recorded and transcribed. Selected parts of the transcription are given.

DISCOVERY EPISODES

In a discovery episode students determine for themselves the existence and dimensions of a social issue. A chart showing crime statistics in the United States for each of the last five years may serve as a springboard for such an episode. As students interpret the statistics, they perceive that violent crimes are on the rise and for the first time (for many of them) realize that crime is a problem in the United States. In discussing the chart they may try to make sense of the statistics and hypothesize about possible relationships in the data. They may wish to search out other information about crime, such as who commits what types of crime and what locales have the highest crime rate. Although the increase of crime may be a well-known social problem for sociologists and others, it may be a new insight for students. When students are able to figure out information themselves and make plausible hypotheses about data before them, they are discovering relationships in their world.

The following discovery episode took place in a high-school government class studying the United States judicial system. The class was composed of 27 high-school juniors with an IQ range of 80 to 140. The socio-economic background of the students was middle class, but the class contained a diverse group of youngsters; some had been in juvenile court and in jail for various offenses and others were school leaders who had never had any experience with the law or juvenile court. The students had been together as a class for about six months and were usually introduced to a new topic by some type of discovery springboard. They had already dealt with the executive and legislative branches of government and had experience analyzing decision-making processes. The course did not use a textbook but relied primarily on case studies, tapping both primary and secondary sources. Social issues had been discussed throughout. When a new discovery episode was introduced, students were asked to react to the springboard, share their information, and develop directions for future study of the issue. The teacher was primarily nondirective, but did moderate the discussion, and actively encouraged students to pursue the logical and value ramifications of their hypotheses and positions. Also, in this particular case, the teacher helped the students with the meaning of certain legal terms.

As a springboard for this episode the teacher asked the students to read the following case study about Gerald Francis Gault.[1] The students spent fifteen minutes doing so in class and then were asked to figure out why the Gaults were appealing to the United States Supreme Court. While the students read the case, they asked their friends or the teacher to explain certain legal terms.[2] Their discussion of the Gault case took place during two classroom periods, comments about which follow the recorded dialogue of each session.

> On Monday, June 8, 1964, at about 10 A.M., Gerald Francis Gault and a friend, Ronald Lewis, were taken into custody by the Sheriff of Gila County. Gerald was then still subject to a six months' probation order which had been entered on February 25, 1964, as a result of his having been in the company of another boy who had stolen a wallet from a lady's purse. The police action on June 8 was taken as the result of a verbal complaint by a neighbor of the boys, Mrs. Cook, about a telephone call made to her in which the caller or callers made lewd or indecent remarks. It will suffice for purposes of this opinion to say that the remarks or questions put to her were of the irritatingly offensive, adolescent, sex variety.
>
> At the time Gerald was picked up, his mother and father were

[1] This case study was excerpted from William F. Eagen and Michael P. Litka, "The Gault Case," Case Study 12 of the *Judgment* series (Washington D.C.: National Council for the Social Studies, 1968).

[2] The legal terms defined during the reading period were: petition, writ of habeaus corpus, affidavit, complainant, probation officer, and detention home.

both at work. No notice that Gerald was being taken into custody was left at the home. No other steps were taken to advise them that their son had, in effect, been arrested. Gerald was taken to the Children's Detention Home. When his mother arrived home about 6 o'clock, Gerald was not there. Gerald's older brother was sent to look for him at the trailer home of the Lewis family. He apparently learned then that Gerald was in custody. He so informed his mother. The two of them went to the Detention Home. The deputy probation officer, Flagg, who was also superintendent of the Detention Home, told Mrs. Gault "why Jerry was there" and said that a hearing would be held in Juvenile Court at 3 o'clock the following day, June 9.

Officer Flagg filed a petition with the court on the hearing day, June 9, 1964. It was not served on the Gaults. Indeed none of them saw this petition until the habeas corpus hearing on August 17, 1964. The petition was entirely formal. It made no reference to any factual basis for the judicial action which it initiated. It recited only that "said minor is under the age of 18 years, and is in need of the protection of this Honorable Court; (and that) said minor is a delinquent minor." It prayed for a hearing and an order regarding "the care and custody of said minor." Officer Flagg executed a formal affidavit in support of the petition.

On June 9, Gerald, his mother, his older brother, and Probation Officers Flagg and Henderson appeared before the Juvenile Judge in chambers. Gerald's father was not there. He was at work out of the city. Mrs. Cook, the complainant, was not there. No one was sworn at this hearing. No transcript or recording was made. No memorandum or record of the substance of the proceedings was prepared. Our information about the proceedings and the subsequent hearing on June 15, derives entirely from the testimony of the Juvenile Court Judge, Mr. and Mrs. Gault and Officer Flagg at the habeas corpus proceeding conducted two months later. From this, it appears that at the June 9 hearing Gerald was questioned by the judge about the telephone call. There was conflict as to what he said. His mother recalled that Gerald said he only dialed Mrs. Cook's number and handed the telephone to his friend, Ronald. Officer Flagg recalled that Gerald had admitted making the lewd remarks. Judge McGhee testified that Gerald "admitted making one of these (lewd) statements." At the conclusion of the hearing, the judge said he would "think about it." Gerald was taken back to the Detention Home. He was not sent to his own home with his parents. On June 11 or 12, after having been detained since June 8, Gerald was released and driven home. There is no explanation in the record as to why he was kept in the Detention Home or why he was released. At 5 P.M. on the day of Gerald's release, Mrs. Gault received a note signed by Officer Flagg. It was on plain paper, not letterhead. Its entire text was as follows:

"Mrs. Gault:

"Judge McGhee has set Monday, June 15, 1964 at 11:00 A.M. as the date and time for further Hearings on Gerald's delinquency.

/s/Flagg"

At the appointed time on Monday, June 15, Gerald, his father and mother, Ronald Lewis and his father, and Officers Flagg and Henderson were present before Judge McGhee. Witnesses at the habeas corpus proceeding differed in their recollections of Gerald's testimony at the June 15 hearing. Mr. and Mrs. Gault recalled that Gerald again testified that he had only dialed the number and that the other boy had made the remarks. Officer Flagg agreed that at this hearing Gerald did not admit making the lewd remarks. But Judge McGhee recalled that "there was some admission again of some of the lewd statements. He didn't admit any of the more serious lewd statements." Again, the complainant, Mrs. Cook, was not present. Mrs. Gault asked that Mrs. Cook be present "so she could see which boy had done the talking, the dirty talking over the phone." The Juvenile Judge said "she didn't have to be present at that hearing." The judge did not speak to Mrs. Cook or communicate with her at any time. Probation Officer Flagg had talked to her once—over the telephone on June 9.

At this June 15 hearing a "referral report" made by the probation officers was filed with the court, although not disclosed to Gerald or his parents. This listed the charge as "Lewd Phone Calls." At the conclusion of the hearing, the judge committed Gerald as a juvenile delinquent to the State Industrial School "for the period of his minority (that is, until 21), unless sooner discharged by due process of law." An order to that effect was entered. It recites that "after a full hearing and due deliberation the Court finds that said minor is a delinquent child, and that said minor is of the age of 15 years."

No appeal is permitted by Arizona law in juvenile cases. On August 3, 1964, a petition for a writ of habeas corpus was filed with the Supreme Court of Arizona and referred by it to the Superior Court for hearing.

The Superior Court dismissed the writ, and the appellants (the Gaults) sought review in the Arizona Supreme Court. The high court affirmed the dismissal.

(FIRST DAY)

Teacher: What do you think of this case? On what grounds do you think the Gaults appealed to the Supreme Court?

Leon: Boy, did he get a raw deal.

Sue: I don't understand why he was sent to jail for so long. Even if he did make a dirty phone call, putting him in jail until he is 21 years old seems like too rough a sentence.

Leon: That's six years.

Bob: Why didn't he have a lawyer? I thought all people accused of a crime was entitled to a lawyer.

Teacher: Bev, do you have a comment on the lawyer issue?

Bev: I want to say something else. What could a person say on the phone that's worth six years in jail?

(*Laughter*)

Petey: It seems to me that six years is too long of a sentence. You get less time for stealing a car and stealing a car is more serious than making a dirty phone call.

Leon: Is the sentence for dirty phone calls six years in jail?

Teacher: What do you think? Al.

Al: I doubt it. But he is a minor and they can do funny things in juvenile court.

Frank: Yeah, did you know that you can be arrested for running away from home? I did that a couple of times and my old man had me hauled into juvenile court. If I was 21, no one could get me for splitting.

Charlie: There are a lot of special laws for people under 21.

Teacher: What are some of the laws that are different?

Charlie: Well, minors can't drink, they have to go to school, they have to do what their parents say.

Lynn: I don't do what my parents tell me to do, at least not all the time.

(*Laughter*)

Charlie: But if you really don't get along, your folks can have you arrested for being . . . uh . . . I think the word is incorrigible.

Frank: I tell you there is a difference if you are a minor. You don't have the same rights as an adult. Judge P_____ has told me that a lot.

Teacher: Frank, are you saying that juvenile court is different than adult court?

Frank: I think they are different. If you are a minor, the judge seems to do what he wants. I've always had a lawyer, though. It helps to have a good lawyer.

Al: Frank's right. Two guys I know were both busted together for smoking dope down by the Center. One of the guys had a lawyer and he got off with a couple months' probation. The other guy got sent to reform school for three months.

Teacher: Why does a lawyer make such a difference?

Frank: Because they know all the ins and outs of the law and they can ask good questions and make sure the judge doesn't screw you.

Lorraine: If that's true, then Gault should have had a lawyer.

Teacher:	Didn't Gerald Gault have a lawyer?
Lorraine:	I don't think so. Just a second, let me check (she looks through the case). Well, he didn't have a lawyer at first, it says that he, his mother, his brother, and the probation officers were there.
Judy:	But he must have had a lawyer when he appealed to the Supreme Court. I think you have to have a lawyer to appeal to the Supreme Court.
Lorraine:	But I don't see anything about a lawyer in this case.
Teacher:	Carol.
Carol:	Aren't probation officers lawyers?
Charlie:	You've got to be kidding. Probation guys work for the police.
Carol:	But they help people too. I know a girl who thinks her probation officer is great. He talks to her and helps her with problems.
Charlie:	All my guy does is tell me to stay clean. I tell him what he wants to hear. He and the judge work together. (At this point all the students start to talk at once.)
Teacher:	Wait a minute, one at a time. Jeannie.
Jeannie:	From the stuff I've read, the probation officer works for the court but also tries to help kids.
Frank:	I tell you, you've got to have your own lawyer. Those probation guys can double-cross you. Look what they did to this Gault guy. They sure didn't help him.
Bob:	I agree with Frank, Gault should have had his own lawyer. That one probation officer, what's his name . . .
Robin:	Flagg or Henderson?
Bob:	Yeah, Flagg. He was even head of the children's detention home. He couldn't be totally representative of Gault's side of things.
Teacher:	Do all of you feel that Gault should have had his own lawyer?
Class:	Yes.
Teacher:	Leon?
Leon:	I bet that's one reason the Gaults appealed to the Supreme Court. I sure would. Doesn't the Constitution say something about right to a lawyer?
Judy:	Yeah, it does.
Teacher:	Where?
Judy:	In the Bill of Rights. Hey, Bob, get that book over there. I think the Constitution is in it. (*Bob goes to the reference shelf and picks up a government book which he hands to Judy. Judy finds the Constitution in the back and starts reading it to herself. Several other students request books and Bob hands out more copies which students begin to read*)
Teacher:	Have you found anything about the right to have a lawyer?
Judy:	No, not yet.

Robin: The Fifth Amendment says (*reading*) "No person shall be. . . deprived of life, liberty or property without due process of law." Doesn't due process of law include a lawyer?

Teacher: Maybe that is an issue you ought to find out about before tomorrow. Those of you who are interested, check out a book.

Comment

During the first day of discussion, the students have raised three major points:

1. The sentence Gault received for the phone calls was excessive.
2. There is a difference between minors and adults in the eyes of the law and juvenile court is different from adult court.
3. The Constitution gives everyone the right to have a lawyer.

The first point is dealt with briefly. Petey defends her position that the sentence was too long by reference to general knowledge that the penalty for stealing a car is less than the one Gault got for making a dirty phone call. The discussion then moves to another hypothesis regarding the legal ramifications of being a minor. Several students have had experience with the juvenile court and cite their experiences, those of others, and general knowledge as evidence that adults and minors are different in the eyes of the law. At this point, the class discussion does not have a central focus. The students are defending their ideas, but are giving somewhat unorganized reactions to the Gault case. The teacher has asked an initial question to get the discussion moving and once asked Charlie to give examples of laws that are different for adults and minors. But thus far the teacher has been primarily a moderator of the discussion, calling on students and rephrasing the points they are making.

As the discussion moves toward the question whether Gault should have had a lawyer, the teacher encourages students to focus on this issue by asking key questions. The students then try to determine if Gault had a lawyer, offer reasons why a lawyer is important, and discuss the difference between a probation officer and a lawyer. The teacher actively encourages students to be sure of their information. For example, the teacher asks Lorraine if she is certain Gault did not have a lawyer and Lorraine checks the case study to make sure her information is correct. When Leon and Judy say that the Constitution guarantees Gault a lawyer, the teacher asks them to indicate where the Constitution makes such a statement. By the end of the period the students are motivated to find out if the Constitution guarantees Gault a lawyer. At no point has the teacher answered a question directly; instead, questions have been redirected to other students. Because these students have had experience with the inquiry process, they do not seem to expect the teacher to give them the answers; they listen to the comments of other students, and when they are stuck they go spontaneously to references to find out answers for themselves. The teacher actively encourages the students to pursue the question of what due process entails and sets the stage for further inquiry the next day.

(SECOND DAY)

Teacher: Did anyone find out if due process means the right to have a lawyer? Judy then Bob.

Judy: Yes, it seems that due process has been an issue in a lot of court cases. Due process means that a person gets those things necessary for a fair trial. Things like being told your rights, knowing why you are in court, and having a lawyer.

Bob: Also due process means being able to ask questions of the person who is accusing you of a crime. And that woman who said Gault made the phone calls to her was never in court.

Teacher: Good point. Alberta.

Alberta: I'm confused. Should Gault have a lawyer or not?

Teacher: Margie. Can your answer Alberta's question?

Margie: He should have had a lawyer. It is due process to have a lawyer and the Constitution says everyone gets due process.

Carol: Then why didn't Gault have a lawyer?

Teacher: Carol has asked a good question. Do any of you have any ideas of why Gault didn't have a lawyer? David.

David: I talked to my father about this case last night. He's a policeman and he said that the courts define what due process means. It has only been in the last fifteen years or so that a person has been guaranteed a lawyer . . .

Ann: But this case took place only a couple of years ago. Just a minute . . . 1964 it took place.

David: I know but maybe Gault didn't know that he could have a lawyer. My father says that if you could afford a lawyer, you could always have one, but it is only in recent times that the court would pay for one if you were poor. Maybe Gault couldn't pay for a lawyer.

Lynn: I read the case again last night and I think the whole thing was screwy. I don't think the Gaults were informed of much and everything happened so fast that they didn't even think of a lawyer until later.

Teacher: What do you mean that everything happened so fast?

Lynn: Well, look. Gault is picked up by the police. His parents found out about it that night. There is a hearing the next day. Hardly anyone is there. He is put in a detention home until the hearing. His folks hardly know what is happening, and then the judge decides to put him in jail until he is 21. The whole thing was messed up. I don't think he got any of that due process.

Teacher: Any reactions to Lynn's points? Judy.

Judy: I agree with Lynn. From what I read about due process, I don't think Gault got due process. Not only a lawyer but also what Bob said about Mrs. Cook not being there.

Teacher: OK, so are you saying that the Gaults are appealing to the Supreme Court because Gerald did not get due process? Judy.

Judy: Yes, I think it is more than not just having a lawyer.

Teacher: Do the rest of you agree with Judy?

Class: Yes.

Robin: Even though I agree that the Gaults probably appealed to the Supreme Court on the issue of due process, what I don't understand is why didn't Gault get his rights. Why did the court act in such a weird way?

Teacher: Al.

Al: I still think if this Gault guy had not been a minor, none of this would have happened.

Leon: What difference does it make that he is a minor?

Frank: I tell you minors don't have the same rights as people over 21.

Teacher: Don.

Don: From what Frank and Al said yesterday, I agree with them. Also I was thinking about it. Isn't it true that until you are a certain age you are treated as a minor in court, and if you are convicted of something it doesn't go on your adult record.

Bev: Yeh, that's true! They are more unofficial in juvenile court. I bet if Gault had been over 21, the court would have handled everything different.

Charlie: In juvenile court they don't think a person has much say. When I was there they listened to my parents, not to me. It was like my parents were as much at fault as I was. The judge told my Dad that he had to do certain things and that I had to do certain things.

Teacher: Any other comments?

Petey: I want to know more about juvenile court. Maybe the reason Gault didn't get due process was because he was a minor.

Teacher: How do the rest of you feel? Do you think we should find out more about the rights of minors in court?

(*Nodding. General agreement.*)

Teacher: OK, let's divide up into groups and do some research on the topic.

Comment

Students have been motivated by the Gault-case springboard and the first day's discussion to find out more about due process and to ponder the case outside of class. At least two students (Judy and Bob) have looked up due process while David has discussed the right to a lawyer with his father, and Lynn has reviewed the basic elements of the case. Whereas the first day the students oriented themselves to the problem and began to clarify terms and concepts and explore the parameters of the case, the students now move the discussion to a consideration of due process. The class is no longer concentrating on fragments of the case but discussing Gault within the context of the larger issue of due process. The issue is redefined, and students begin to fit elements of the case into a framework. Bob says that Gault also did not receive due process because he was unable to confront and cross-examine the witness against him. Lynn expands Bob's observations by pointing out that the entire case was handled in such a way that Gault's parents did not know where he was or what the charges were against him.

It is interesting to look at the relationships the students begin to perceive. Margie follows the logical consequences of the Constitution's guarantee of due process, incorporates Judy's information that due process includes having a lawyer, and concludes that Gault should have had a lawyer. Also the students consider the relationship between the Supreme Court's recent interpretations of the meaning of due process and the year in which the Gault case took place. Through redefining terms, searching for more data, responding to and building upon one another's ideas, and drawing logical conclusions, the students have been able to reach a consensus. They conclude that the Gaults appealed to the Supreme Court because Gerald was denied due process of law.

In a sense, the students have solved the initial problem presented by the springboard. Even so, some members of the class still feel that there is an important element missing from their solution. Robin doesn't have a sense of closure; she cannot understand why all of this happened to Gerald Gault. Al goes back to an issue he raised during the first day's discussion and which he considers of crucial importance—the difference between minors and adults in the eyes of the law. He really wants this idea examined and now that the class is satisfied with their conclusions regarding the issue of due process, they are interested in investigating this second aspect of the case. This change in orientation and desire to pursue ideas in depth is a phenomenon often observed in discovery episodes. As students discover an issue, they are motivated to know more about the reasons why events occur. Their discoveries often lead to an expanded awareness of the world and a desire to analyze and understand the issues of our time.

The teacher in this class has been effective in decreasing the students' reliance on her for answers. Almost all of her influence is directed toward encouraging student thought and participation. On the second day she uses the following six techniques:

1. Reinforcing students for offering ideas. For example, the teacher tells Bob that he has made a good point.
2. Redirecting students' questions. The teacher does this twice, once when Alberta says she is confused and a second time when Carol asks why Gault didn't have a lawyer. Learning to redirect students' questions is important in teaching through inquiry. Most teachers are greatly tempted to answer students' questions themselves, but to constantly do so can be fatal to the inquiry process for it encourages students to rely on the teacher for answers.
3. Asking students to respond to other students' ideas. The teacher asks the class's reaction to points made by Lynn and to Petey's suggestion that they find out more about juvenile court. Using this technique accomplishes three goals in the inquiry process: getting more alternatives out on the floor for discussion, focusing the discourse on one issue at a time, and testing to see the extent of consensus that has been obtained.
4. Asking students to explain or defend their ideas. Optimally, students will spontaneously support and explain their observations, but at times it is necessary for the teacher to step in and encourage students to perform this operation. Here the teacher asks Lynn to explain what she means by saying "everything happened so fast."
5. Restating and summarizing students' ideas. The teacher performs this operation several times and uses it not only to help the class focus on the essence of a student's comments, but also to pull together several students' ideas. By asking, "OK, so are you saying that the Gaults are appealing to the Supreme Court because Gerald did not get due process?" the teacher is crystallizing the consensus that is becoming apparent in the class.
6. Suggesting courses of action and investigation. In both the first and second day of discussion the teacher is sensitive to the students' desire for more data, and in a non-authoritarian manner encourages avenues of further study. The first day students are encouraged to read about due process and the right to a lawyer, and the second day the teacher suggests that the class get into groups to gather more information about juvenile court.

The inquiry process requires that a teacher assume a number of roles.[3] Two important roles are those of a questioner in the discussion

---

[3] For a detailed discussion of the roles of the inquiry teacher, see Chapter 2.

and a sustainer of discussion; certainly, the teacher in this discovery episode demonstrates these skills in action.

ANALYTICAL EPISODES

In analytical episodes students attempt to establish the causes or underlying dimensions of a social issue. These episodes focus on cause-and-effect or other explanatory questions. Why did an event occur? Why was a decision made? Why did the stockmarket crash in 1929? Why was Scopes brought to trial for teaching evolution in the schools? Many historical questions regarding policy decisions and social events remain controversial and unresolved, and thus wide open for student inquiry. Even if the majority of social scientists concur on the analysis of an issue, the process of analyzing and figuring out why events occurred encourages students to think and reason as social scientists and policy makers.

The ability to analyze current social issues is a skill that is important to all citizens of our society. If we are able to understand how we got involved in Vietnam or why we have polluted our rivers, we are in a much better position to understand the sources of conflict and controversy and suggest meaningful alternatives to resolve the issues.

Comparative analysis of social issues allows students to make generalizations regarding social phenomena. For example, a comparative analysis of the events leading up to the Civil War or World War I can be effective in helping students to generalize about the causes of wars. Comparisons of social issues also allow insight into the situational differences in issues and the varying outcomes of social controversy.

Not only may students develop generalizations about a category of issues, but in analytical episodes they may also test the adequacy of generalizations. In a high-school psychology class, for instance, students might examine the validity of Freud's theory regarding defense mechanisms by applying his ideas to a number of case studies and seeing to what extent Freud's principles explain the behavior that occurred.

In contrast with discovery episodes, analytical episodes tend to be more sequential and orderly in their development. The dimensions of the problematic springboard are more defined and the process is likely to follow the classical inquiry model of forming a hypothesis: defining terms, testing the hypothesis, and arriving at defensible conclusions. In some ways these episodes contain fewer instances of divergent thinking and valuing; the major emphasis of analytical inquiry is usually intellectual, and the operations are cognitive rather than emotional or affective.[4]

[4] For a discussion of the differences between analytical and creative thinking see Byron G. Massialas and Jack Zevin, *Creative Encounters in the Classroom* (New York: John Wiley & Sons, 1967), pp. 7-16.

The analytical episode reproduced below occurred in an eleventh grade U.S. History class in a large city high school. The episode took place at the beginning of the school year; at this point in their education, the students in the class had had very little experience with the inquiry process. The teacher was working on encouraging student discussion and striving to teach students inquiry skills.

The students in the class were primarily children of first- and second-generation immigrant families and of average intelligence. The class was using a standard history text, but it was also working with materials that supplemented the text. Just prior to this discussion the students had been reading a number of materials on immigrants and blacks after the Civil War.

The class was contrasting the problems faced by immigrants from the middle of the nineteenth century into the twentieth century with those faced by post-Civil War black freedmen as they immigrated into northern cities from the South. Some students had interviewed grandparents and relatives regarding the problems they encountered as immigrants while other students had talked to black teachers and friends in the school regarding the barriers blacks had to overcome. In the dialogue below the students use both historical and current information in analyzing the problem presented to them.

Teacher: The problem today is to contrast the problems faced by immigrants from about the middle of the nineteenth century into the twentieth century with problems faced by black freedmen. Which group faced the most problems? Yvonne, you mentioned that one of the immigrants you interviewed had trouble with language.

Yvonne: Yes, he was from Lithuania.

Teacher: OK. So let's on the one side list immigrant problems and on the other side, problems of freed slaves. (*Writes on board*) Problem of language for immigrants. How about freedmen, Pat, did they have the problem of language?

Pat: Well, they had the problem of literacy. A lot of them, they'd never been to school in their lives. And they aren't any better off if they can't read or write.

Teacher: OK. Is there a problem with language as contrasted with literacy for the freedman who, say, tries to go to the city to hold a job? Doesn't the fact that he speaks English put him at an advantage over the immigrant? How about it? Fred?

Fred: But the slave culture had developed their own language, you know. The accents that they had and everything. You'd really have to listen to them when they talked to make out what they're saying. It's slang.

Pat: Even today a kid who comes from a ghetto or a southern farm has a problem of a limited vocabulary.

Teacher: So the language problem can exist for the black today also. Of course, it probably wasn't as acute as for our Lithuanian friend who doesn't have any English words at all. Lynn, what are some other problems that each faced?

Lynn: Housing problems.

Teacher: Why housing?

Lynn: Like the Negroes, they, they . . . most people don't like them to live near them and that. And then some people don't like people from a foreign country to move into their neighborhood because they don't know what they're like and that and how they keep up their neighborhood.

Teacher: How about the immigrant who came to the city, like New York, Detroit, Cincinnati? Could he afford much in the way of housing? I'm speaking of the typical immigrant, not the person who is highly trained and fits very easily into American life.

Lynn: They probably couldn't afford much in housing because they probably didn't have much when they arrived.

Teacher: What part of the city would they live in then?

Lynn: In the older part of the city I imagine.

Teacher: John. Do you want to make a comment?

John: It seems that if an immigrant wasn't very literate when he came over, the only job he usually held was in a factory and so it seems they'd naturally tend to live around big factories.

Teacher: That's a very good point. Housing in the vicinity of factories in the days before zoning laws. What would such housing be like?

John: It wouldn't be pleasant. It would probably be something like the project housing we have today. It would be built, probably financed by the factories, you know. It would probably be crowded and cheap.

Teacher: So the immigrant from abroad faced lousy housing. What about the black immigrant from the South? Is there any difference between the black man and the immigrant? Mike?

Mike: I don't think the people from the United States would resent an immigrant living next to them as much as a Negro. The Negro is a black and the immigrants we're talking about were white.

Teacher: In other words you could move if you were white.

Mike: An immigrant could change his name and become more literate, but a Negro can't change his color. Most people feel that no matter what your name is, if you're black you're not on the same level as the white man.

Teacher: In other words no change of names is going to change the color of a man's skin. Judy.

Judy: If you are an immigrant, particularly first generation, and you're eager to get ahead, you can drop the accent, the language, drop your name and assume a completely different identity and emerge into the culture.

Don: About the problems of the freedman. They have trouble with respect. The whites wanted respect from the black man, but the white man doesn't give respect to the black.

Teacher: That's a very good point. Self-esteem for the immigrant is a far easier thing than it is for the black. Let's see. Where are we? Housing is a problem for both because of money, but immigrants can move easier than blacks. Jobs. Immigrants tended to be restricted to jobs in factories because of language. Yvonne.

Yvonne: Also the blacks were restricted in jobs. The Black Code in the South prevented Negroes from becoming artisans or developing skills. So Negroes have problems, too.

Teacher: OK, Pat?

Pat: Well, I think one big thing is the Negro had been in America. The white has his ideas set down on what he thinks of the Negro. A lot of them probably look down upon them because they might have even owned a few slaves, and after they were freed, they didn't change their mind about them all of a sudden. They still had this bias against them. But with the immigrant if an immigrant moved next door, I think they would have been unsure about them. I mean they didn't have any set ideas about them, more than likely. Like if an Irishman moved next door, they'd give him more of a chance than they'd give a Negro.

Teacher: Umhum. That's an interesting point. In other words many people withheld an opinion until the immigrant proved himself or made some sort of impression on them. John?

John: Well, I'm not sure I agree. Wouldn't they already have an opinion formed on an immigrant, too. Thinking he was inferior, you know, he's not a regular American.

Pat: Why? Just because he comes from a different country?

John: This is what I thought happened. Like if they had Czechs come over, Slavs or something like this and they worked in the factories for lower wages and so they were looked down on. Weren't they also considered inferior?

Teacher: They were inferior somewhat in relation to the differences they had with Americans. If a German immigrant came in and had the ability to read and write and happened to be a Protestant German, he could be accepted into an American Protestant church. In terms of competition for jobs, wherever immigrants threatened jobs for American whites, they were not appreciated. You're right as far as strangeness of language. Wherever there was a language barrier as there was in most cases, people tended to be somewhat suspicious.

At the time of the major wave of immigrants, though, America was just peaking in terms of industrialization and so unskilled jobs were numerous and easily available. At that same time the Black Code in the South prevented Negroes from going into factories. What about today's black immigrants from the South? Are there jobs in factories today? Ben?

Ben: Well, today factory jobs require more training and there are less jobs available.

Teacher: Good. Jobs are much more difficult today. The Ford Motor Company and some other big corporations are making efforts to train, not only blacks but whites and blacks in the ghetto who lack skills. But a person can't automatically get off the boat, as it were, and go into a factory and start making a living because things are a bit more complicated today in terms of skilled and unskilled work. Can we add anything else in the way of problems faced by immigrants and blacks? OK, Pat.

Pat: How about education?

Teacher: OK, how about it?

Pat: Well, it would be hard in the schools if you didn't speak English.

Teacher: Since my wife's parents were Italian immigrants, my wife could not speak a word of English when she began public school. What would be the problems for a kid coming into kindergarten or first grade who couldn't speak English. Pat?

Pat: It would be hard to make some friends and you wouldn't learn anything if you couldn't understand the teacher.

Teacher: Lou?

Lou: I went to Saint "X" and they spoke Polish there. Some of the teachers understood Polish and helped the kids.

Teacher: OK, good. Many of the Catholics set up their own parochial schools. As a kid I attended Polish parochial school. The parochial school was a source of education to the immigrant. There were German parochial schools, too. Many immigrants, though, didn't go to special schools and had trouble and often dropped out of school. So let's put education down as a problem. Let's talk about education for the black. Jack?

Jack: During slavery and after the Civil War there was almost no education for blacks.

Teacher: No education. And then when the blacks began to go to school what was the problem? Yvonne?

Yvonne: The schools were segregated in the South. There were separate schools for blacks and whites and the blacks didn't get as good an education.

Teacher: What about the North? Is education equal today in the North? Mike?

Mike: I don't think so. I don't think we hold as much prejudice against the black as the people in the South, but I think we still hold more than we should. Most of the black kids in the North who live in the cities live in the ghetto. The schooling in the ghetto isn't quite as good. I've heard that the schools are old and the teachers aren't as good. Also there seems to be more of a problem of broken homes and not as much support for black kids.

Teacher: So a good home life, a solid home life with parents encouraging you obviously is going to result in better acomplishment on the part of any student. Why is it that the father is absent in so many Negro families? Bill?

Bill: Well, maybe it was because he didn't have a good education, you know, in his youth when he got married and then couldn't find a good job and, you know, maybe he just couldn't make ends meet so he just cut out.

Teacher: It's the simplest solution, isn't it? When you've got problems heaped on your head to just cop out, just leave. Is there anything else that pulls a black male out of the family? What about life under slavery? Was stable family life encouraged? Yvonne?

Yvonne: No, they were pulled apart usually. Slavery made it necessary at times to break up families and if your families were too tightly knit, it made messy problems. You couldn't make slaves work as well if they were separated and pining for a lost father or mother.

Teacher: Ray?

Ray: Well, I think another reason why the white slavists wouldn't want a family united is because if the kids, if a Negro male is brought up, you know, with his father always teaching him all the things and everything, then he might know too much when he's older and then he might want to do something about the condition he's in.

Teacher: That's kind of a subtle thing but it makes a lot of sense. Yvonne?

Yvonne: You could say one thing that the immigrants, they seem to stick together, their families seem strong and that might be one reason for the immigrants coming farther ahead than the blacks nowadays. Kids grow up and tend to take care of their parents because they figure, well, they took care of me when I was a kid so I should take care of them when they're old.

Teacher: So where are we? Do you feel that the black freedmen or the immigrants had more problems to overcome? John?

John: In a way the blacks were immigrants, too. They immigrated from the South. It seems that both groups of immigrants had many of the same problems—language, housing, jobs, thought of as inferior. I think the blacks had the most problems, though. The thing about the family and the different color of their skin are problems blacks have that the regular immigrants don't.

Teacher: Marie.

Marie: The blacks' and immigrants' problems may be very similar at first, but after a couple of generations white immigrants can fit right into society. I don't think I have the problems my grandfather did when he came from Poland. But blacks' problems last longer. Because they are black, they are still not accepted. They still are discriminated against. Some problems a person can overcome himself through work and time but other problems depend on changing the society and attitudes of others.

Comment

In contrast with the teacher in the discovery episode presented earlier, the teacher in this class is much more directive. The class depends on him to guide the discussion. The teacher effectively uses student ideas to move the discussion and generally asks questions that encourage students to offer data that may be used to analyze the social problems surrounding the influx of immigrants and blacks into northern cities. The students' ideas and thinking, though, are not constrained by the teacher. For example, at one point, the teacher suggests that since a freed black spoke English, he had an advantage over the immigrant; instead of agreeing with the teacher, several students point out that the English of the black culture is different from that of the dominant white culture and conclude that the black had language barriers also.

The teacher expects students not only to suggest possible difficulties encountered by immigrants, but also to defend the points they raise. Lynn states that both groups faced housing problems; when she doesn't defend her answer the teacher immediately requests additional explanation and evidence. The class then examines the housing situation, concluding that the immigrants and blacks probably lived in older sections of the city next to factories because they faced discrimination in better neighborhoods, didn't have the money to pay for good housing, and tended to work in factories. The teacher in this analytical episode is actively teaching the inquiry process to students by the types of questions he asks and by helping them to categorize and relate their ideas. In classes that are not familiar with inquiry, it is often necessary for teachers to be more active participants initially and then gradually encourage the class to depend less and less on them to monitor the process.

Although the amount of teacher influence in this episode may in part be attributed to the students' relative inexperience with the inquiry method, it may also be one of the characteristic differences between analytic and discovery episodes. In their study of classroom dialogue, Massialas and Zevin concluded that teachers have a tendency to ask more questions of students in analytical episodes than they do in discovery

episodes. The questions, they observed, are often used to establish the
sequence of the inquiry process and culminate at a point at which students are using principles to explain the evidence that has been presented.[5]

The discussion in this episode follows a fairly orderly sequence of
steps:

1. A student offers a hypothesis that a given problem was encountered by
   immigrants or by freed blacks.
2. The class probes the hypothesis and suggests possible implications of the
   problem.
3. The students compare the blacks and immigrants to see if both encountered the barrier to the same degree.

Guided by the teacher, the class analyzes the problems faced by immigrants and blacks in the areas of literacy, housing, discrimination,
jobs, education, and family stability. The students recognize that these
problems are interrelated. For example, difficulties with the language
make it difficult for immigrants, black or white, to get a good education
and a good job. Without a good job, they don't have the resources to
acquire good housing. The class is also astute at picking up differences
between the opportunities presented European immigrants versus the
opportunities open to migrating blacks. They point out that there was
more help educationally for the white immigrants; the immigrant groups
and the Catholic Church established schools to meet the specific educational needs of immigrants. The students are also cognizant of the fact
that once white immigrants learn basic skills they can be assimilated
into the dominant culture, but even if blacks learn the skills they still
face barriers because of the color of their skin.

At the conclusion of the dialogue two students offer generalizations
based on the data presented and discussed. The first generalization is
that immigrants, whether they be whites from Europe or blacks from
the South, face many similar problems. The second generalization is
that immigrants who have racial characteristics similar to the rest of
society are more easily assimilated into that society than immigrants who
are racially different.

PRESCRIPTIVE EPISODES

Prescriptive episodes focus on determining the most desirable alternatives for resolving a social controversy. The goals of instruction are to

[5] Massialas and Zevin, *Creative Encounters,* p. 71.

clarify the problem, to seek resolutions to value conflicts, and to determine defensible alternative solutions to the problem. In some cases the accepted solutions are followed by some form of individual or group action. Prescriptive episodes present situations that require students to make personal value judgments regarding past and present social problems. Though cognitive reasoning is important, more operations falling in the affective categories of the *Taxonomy of Educational Objectives*[6] are apparent in the discussion.

In prescriptive episodes, students are asked to make policy judgments and take value positions on issues. Whereas a hypothesis attempts to describe or explain social phenomena, a position statement asserts explicitly or implicitly that something should be done because it is desirable. Fred Newman and Donald Oliver argue that questions involving policy judgments rest on value conflict and that when one makes a policy choice one is also choosing between competing values and must justify the choice.[7] They suggest several possible strategies for justifying or challenging values:

1. Using a respected or venerable source.
2. Predicting a valued consequence.
3. Relating the specific value to a higher order general value.
4. Finding inconsistencies or contradictions in value commitments.

When a person uses a respected source, such as the Constitution or the Pope, she is justifying her value by showing that an authority agrees with her. If the participants in the discussion accept the values of the authority, then there may be some agreement on the value choice. The trouble with this type of value defense is that the sources themselves often contain contradictory values, and those involved in the dispute may disagree as to which sources are most respected. When one justifies a policy choice by stating that it leads to a valued consequence, one must be able to show that the valued consequence has a good probability of occurring and that the consequence is desirable. For example, a person might have argued that the Vietnam War should end because it was creating deep divisions in American society and that if the war ended these divisions would begin to heal. Justifying a specific value by showing that it is related to a higher order value is the type of defense a person uses when he says that individual freedom implies the right to free speech.

[6] David R. Krathwhol, Benjamin S. Bloom, and Bertram B. Masia, *Taxonomy of Educational Objectives: 2, Affective Domain* (New York: David McKay Co., 1964), pp. 49-53.
[7] Fred M. Newman and Donald W. Oliver, *Clarifying Public Controversy* (Boston: Little, Brown and Co., 1970) pp. 44-46.

One way in which to challenge the value positions of others is to show that their value choices are inconsistent. In the controversy over busing, white senators who advocate busing have often been attacked as hypocrites because they live in the District of Columbia and send their own children to private schools instead of sending them to the district's predominantly black public schools. The implication is that these senators ask others to accept values which they themselves do not live by.

Resolution of value conflicts is perhaps the most difficult aspect of prescriptive episodes. Definitional conflicts and factual conflicts usually are resolved within the class by sufficient analysis and research. But sometimes it is impossible to resolve value conflicts. If this is the case, then the class as a whole will probably not agree that one course of action is better than another. Nonetheless, the various alternative solutions have been made explicit in terms of their underlying values and the students have come to recognize how their values affect their individual policy choices.

In the following prescriptive episode, the class is discussing the desirability of the military draft and examining possible alternatives. The students are members of a tenth grade world history class in a racially mixed city high school. About 40 percent of the students are black. The students are average in intelligence and are used to discussing social issues. This discussion took place at the height of the Vietnam War when the selective service draft was still in effect. There were several proposals before Congress to have a draft lottery or to substitute a national service system for the draft. The national service proposal required that all Americans give two years of service to their country. At the time of this discussion, though, the issue regarding the selective service draft was still a current event. None of the proposals to modify the draft system had been passed by Congress.

Teacher: Bob, which do you think would be more democratic?
   Bob: The National Service Program would be because all physically fit people would have to serve; there's no discrimination as to rich or poor, black or white.
Teacher: Steve?
   Steve: It would be less democratic because everyone would have to serve, everyone would have to give up their liberties; there would be no way, no way you could get out of it.
Teacher: Why is the system less democratic? You said it's less democratic. Why?
   Steve: Because you are forced to do it. You don't have a choice. Maybe you don't want to go in the Peace Corps or Vista or even in the armed services, but this way you have to do it. The Thirteenth Amendment strictly forbids involuntary service.

Teacher: All right, Rick, what?

Rick: Well, I think the National Service is even more democratic than the draft. The draft and the National Service are both involuntary servitude. You have to go in if you are drafted. At least in the National Service you have a choice between the armed service, Vista, and the Peace Corps.

Joan: But the draft doesn't force everybody to go in because you can always get a student deferment. People who don't want to go in usually have an argument and they say, okay, you don't have to. In the National Service you are forced.

Rick: But for the draft to be democratic, all people should have the same opportunity to get a deferment or stay out. This isn't what happens. I was reading that poor people and blacks get drafted rather than rich people. They can't get student deferments because they can't afford to go to college.

Teacher: It seems to me that we have to decide what we mean by democratic. Joan, you were saying that the draft is more democratic because you are not forced. What do you mean by democratic?

Joan: Everyone is subject to the draft equally, but individual circumstances are taken into account so if you have a good reason you are not forced to go. If a lower class person is going to college he can get a deferment just as easily as an upper- or upper-middle class person going to college.

Teacher: Yes I'd say that's true, but don't more upper-class children go to college than middle- and lower-class children? Melba?

Melba: Well the upper-class people have got enough money to send their kids to college. They're going to be something important. The lower class don't have much chance to go to college, so they draft them first, before the people who are richer.

Carol: I disagree with Joan. Lower-class people may have to work and may not get as good grades.

Teacher: Jeff?

Jeff: Well, my brothers, they got deferments because they were getting fairly good grades in college. Anyone who gets good grades can be deferred.

Teacher: Dennis?

Dennis: Well, there wouldn't be as much fuss about the Selective Service if there wasn't a war, really, because you know they wouldn't be worried about going over and getting killed.

Teacher: Steve?

Steve: Who really started knocking the draft? . . . ah, was it wives of guys who had to go over, or the guys themselves? Because five years ago you didn't hear anything about how bad the draft was and we were still drafting for Vietnam.

Teacher: Yeah, I think what Dennis said applies here. Maybe when more people started getting killed in the war and the war was getting more attention, people began to think that it wasn't fair and people shouldn't be drafted to fight a war they didn't think was right.

Don: I'm not sure the National Service would help the situation. What if a person is already in the National Service thing like in Peace Corp or Vista; if a war came along he wouldn't have to fight. He probably would not get drafted because he would be serving his time. What if they need more people for the Army. People would still be forced into the Army.

Teacher: So you feel the National Service could be as undemocratic as the draft. Jeff?

Jeff: Well, I believe there'd have to be some force. I mean nobody really wants to go out and fight unless they're a little weird, you know, or unless they're really patriotic or something. I don't really believe that 99 percent of all Americans are patriotic toward their country.

Teacher: You don't think so. Why not?

Jeff: Not enough to go out and die. Say if the guy's a family man, you know, he's well off. Why should he want to go out and die for the country instead of staying alive to see his kids through college?

Teacher: Sharon?

Sharon: He said that 99 percent of the people aren't patriotic. I don't know about 99 percent, but if people are really patriotic, why are they protesting and why are they burning draft cards. Why are they doing such things like that?

Teacher: Are all draft-card burners really unpatriotic?

Sharon: Well, why aren't they giving their lives for their country? Don't they want to stop communism?

Teacher: What about these draft-card burners—she says they're unpatriotic. Is there anyone who disagrees? Janet?

Janet: I think they're just against the draft and they're not really unpatriotic.

Faye: No, I don't think that that they're not being patriotic. I think that they don't believe in the war and don't think we have any business in Vietnam.

Teacher: Doesn't that make you unpatriotic if you don't believe in the country's war?

Faye: No, because they believe the country's wrong being in Vietnam and they're trying to move our country from wrong.

Teacher: Mark?

Mark: Yeah, it probably could be because they're scared too; you know, scared of dying. I think a lot of them burn their draft cards because they are scared.

Teacher: You don't feel that they are doing it for patriotic reasons?

Mark: No, I don't think so.

Teacher: All right, Gayle.

Gayle: Well, when a person burns their draft card, they're a little bit patriotic because they're really risking their lives protesting like that because sometimes they get beaten up by the police, you know, for doing that. And they're willing to spend I don't know how long in jail for doing it and that's just as bad as going to war.

Teacher: Yeah, how 'bout that. They're risking police sentence, police records, jail sentences, and everything else. Jeff?

Jeff: Well, the draft cards are from the government. When you burn up the draft card, you're actually defying the government. And therefore, you're unpatriotic.

Teacher: That's the definition of unpatriotic—whenever you defy the government, you are unpatriotic.

Jeff: I think in a sense the United States is at stake like in the war in Vietnam. I mean the spread of communism could keep on going and, ah, I know there could be arguments towards that but if the United States is at stake in some of this then it's being unpatriotic to burn your draft card.

Pat: Well, I think we should define patriotism first, I mean, a lot of people think, you know, some people think that burning your draft card is being unpatriotic—well, what is patriotism?

Teacher: All right, what is patriotism? What do you think it is?

Pat: Well, if you have a love for your country and you're willing to die for a good cause, I mean, and stand up for your country and what it believes in and your beliefs.

Teacher: Yeah, but what if your personal beliefs conflict with the country's beliefs, then which becomes right your own beliefs or your country's beliefs?

Joyce: Your own.

Teacher: I'm just curious. How many believe that your own personal beliefs and morals should come above what your country's belief and morals are? Then all of you people should probably be on the side of these draft-card burners because aren't they following their own personal and moral beliefs?

Dave: They are not all following their beliefs. Some just want to get out of the draft. They are scared.

Darryl: But those that are standing up for their beliefs are doing the right thing. Standing up for what you believe in, that's the most important thing. If you back down from your beliefs, you're not much of a person.

Teacher: OK, Willie.

Willie: I think that some of those who burn their draft cards, they're thinking about the country never does nothing for them, you know, to better their conditions, so why should they try to better the country's conditions.

Teacher: Well, is the only reason you should work for your country be-

	cause of what your country can do for you? Doesn't everyone who's a citizen here and enjoys any rights and privileges, shouldn't they have an obligation to serve their country in some way, male or female, and isn't this the most democratic way? Venessa?
Venessa:	Well, you said that everyone has an obligation to serve their country if they're a citizen, well just about everyone does, like women, they teach, or a nurse, or something, and that's helping the country because you're helping to develop the minds of the future Americans and, ah, and no matter what you do, you're helping a lot, like people, even men who worked on, at the plant down here, they help build cars that will help everybody in the country so everybody serves their country, no matter if they go to the service or not.
Teacher:	Yeah, I think you've got a good point, everybody helps to serve their country. However, some of us who serve here at home, but we benefit more, don't we? I mean after all, I might be serving my country, but, right? I'm getting paid for it, right? Wouldn't it be better for people to serve their country and get less for it?
Venessa:	No, because you have to live.
Joyce:	You have to have some money, I mean, a person could, you've got a family and you've got to support your family.
Teacher:	All right, you've been talking about practical considerations, what about the family, what about the money angle, what will people do and so forth, but what about the moral angle—which is more morally right—continue the Selective Service as it is or to have a a national draft where everybody serves? Which is more morally right do you think? Chris?
Chris:	Well, I don't know which one it is, but one of them sounds like, you know, everybody has to go—it sounds kind of communistic— you know what I mean. It's like in Russia—the government, the government is the ruler of everything, you know what I mean, and half of the stuff that they make, the supplies and all this car business and all this, have to go through the government, and the other half, I don't know where it goes, but it sounds more like . . .
Teacher:	Carl?
Carl:	Well, it might sound like it's communistic, but it's still under a National Service, you still have a choice of what you want, if you want to go into the Peace Corps.
Teacher:	So that makes it democratic if they give you a choice? Rick?
Rick:	Well, of those two, I think the National Service Program is best. In another current events, we had something about a lottery, and I think that would be better than any of them.
Teacher:	Why?
Rick:	'Cause that shows no favoritism toward anybody and you can get just as many guys as you need. I can't see anything wrong with that system.

Steve: I agree with Rick. With the National Service you've still got to go in. There is no choice about that. With the lottery there is no discrimination and no deferment, so it is the most democratic of all.

Teacher: What do the rest of you think?
         (A number of students indicate their agreement with the lottery.)

Comment

At the outset of this discussion, students quickly get involved in a definitional dispute over the meaning of "democratic." As the students debate over whether the National Service System or the draft is more democratic, they realize that they are using different definitions. Joan offers a definition that the rest of the class seems to accept—that democratic means being subject equally to the draft. The students then discuss whether upper- and lower-class children are equally subject to the draft. Before this issue is resolved, Steve steps in and asks why there is so much fuss about the draft. The question of the draft is then placed in the context of the larger social controversy over Vietnam. The conflict over the draft is seen as a reflection of personal values and attitudes toward the war.

Students then begin to take positions on the draft and the war in Vietnam. Sharon argues that it is the duty of all citizens to submit to the draft, be willing to die for their country, and "stop communism" in Vietnam. This student obviously values stopping communism. Other students who support Sharon's position believe that citizens should not defy their government. The opposite position is taken by another group of students who feel that those who resist the draft are doing what they believe is right for the country. The teacher brings the value conflict to a head by asking, ". . . But what if your personal beliefs conflict with the country's beliefs, then which becomes right—your own beliefs or your country's beliefs?" The students wrestle with this value conflict; some, such as Darryl, choose one value over another. Darryl argues that standing up for one's beliefs is inherent in a higher value—that of being your own person. Willie seems to side with Darryl, but for another reason; he questions the value of serving your country if your country is not serving you. Other students, such as Dave, discount the value conflict by stating that people who avoid the draft are not pursuing their own beliefs, but are simply scared. In this class, the value conflict over following one's own beliefs or the country's beliefs is not totally resolved, but the students have clarified and made public the values underlying the social controversy over the draft.

When the students return to the question of whether the draft or the National Service is more democratic, they are still not satisfied with either policy alternative. Finally Rick offers another alternative, the lottery, which he feels is more desirable than any solution that has yet been suggested. He defends his position by stressing that the lottery is impartial, something he values, and that it is practical because the military gets the number of men it needs.

This prescriptive episode began with the students trying to make a policy decision between the draft and the National Service, using the criteria of which is the more democratic. The discussion then moved to a consideration of the pros and cons of both systems and a recognition of the value conflicts present in society concerning the draft. The episode concludes with a rejection of the original policy choices and an acceptance of a different alternative. It is interesting to note that a year later Congress agreed with the alternative the students in this class thought was best and passed the draft lottery proposal.

SUMMARY

Inquiry into social issues need not be limited to current social events. A historical issue may also be discussed using the inquiry style of teaching if it is presented as a problem to be resolved. Each inquiry episode begins with a springboard that establishes a problematic situation of interest to the students. During the course of the discussion the students attempt to resolve the issue and come to some conclusions or generalizations regarding the problem.

Inquiry lessons may be grouped into three categories: discovery episodes, analytical episodes, and prescriptive episodes. In discovery episodes, students are asked to react to a springboard, share information, come to some conclusions about the implications of the springboard, and develop directions for additional study. A value of the discovery episode is the interest students usually develop in the topic and their consequent motivation for its continued study. In this type of episode, teachers must be very nondirective, for once the students think that the teacher has "the answer," closure sets in and their desire to explore the topic decreases. The teacher's major role is to ask questions and to sustain the discussion by restating and summarizing students' ideas and suggesting courses of action and investigation.

In contrast with discovery episodes, analytical episodes are usually more sequential and orderly in their development. The dimensions of the problem as presented by the springboard are more defined and the process of resolving the problem is likely to follow the classical inquiry model of forming a hypothesis, defining terms, testing the hypothesis, and arriving at defensible conclusions. In analytical episodes the class usually reaches a sense of closure when they are satisfied with their conclusion. The teacher is usually more directive in these episodes. The teacher makes sure that the class is focused on the problem and that students defend their hypotheses. The teacher asks questions to establish the sequence of the inquiry process and to ensure that the discussion culminates in generalizations or conclusions that are well supported.

Prescriptive inquiry episodes are the most value laden. They focus on determining the most desirable alternatives for resolving a social controversy. Springboards for these episodes require students to make value judgments regarding the social problem. Because students may hold different values, prescriptive episodes often generate heated discussions. The teacher must see that students are aware of and justify their values. In some episodes, it is impossible to resolve value conflicts and decide as a class on the best alternative. Nonetheless, the various alternative solutions are made explicit in terms of their underlying values and the students come to recognize how their values affect their individual choices.

5

selecting
motivating springboards

In spite of all the attempts in the sixties on the part of the federal government and private foundations to raise the quality of textbooks and materials available for children in American schools, many of them have not shown a marked improvement. Many materials are flat, they avoid controversy, they discriminate against ethnic and social minorities and women, and their information is out-of-date.

A major review of standard texts used in elementary and secondary schools conducted by a panel of fourteen educators and social scientists pointed "to the ethnocentrism, middle-class bias, Anglo-Saxon and white racial emphasis, Adam Smith economics, Protestant Christianity, and sexual purity" prevailing in school textbooks." [1] Texts did not encourage students to raise questions and to provide their own positions or interpretations of an event. One of the reviewers, summarizing the findings of the others as well, concluded: "Textbooks generally present an unrealistic picture of American society and government. Many social problems that exist today are not discussed. . . . America is presented as the champion of freedom, good will, and rationality, while all other nations are depicted as aggressors or 'second-raters.' . . . Controversial issues are not dealt with in an ethically and intellectually responsible manner. Nowhere do authors outline a defensible model for dealing with social cleavages and value incompatibilities."

Another study conducted under the auspices of the Anti-Defamation League of B'nai B'rith confirmed these findings. While the study acknowl-

[1] C. B. Cox and B. G. Massialas, eds., *Social Studies in the United States: A Critical Appraisal* (New York: Harcourt, Brace & World, Inc., 1967), p. 313.

edged that there have been some improvements over the past years, it concluded: "A significant number of texts published today continue to present a principally White, Protestant, Anglo-Saxon view of America's past and present, while the nature and problems of minority groups are largely neglected." [2]

A more recently published study of elementary school textbooks and social studies curriculum guides developed by school systems again pointed to the inadequacies of these materials. In his conclusions, the author of the study stated: "Through sins of both commission and omission, it is clear that the material on the United States, the U.S. government and citizenship, and on race and social class constitutes at best a sugarcoating of history and at worst a rewriting of history to eliminate unpleasant facts. The material on foreign countries and peoples includes both some rewriting of history and a distinctly ethnocentric viewpoint." [3]

While very recently there have been attempts in educational materials to introduce some social controversy in a planned manner—for example, the World Law Fund cases, the Prentice-Hall series on Crucial American Problems, the Harvard public issues series, and those of the Sociological Resources, Inc.—these materials are basically *supplementary* and are usually not listed in state or local adoption lists. In the mid-seventies, the social issues component on such topics as racial and ethnic minorities and the role of women in society has not yet really penetrated the hard-cover textbook market in social studies and related fields. This component largely remains outside the mainstream of social studies instruction of American schools. [4]

It is difficult to explain why the materials available to teachers have not made substantial improvements in the deficient areas. Perhaps the fact that materials are published by national private organizations intent on appealing to a variety of interest groups explains their blandness and the absence of any issue that might be thought of as controversial. That many states have strict adoption rules requiring, among other things, hard covers for textbooks and subscribe to a rigid printing format are also contributing factors. Publishers, however, are perhaps more guilty than any other group, including school administrators and teachers, being un-

[2] Michael B. Kane, *Minorities in Textbooks* (Chicago: Anti-Defamation League of B'nai B'rith by Quandrangle Books, 1970), p. 138.

[3] Robert J. Goldstein, "Elementary School Curriculum and Political Socialization," in *Political Youth, Traditional Schools*, ed. B. G. Massialas (Englewood Cliffs, N.J.: Prentice-Hall, Inc., 1972), p. 30.

[4] See extensive reviews: William W. Joyce, "Minorities in Primary-Grade Social Studies Textbooks: A Progress Report," *Social Education* 37 (March, 1973): 218-233; and Irma Garcia, "The Colonialist Mentality: Distortions and Omissions in Children's History Books," in *Interracial Books for Children*, special issue on Puerto Rican materials, Council on Interracial Books for Children, Vol. 4, Nos. 1 and 2 (1973), p. 3.

duly concerned that books with "sensitive" topics will not sell. One publisher, for example, took out of its printed books several pictures of Bushman women because their bare breasts were shown. In this case management felt that the pictures, although they were vividly representing life among the tribes in Africa, might be offensive to some communities—something that could result in loss of sales. Though all publishers—and authors—do not operate this way, it is a fair observation to state that the profit motive has the highest priority among them, not teaching and learning. If this condition continues, it will probably result in greater pressure from educational associations and teacher unions to ask states to provide educational not corporation, rules for textbook publishing. If the pressure is strong enough, it could lead to a replication of the system that exists in many other countries: the nationalization of the textbook industry. In the United States, such public action could result in school districts, especially the larger ones with research-and-development capabilities, producing their own instructional materials.

There are no magic solutions to the problem of the exclusion of issue-centered materials from the host of those produced daily. The problem will persist unless the teachers themselves—not the textbook publishers or the authors—take it upon themselves to prepare packages of materials that are issue-oriented and make sure that a good many of the issues relate to the particular problems of their region. School corporations should release those interested teachers with imagination and skill to begin to develop materials for school use. In selecting these materials and preparing them for classroom use, the teachers may keep the following questions in mind:

1. Does the material deal with a current social problem in which students of that age have a personal involvement?
2. Does the material deal realistically with the situation?
3. Does the material enhance multi-ethnic understanding?
4. Does the material enable the students to develop their own ideas or positions about the problem at hand?
5. Does the material facilitate student discovery of important concepts and generalizations from the arts and sciences and from personal experience?
6. Does the material include questions that encourage students to conduct further inquiries of their own?
7. Does the material encourage students to provide defensible grounds for their position or hypothesis?
8. Does the material encourage students to clarify key terms and concepts so that communication problems can be reduced?
9. Does the material encourage students to be inquiring activists—to de-

velop the skill and the affective determination to be personally involved in social action?

10. Does the material contain possible areas for valuing, feeling, and value clarification? [5]

In the chapter sections that follow, we shall try to go into more detail on what constitutes a springboard for study and discussion and the different types of springboards that could be developed by teachers for use in the classroom.

DEVELOPING AND USING SPRINGBOARDS

One of the most important tasks of the social issues, inquiry teacher is to plan for learning activities that involve the use of springboards. Springboards are thought-provoking materials on a subject that motivate students into conducting an inquiry. Springboards are ordinarily used in the opening phases of a discussion on a topic—their main function being to get students involved and to generate relevant hypotheses or position statements.

Springboards introduced into the classroom can take many forms—documents, magazine articles, graphs, poems, maps, cartoons, advertisements, newspaper editorials, pictures, musical productions. An example of a series of multimedia units used as a source of springboards is a published program entitled *World History Through Inquiry*.[6] Drawing from several disciplines and in the context of world history and cultures, each unit in the program focuses on different aspects of society and provides a variety of printed and visual materials for students to examine and discuss. Let's take, for instance, the unit entitled, *Man and His Environment*, parts of which emphasize population-related themes. The unit has seven exercises, one of which begins with a *map game.* Students are given maps of "Bonaria" showing climate, natural vegetation, minerals, and landforms and are asked such questions as:

[5] For a more elaborate set of criteria for selecting materials, see Cox and Massialas, eds., *Social Studies*, pp. 8-9. For detecting racial biases in texts, see *Checklist for Selecting and Evaluating U.S. History Textbooks*, prepared by NEA Teacher Rights, National Education Association, 1973; and *Basic Content Analysis Evaluation Textbook Form* (New York: Council on Interracial Books for Children, 1973), p. 94. The last includes criteria for evaluating treatment of the following minorities: African Americans, Asian Americans, Mexican Americans, native Americans, Puerto Rican Americans, American women.

[6] Byron G. Massialas and Jack Zevin, *World History Through Inquiry* (Chicago: Rand McNally & Co., 1969, 1970).

If Bonaria were inhabited by (a) hunters, (b) herders, (c) farmers, (d) industrial people,

1. Where would each group be most likely to live?
2. What might happen if hunters moved to the area first and then herders came? Then farmers? Then the industrial group? What would the pattern of settlement be if all the groups tried to live in the area at the same time? [7]

The same exercise contains five *case studies* of population movements—of the Semang (hunters and gatherers), of the Turkmen (nomads), of the inhabitants of Easter Island, of the forced exchange of population between India and Pakistan, and of migratory workers from southern Europe. The case studies provide students with the opportunity to test and further refine the hypotheses generated in the map game on the settlement of Bonaria. These hypotheses aim at explaining why people move from one place to another and at establishing some of the social consequences of such movements.

In another situation, a class was presented with *charts* that showed birth and death rates in four different but unidentified countries over a period of seventy years. Given an inquiring posture represented by the teacher who introduced this springboard, the students became quite involved in trying to figure out from limited information how birth and death rates can be used to understand events in a nation's history. [8]

Statements that present opposing or incompatible positions or interpretations also form excellent classroom springboards. [9] Continuing with our population theme, the teacher may ask students to read *two articles* on population and world power; for instance, one written by Colin Clark and the other by Kingsley Davis. [10] The Clark article argues that population means power, and it offers some statistical data to support that position. The Davis article suggests a more complicated relationship between population and national power than ordinarily is assumed and cites some factors that could make a substantial difference

[7] Ibid., p. 37; *Man and His Environment*, p. 4.

[8] The springboard as well as the actual classroom dialogue that followed are given in Byron G. Massialas and Jack Zevin, *Creative Encounters in the Classroom: Teaching and Learning Through Discovery* (New York: John Wiley & Sons, 1967), pp. 106-124.

[9] A useful compilation of articles for teachers and students is Daniel Callahan ed., *The American Population Debate* (Garden City, N.Y.: Anchor Books, Doubleday & Co., 1971).

[10] Colin Clark, "World Power and Population," *National Review* (May 20, 1969): 481-484. Kingsley Davis, "Population and Power in the Free World," in *Population and World Politics*, ed. Phillip Hauser (Glencoe, Ill.: The Free Press, 1958), pp. 193-213.

in determining that relationship: "(1) the relation of population to resources; (2) the state of mortality and morbidity; (3) the level of fertility; (4) the age structure; (5) the rate of internal migration; (6) the degree of urbanization." Given a supportive psychological climate, this springboard should elicit a number of hypotheses and positions from the students, some of which may depart from those advanced by the two authors. This exercise can also demonstrate how disagreements exist in any field of endeavor and point to the need to exercise independent judgment based on logic and reliable evidence. The need to secure additional data that are relevant and up-to-date should become obvious.

One might follow up the initial springboard by showing how different nations feel about population growth. Is a large population a strength or a weakness? Here the introduction of material from various countries on population policy could serve as the springboard. For example, President Nixon's *Message to Congress* of July 18, 1969, called attention to the need for a United States population policy.[11] With regard to the domestic scene, the President posed the following questions: "How . . . will we house the next hundred million Americans?" "What of our national resources and the quality of our environment?" "How will we educate and employ such a large number of people?"

In contrast with the message, material from countries that have an explicit population policy may be introduced.[12] *Articles* from the Soviet press could be used here. For example, a discussion of the national effects of being a bachelor is presented in articles in *Literaturnaya Gazeta* of April 21, 1971.[13] The articles are introduced with the following editorial note: "To increase the birth rate is one of our country's urgent problems. Statistics bear this out. Whereas 5,300,000 were born in the USSR in 1960, fewer than 4,100,000 were born in 1969." Another article, originally appearing in *Voprosy Ekonomiki* of February, 1971, states in part:

> Many socialist countries are now pursuing an active demographic policy, proceeding from their specific conditions. Thus, in the European socialist countries demographic policy is aimed at raising the birth rate. The basic instruments of such a policy are the propaganda of demographic and medical information, agitation and financial support for actions corresponding to the national interest.

---

[11] "Problems of Population Growth," Message from President Nixon to the Congress. A reprint from *The Department of State Bulletin*, Aug. 11, 1969.

[12] See, for example, "Government Policy Statements on Population: An Inventory," *Reports on Population/Family Planning* (Population Council), February, 1970. See also the Population Council's occasional publication, *Country Profiles*.

[13] See, "Marry Early, Down with Bachelors!" *The Current Digest of the Soviet Press* 23 (May 11, 1971): 35-37.

The implementation of a more active demographic policy aimed at encouraging the birth of two or three children is necessary in our country, too.[14]

Questions raised regarding the two sets of material might include: What is the position on population represented in the statements from the U.S.A. and the U.S.S.R.? Do they agree with each other? Why or why not? Does each produce sufficient evidence to justify the position taken? What is your own opinion on the issue? What would you recommend as a national policy? Why?

Springboards can also take the form of a *series of hypotheses* introduced for purposes of classroom investigation. Here is an example of three provocative propositions taken from an article written by Myron Weiner:

> . . . as population continues to increase more rapidly than ability to satisfy needs and desires, political unrest, perhaps leading to the violent overthrow of existing governments, becomes almost inevitable" [quoting Harold Dorn].
> . . . if one ethnic group in a society has a higher population growth rate than another, there may be a change in the distribution of power even if there are no accompanying economic changes.
> . . . modern revolutionary movements are associated with an increase in the number of young adults.[15]

Given these initial stimuli, the task of the class is to ascertain the validity of the hypotheses. This process involves a conscious effort to clarify the meaning of the key concepts and to gather relevant data that support, reject, or modify the original propositions. In many cases the students may conclude that there is not adequate evidence within their reach to check the validity of the hypotheses. In others, meaningful modifications may evolve from student inquiry, thinking, and interaction.

Springboards can also present issues that are highly controversial. A controversial issue is a component of a larger social problem in which the individual is personally involved. As we mentioned before, controversial items, when presented in the spirit of inquiry, form excellent springboards. They generate wide classroom participation, they provide the opportunity to take positions on an issue drawing from personal resources, and they open up the way for value clarification. The educative

[14] "Demography and the Manpower Problems," *The Current Digest of the Soviet Press* 23 (June 1, 1971): 5-8.
[15] Myron Weiner, "Political Demography: An Inquiry into the Political Consequences of Population Change," in *Rapid Population Growth: Consequences and Policy Implications,* ed. Roger Revelle (Baltimore: The Johns Hopkins Press, 1971.)

aim of controversy is to air important social concerns in the classroom and to give to the individual student the intellectual and psychological capability to form *defensible* positions on pressing social problems and, where possible, to act on them.

One does not need to search far for controversial material on many current topics. The local newspaper provides a good source. The following constitutes a small sample of titles of relevant articles that appeared in newspapers in Florida in a period of less than a month.

"On Male Patients: New Sterility Method Tested"

"Sterilization Urged for the Defective"

"Multiple Fathers Possible in France"

"Teenage Pregnancy and Suicide"

"A Court Responds"

The last item on the list is an *editorial* published by the *St. Petersburg Times* on Oct. 4, 1971, which takes a position against the validity of an abortion law passed by the state of Florida in 1968 (Statute 797.02). The editorial states in part:

> Floridians have an example to ponder this week of what happens when the Legislature fails to modify a law that is harsh, outdated, and unresponsive to present needs.
>
> Such a law is the Florida statute prohibiting abortion. It not only does that, but it also leaves a minister—who advises a woman with a problem pregnancy on how to obtain a legal abortion in another state—liable to prosecution and imprisonment at Raiford.
>
> Last July, the Supreme Court warned the Legislature that the law was "not responsive to the realities of medical science."
>
> A new law should leave the abortion decision to the woman and her doctor.
>
> A report from New York City's health services administrator shows the favorable effects of the first 14-month's experience under the state's abortion law. Health chief Gordon Chase revealed a decline in incomplete (illegal) abortions—those cases hospitals receive after abortion has begun elsewhere—from 480 a month July-December, 1970, to 243 a month July-August, 1971. Also, against a previous upward trend, there was an actual decline in illegitimate births during the first five months this year.

The excerpted editorial takes a clear position on abortion laws as represented by those in force in Florida. The task of the class where the item is introduced as a springboard is to clarify the stated position and to probe into and further explore the grounds upon which the position

rests—that is, to examine the supporting facts and the general value principle which relate to the object that is to be rated. Members of the class
may challenge the position and introduce their own positions and the
grounds that support them.[16] The springboard may also provide the initial
idea for subsequent systematic discussion of abortion from the legal-social
point of view—the measures that a state should justifiably take to protect
the general welfare of society versus the rights of the individual to self-
determination. One teacher in a Florida Catholic junior high school has
had students debating the issues of population management and abortion
using factual material and a variety of viewpoints on policy for exploring
their personal positions and statements. Material such as *Options*[17] may
provide the springboard for examining the issue from a moral, ecological,
or economic point of view.

Controversial issues can also be introduced in the form of brief
statements. The statements or propositions below may serve a springboard
purpose: [18]

> A married couple has the right to have as many children as it can afford.
>
> The government should control the dispensing of all birth-control mate-
> rials.
>
> Eliminating all unwanted pregnancies in the U.S. would bring about
> zero population growth (ZPG).
>
> A married woman should be able to have an abortion without her hus-
> band's consent.
>
> Population control would cause the genocide of blacks.
>
> The communal life should be legalized.
>
> A woman should have complete choice over what happens to her body.
>
> Abortion should be permitted for married women but not for single
> women.
>
> Nobody ever dies of overpopulation.
>
> Overpopulation is not a problem in my community; there is plenty of
> room for me and the six children I plan to have.

[16] An excellent source of ideas for the teacher in handling value questions in
the classroom is *Values Education: Rationale, Strategies and Procedures,* ed. Lawrence E. Metcalf, 41st Yearbook (Washington, D.C.: National Council for the Social
Studies, 1971).

[17] Kathryn Horsley, Parker Marden, Byron Massialas, Jerry Brown, *Options: A
Study Guide to Population and the American Future,* Washington, D.C.: The Population Reference Bureau, Inc., 1973.

[18] Taken from a list on "Issues Related to Family Planning and Population
Education" prepared by a group of participants in the Institute on Family Planning/
Population Studies co-sponsored by Florida State and Florida A & M universities in
the summer of 1971.

All these statements contain challenging ideas that should immediately elicit a great deal of heated discussion. They focus mainly on fertility factors, but mortality, urbanization, or migration factors could also be considered. After an initial exchange of ideas on these statements, it would be the task of the teacher and the students to probe into their underlying assumptions and see to what extent they are justified. A thorough examination of each topic should follow.

Springboards need not be confined to conventional social studies materials only. They can be drawn from several fields of human endeavor including art, music, and literature. As with all springboards, the main questions to be raised in collecting the material would pertain to the extent to which it can be used to stimulate discussion on a current or historical social issue. For example, in using folksongs as a springboard, it might be asked what notions of male and female roles in the family do they convey? What are their notions of children? Of procreation? Do they have a pro- or anti-natalist bias? Why? What images of family in relation to society have folksongs conveyed over certain periods? Has there been a corresponding movement in other forms of artistic expression?

A popular singer, Cat Stevens, raises the important issue of the relationship between people and the environment in his song, "Where Do The Children Play?" He says that although we have made tremendous technological advances, such as reaching outer space and building huge airplanes, we have not provided space for children to play. What shall we do about it? Shall we continue our climactic technological build-up while, in the meantime, we are not attending to some basic conditions of society that give meaning to life? This type of popular song can be very effective, especially if the original record is played by the teacher.[19]

Classroom Examples

How can the teacher introduce controversy and social science concepts into the classroom? How do students react to springboards? Below are some excerpts of dialogue that followed the introduction of population-related springboards. Attention will be given to the kinds of questions the teacher raised to initiate discussion.[20]

[19] "Where Do The Children Play?" by Cat Stevens, © 1970, Freshwater Music Ltd. (England). Controlled in Western Hemisphere by Irving Music, Inc. (BMI).

[20] The springboards were used in high-school social studies classes with "average" students. Many thanks are due to Will Veal for teaching this material.

Discussion 1 [21]

Teacher: If we implement a policy of ZPG, what other considerations must be taken into account?

Arlene: Well, like they could control the growth of the United States, but what about the other people coming in all over the nation into the United States?

Mark: Limit it?

Arlene: Yeah, we could do that.

Bill: Stop the total inputs from different countries.

Maria: You'd have to be careful what occupation you chose like . . . an occupation that wasn't needed . . . There wasn't going to be a need for more buildings and you're going to be an architect—that wouldn't be a very good choice to study to be an architect . . . rather pick another field that doesn't rely on population growth.

Teacher: What other occupations?

Ursula: Well, I don't know.

Mark: Probably most producers would have to cut down. There wouldn't be as much growth in production as there is now.

Teacher: Why?

Mark: Because the population wouldn't be growing.

The discussion above explores consequences of ZPG. The teacher introduces the original material by asking "hypothesis generating" questions. In response to questions such as these the students suggest that immigration is an important factor in population growth. They also point to possible consequences of population changes. The teacher constantly asks "clarification" questions and questions that call for the "grounding" of claims.

Disscussion 2 [22]

Teacher: What lessons might *In the Ghetto* have for society as a whole or the world?

Don: It's a model for us to look at.

Teacher: Yes, it could be a model.

Becky: Well, the ghetto's real crowded and it might show that the world gets that crowded and it's like that everywhere and not just in parts.

[21] Based on James E. Carlson, "Economy—Ecology—and Zero Population Growth," *Architectural Record* 148 (August, 1970): 59-60.
[22] Based on the Elvis Presley record, *In the Ghetto*, RCA Victor, 47-9741.

Billy: I think it said something like when he gets hungry enough, you know, he steals a gun or a car or something, you know. He's tired of living that way so, you know, and the world get like that. I guess he gets used to the bad or something.

Teacher: Anything else?

Arlene: I guess the middle-class family thinks that whenever there's a child born and they're related to it, they have good feelings like they're happy or they're concerned for the mother and baby or they have a feeling of pride and then like somebody in the ghetto that has a baby that doesn't have any money to support it or anything they feel sorry for the baby and they pity him because they can't afford him but they still love him and they feel sorry for him because they know that he probably won't make it . . .

Maria: You should have kids if you can afford them, and want them, you shouldn't have kids if you don't want them. She couldn't take care of him—look what happened—he stole a car, stole a gun . . . So if she couldn't take care of them, she was sad when she had them. How would you feel if you were unwanted and didn't have anything to eat or nothing else to do but go out in the street and steal?

Don: Well, I can't say that won't happen in each case. Some kids might try to better themselves.

Maria: Yeah, that could happen, but the better percent of them turned bad.

The dialogue above is again initiated by the teacher who uses a hit song on the ghetto as the springboard. The teacher begins by asking the students to hypothesize about the significance and the implications of the song. Inescapably, value judgments issue from an open kind of discussion, such as Maria's position that "you should have kids if you can afford them and want them." It is the teacher's responsibility to create the supportive conditions that bring out these value positions and provide the opportunity for all to examine them critically.

Discussion 3 [23]

Teacher: After Garret Hardin's article, do you feel that society has a right to limit the number of children a couple or a person can have?

Dale: I think he attacked planned parenthood and birth control and women in particular.

Bert: How do people attack women?

Dale: How? In every nation women want more children than the community needs. Birth control must be exerted through females. Biology makes women responsible.

[23] Based on an article by Garrett Hardin, "Parenthood: Right or Privilege?" *Science* 169 (July 31, 1970): 427.

Bert:	His reasons then why attacking womanhood?
Dale:	Aren't men responsible, too?
Teacher:	Is it primarily a woman's responsibility?
Girls:	No, I don't think so. No.
Billy:	The woman has to take the birth-control pill, the woman has the kid, right?

(Heated exchange)

Dale:	I think his major point is right. He said society would have to exert more control measures and, as this last paragraph says, if it's a right you can't control people, if it's a privilege you can.
Teacher:	Is it a right? Is it a right for a person to determine how many children he or she is going to have?
Class:	Yes.
Jim:	To some extent.
Teacher:	To what extent, Jim?
Jim:	You know, if everyone went out and had twenty kids then there would be starvation and all that kind of stuff, so it wouldn't work out that way.
Billy:	I think it's a right, but it depends on the person, I guess the parents know how many kids they can support and how many they want.
Alicia:	It's a right but it shouldn't be taken advantage of like people who go out and have a whole bunch of kids when they know that the world is going to be overpopulated if they don't cut down, that's when it kind of ends.
Teacher:	What basic American values come into conflict, if any, when you talk about limiting the number of kids a person can have?
Jim:	Well, the first thing is personal freedom. This is supposed to be the land of the free, and if people tell you to do something, you usually object.
Annette:	I don't think it's right for somebody to come up to you and tell you how many you can have, 'cause the person, whoever it is, is able to support the family—it's all right for them, you know, to have any amount.
Teacher:	Do you think this is a practical approach? How can it be enforced?
Mary:	I think it should be enforced like you have a fine if you had so many kids . . .
Brenda:	That wouldn't work because the rich people then could afford to have kids but the poor people then couldn't afford to pay the fines. But like in certain amounts, you could take their income tax and use that and take so much from the rich and so much from the poor. Take a certain percent.
Becky:	It says here persuasion is going to have to be used. I don't think

            that's right. I don't think you can force people to have just so many children. You're going to have to talk to them and explain to them.

Annette: I think that people should try to persuade people to just, instead of having so many kids, to get some from the adoption place. Adopt some instead of having so many of their own.

Teacher: Are there any groups of people that should have a different kind of status than others, as far as the right to have children?

Maria: I don't know; it seems like it's going to be needed that someone that has had twenty kids should not keep on having kids so the ones that hadn't had any would be able to have them. Maybe it's not necessary to tell people how many kids they can have 'cause having kids used to be a right, because there were ways of taking care of them. The way it's getting there are so many kids and things are getting all messed up. You should try to protect the kids coming in from having to get into this world that's polluted.

Ramey: I don't want to bring my opinion in this but, it seems to me that it would be hard for anybody to make a law concerning who can have children and who can't. That's a right. It's a little different than saying that you can't go straight ahead through a red light. That's protecting yourself and protecting other drivers. But, indirectly it is protecting everybody in the country, when you're saying we shouldn't have a lot of kids, but I don't see how you can tell somebody: "NO, you can't have a child."

    In this sample discussion the teacher opens up the session with a "position" question. The question centers around the idea of whether a society should regulate the number of children one may have. Students are encouraged to state their own positions on the issue and agree or disagree with another person's position—in this case Garrett Hardin's. The teacher, as in the previous examples, constantly asks that positions be defended and clarified.

Discussion 4 [24]

Teacher: Do you agree with Dr. Odum's position that every pertinent society owes every person a quality environment?

Jim: I think it does. Every child that's born has a right to live in the same world that you were born in. If it was good to you, you shouldn't destroy it for the next generation.

Alicia: I don't think society really owes it to 'em. I think it's up to the people themselves, what kind of environment they live in.

Dale: When you talk about society owing somebody a right, I kind of

[24] Springboard condensed from Eugene P. Odum, "Optimum Population and Environment: A Georgian Microcosm,' *Current History* 58 (June, 1970): 355-359.

wonder what you mean by society. Don't you mean that other people owe somebody else a right to live? That won't happen. People have to earn the right.

Teacher: Can an individual earn the right for quality environment, starting at birth?

Dale: No.

Teacher: I'll agree with you, basically, that many rights have to be earned. But is this something that we have a right to withhold until they do earn it?

Dale: I don't think anybody—has the right to take away anything from anybody else.

Jim: I was just going to say, you might say that a person can earn the right if he just contributes to not tearing up the world, he sort of earns it.

Teacher: What are some values or behaviors which must be changed from our present social system if we are to make sure that every person who is born in the future has a quality environment?

Dale: We have to prevent or slow down pollution.

Roger: Like in Georgia, they can produce enough food for maybe 12 million people if it was consumed directly and not made into other products.

This discussion, which deals with population and the quality of life, is again initiated with a position question. In this case the students take different positions on the issue, each one trying to justify his own with whatever evidence he can marshal.

Classroom springboards are motivating episodes that usually contain puzzling or emotionally charged situations. Most often, a springboard leads to student involvement through open or guided discovery. Much of the research available on discovery teaching and learning suggests that there are several positive effects related to student behaviors and attitudes.

In a study of inquiry teaching conducted in a tenth-grade world history class, students were frequently exposed to a wide repertoire of discovery episodes, usually initiated by historical documents from which the various origins, referents, and authors had been deleted.[25] The investigators of the study pointed out that students had no "pre-knowledge" of the problem at hand. The results clearly demonstrated that:

1. Without exception the students were able to participate directly in the processes of discovery and inquiry.

2. A new psychological climate was created in which students became in-

     [25] Byron G. Massialas and Jack Zevin, "Teaching Through Discovery," *Social Education* 28 (November, 1964): 384–387.

creasingly independent and began to question the authority of secondary historical sources. They generally adopted an attitude of intelligent doubt, and they tended to propose new ideas and explanations that had to be defended.

3. Discovery was highly motivating in that students became personally involved with the materials and problems under investigation. This was because discovery is like a game which reinforces the element of perplexity and incentive to explore.[26]

These results tend to support the four advantages of discovery learning proposed by Bruner: greater intellectual potency, intrinsic motivation, facility in processing and retrieving information, and the learning of heuristic processes.[27]

In his study on personality and learning, Jerome Kagan discusses the merits and the disadvantages of discovery learning. Among his stated advantages are that it requires high involvement and attention, stimulates students to make intellectual efforts, increases autonomy and the expectation of success, and promotes more independent attitudes.[28] The disadvantages Kagan discusses include such factors as the lack of initial motivation on the part of many students, the extra time required, the absence of appreciation by younger children of cognitive problems and the joy of discovery, and the tendency by impulsive children to settle for a wrong conclusion.[29]

Kagan concludes that the discovery method is possibly most appropriate for highly motivated, older children who have high tolerance for conflict and who are already inclined to use a reflective strategy in their thinking. Discovery, according to Kagan, is least appropriate for younger children, especially those below the age of nine who do not have high motivation to master intellectual tasks and who tend to be impulsive. However, Kagan, ignores the possibility of any resulting change in students' abilities and attitudes after receiving instruction designed to encourage and develop their discovery skills. He does suggest that discovery could be motivating because it uses "surprise" to capture the attention of all children, at least temporarily, and he argues, "Novelty is one of the educators' most effective weapons against pupil apathy, for surprise temporarily recharges the attention system." [30]

[26] Ibid.

[27] Jerome S. Bruner, "The Act of Discovery," *Harvard Educational Review* 31, No. 1 (1961): 21-32.

[28] Jerome Kagan, "Personality and the Learning Process," *Daedalus* 94 (Summer, 1965): 560.

[29] Ibid., p. 561.

[30] Ibid., p. 562.

SUMMARY

A country that has many ethnic and interest groups, each with its own cultural norms, needs to have its schools provide a fair picture of each group's problems and contributions. Unfortunately, not only have schools failed to provide materials on the various ethnic and interest groups but they have offered very little—in fact, virtually nothing—that has to do with crucial social problems. Thus children and youth have very rarely been given the opportunity to deal directly and honestly with the vital issues that society is facing and is trying to resolve. The most important of these issues is the relations among different groups.

With the new movement to open up the schools to reflective inquiry, the social issues of our time are gradually finding their way into curricula. Because materials for classroom use are scarce, teachers should develop their own, using newspapers, magazines, musical productions, radio and TV programs, and similar sources. The materials that provide the bases for the four discussions presented in this chapter are good examples. Such resource materials serve as springboards that motivate students to ask challenging questions and to discuss and take stands on social issues.

6

social-inquiry teaching:
some practical examples

To conduct social inquiry in the classroom, the teacher must employ a number of skills and techniques, several of which are related to the planning of motivating inquiry exercises and the use of various learning activities and materials. The practical examples of discovery strategies given in this chapter have been taken from teaching situations in both elementary and secondary classrooms. Their purpose is to define the inquiry process further and to serve as guides to teachers planning inquiry lessons.

It was suggested in the previous chapter that the concept of springboard to introduce inquiries into general or specific topics be illustrated through use of a variety of materials. The exercises that follow also illustrate how springboards can be used to facilitate social inquiry through discovery learning, they are practical examples of discovery episodes for elementary and secondary students and they deal with different content areas and subject matter. Examples are also included that recommend use of a number of materials including documents, letters, case studies, music, poetry, cartoons, open-ended stories and pictures, court cases, role-playing and creative dramatics, art work, games, maps, charts, folk tales, graphs, articles, advertisements and editorials. These classroom samples also provide actual examples of such inquiry-oriented processes as defining problems, making hypotheses, collecting and analyzing data, testing hypotheses, and drawing conclusions. The types of questions and activities useful in promoting social or probing inquiry receive particular emphasis.

PUZZLING DOCUMENTS AS SPRINGBOARDS

The creative inquiry teacher is always on the lookout for historical and contemporary documents that include discrepancies in their accounts or that lack crucial facts and conclusions. The documents below demonstrate how a puzzling springboard can help students define social problems, hypothesize, and express their feelings and values. The following lesson sequence, based on original documents—including a description of an abandoned town, two letters threatening violence to a religious sect, a plea for freedom by Massachusetts slaves—has been used with fifth and seventh graders as well as with pre-service and in-service teachers as demonstration lessons. In American history classrooms the lesson sequence has been used to initiate inquiry into the topic of migration, especially westward migration.

The Colonel's Account

AN UNUSUAL GHOST TOWN [1]

by Colonel Thomas Kane

A few years ago, I took a steamboat up the Northern Mississippi in the fall when its waters were low. I had to go by land past a dangerous part of the river, the shallow rapids. My road went through a very beautiful part of Iowa. This area had become a home for horse thieves and other outlaws. I got off the steamboat at Keokuk, Iowa. I rented a carriage and stopped for a bite to eat. It was several miles to where the water was again deep enough to catch another steamer. I drove the carriage through this barren land of bandits, vagabonds, and lazy settlers. They had done nothing to use or beautify the land.

I was coming down the last hillside of my journey when I saw a beautiful place. On the bend of the river was a city shining in the fresh morning sun. It had bright new houses and rich, green gardens. The town was settled around a hill on which I could see a large marble temple. A high steeple was shining white and gold in the sun. A sign read, "Church of Saints." The city covered several miles. Beyond it, in the background, there was plowed land looking

---

[1] Thomas Kane, *Journal of the Historical Society of Pennsylvania* (Philadelphia: King and Basid, Printers, March 26, 1850).

like a checkerboard of green, brown, and yellow squares. Someone had been hard at work here. It was a very beautiful sight.

I was curious to visit this place. I borrowed a boat and rowed across the river to the city's wharf. No one met me there. I looked and saw no one at all. I could hear no one move. The only sounds to be heard were the buzzing of flies and the water ripples hitting against the beach.

I walked through the empty streets. The town lay as if in a dream. It was clear that the city had not slept for a long time. There was no grass growing up in the streets and there were still some footprints in the dust.

There was no one there to stop me. I went into empty workshops and stores everywhere. The spinner's wheel was still. The carpenter had left his loaded work bench. Fresh bark was still in the tanner's vat. Freshly chopped wood stood piled against the baker's oven. The blacksmith's shop was cold, but looked as though he had just gone off for a holiday.

No one called to me from the open windows. Not even a dog barked at me. I walked into some houses. I found nothing but cold ashes on the hearths and squeaking floorboards.

On the outskirts of town was the city graveyard. There was no new sign of plague on the tombstones. It did not look any different than any other graveyard I had ever seen before. A stone read, "Nauvoo, Illinois."

Beyond the graveyard, out in the fields, I saw in one spot an orchard of ripe fruit trees. I could also see the still-smoldering ashes of a big barbeque fire. It was the latest sign of life there. Field after field of heavy-headed yellow grain lay rotting ungathered upon the ground. No one was there to get the rich harvest. As far as the eye could see rich fields stretched across the country in the hazy autumn air.

Such a ghost town I had never seen. I kept wondering. Who had lived there? Where had they gone? Why had they left?

After the students had read the story above, the teacher initiated inquiry into migration by asking open-ended questions that helped define the problem (on the basis of data questions), stimulate student thinking (on the basis of hypothesis questions), and generate student reaction and feeling (on the basis of feeling questions):

(PROBLEM DEFINITION)

1. What is this story really about?
2. What seems to be the problem here?
3. Why is this story entitled "An Unusual Ghost Town"?
4. Is there anything unusual about Nauvoo? Explain.

(HYPOTHESES QUESTIONS)

1. Why are there no people in Nauvoo?
2. Why might Nauvoo be a ghost town?
3. Why do ghost towns appear?
4. Why do people move from place to place?
5. What things might make you and your family move? Why would they make you move?

(FEELING QUESTIONS)

1. How might the people of Nauvoo have felt about moving away? Explain what you mean.
2. How might you feel if you were in a ghost town by yourself? Why?
3. If you were to move away from where you live now, how would that make you feel? Why?
4. Have you ever moved in the past? How did that move make you feel? Why?

The upshot of the second set of questions was that a number of students hypothesized about the motives behind this particular migration as well as those behind any human migration. Some of their hypotheses included:

People may move because they are attracted to new places.

People are often attracted to new locations by powerful economic forces, such as gold, riches, land, employment, and profits.

People may be attracted by opportunities to experience religious or political freedom, to start a new life, or to gain more political or social power.

People may be induced to move by such factors as a better food supply, more resources, family ties, friends, weather, schools, and adventure.

People may migrate because they are being driven away from their homes by war, famine, fire, flood, plague, and fear.

Many people move to secure employment.

Religious and political persecution often leads to migration.

People may not move for some of these same reasons.

Students were encouraged to provide evidence in support of their hypotheses, and they cited books, periodicals, television, movies, and personal experience. Students who had already heard of Nauvoo were used as resource people to collect additional information and to prepare a skit or "news report" with further facts about the migration under study. On the following day students were asked to examine two short, original letters concerning the Mormons of Nauvoo. These letters, reprinted below, offered some data with which to test the student hypotheses of the previous day, and they served as springboards into other areas of social inquiry such as religious persecution, Mormon migration, and the determination of human values.

Two Letters to the Mormons

April 8, 1845

To: Brigham Young
      President of the Mormon Church

If you can get off by yourself, you may find peace. But surrounded by such neighbors, I do not think you will be happy here. I was told by Joseph Smith last Summer that he was thinking about a move then. If he were alive, he would have begun to leave before now.

I advise you to go. California now has open land for a new life. Few people live there. Why don't you go out there and take over some of the country? You can start your own government there. You could stay there a long time before you would be disturbed by other settlers.

T. Ford
Governor of Illinois [2]

October 3, 1845

To: Mormons of Nauvoo

You have told us that you will be willing to go. This committee and our whole community expect you to leave Illinois with your whole church group. If you do not, then we are sure something will happen. We hate violence and bloodshed, but we will use them to make you leave.

We think that you should leave. Start getting ready now. Then you can leave in peace. To keep law and order until then, armed men from the state militia (army) will stay here.

With many wishes that you find the peace and good life which you want in the west.

The Quincy Committee
John J. Hordin   W. B. Warren
S. A. Douglas   J. A. McDougal [3]

---

[2] William A. Linn, *The Story of the Mormons* (New York: Russell and Russell, Inc., 1902), pp. 340-341.
[3] Ibid.

The teacher initiated further inquiry by asking the students to interpret the meaning of the letters and state possible relationships with the "unusual ghost town." Concepts serving as cues for the formulation of testable statements and value positions included oppression, persecution, political freedom, religious freedom, prejudice, beliefs, and conflict.

(PROBLEM DEFINING OR DATA QUESTIONS)

1. What are these letters about?
2. What do they tell us about the people of Nauvoo? About their neighbors?
3. What new information do these letters provide us?
4. What problems or issues are involved here?

(HYPOTHESIZING QUESTIONS)

1. Which of our hypotheses are supported by the new data?
2. Which hypotheses are not supported?
3. What other information do we need? How can we get it?
4. Why do many people move? Why might the Mormons have moved west?
5. Why might the Mormons have stopped in Salt Lake Valley?
6. The Mormons sang many songs on their way west. What ideas and words might we find in these songs? Why do you think so?
7. Would songs be good sources of information about how people feel and think? Why or why not?
8. Have other people moved for similar reasons? Explain and give examples.

(POSITION AND FEELING QUESTIONS)

1. How do these letters make you feel? Why?
2. How must the Mormons have felt? Why do you think so?
3. How would you have felt after getting such a letter? Why?
4. Do you think the Mormons should have moved? Explain your position.
5. What should people do when they are threatened? When denied their religious freedom and rights? Why? What are the implications of that position?
6. How should people treat others who do not share their own religious and political beliefs? Why?
7. How would you resolve religious conflict? Why would you do it that way?

At this point students were asked to write down topics and unanswered questions that they would like to study during subsequent sessions. They were encouraged to put down subjects that were interesting *to them.* Some of the following topics were identified and explored by a seventh-grade history class:

> What is polygamy? Are Mormons still allowed to practice it? Was this a cause of their moving?
>
> Did all the Mormons leave? Did some stay and fight? Were they pacifists?
>
> What violence occurred? Did the Mormons move many times? Why? Why did they stop in Utah and not go to California?
>
> Where did the Mormons come from? What did they believe?
>
> How did they make a living? What were their customs?
>
> What was the gold rush? How did it begin?
>
> What cities have been wiped out by plague?
>
> What happened to Nauvoo? What is it like today?
>
> How did they get to Salt Lake? What was the trip like? What was the new Mormon colony in Utah like?
>
> What was the Quincy Committee? Why did its members write the letter?
>
> Why didn't the Illinois and national governments help the Mormons?
>
> Why do ghost towns happen? What ghost towns have been famous in our history?
>
> Why are people prejudiced? What is happening in Ireland?
>
> How has prejudice affected American history?

These topics served as ideas for student research and study and for projects related to migration and the study of the West. In this particular class the teacher allowed students a good measure of freedom in selecting, planning and researching projects and in presenting their findings. She assisted students in their individual and group study by serving as a resource person—that is, she located books, films, filmstrips; gave short presentations of information; and asked inquiry-oriented questions. Other data sources and springboards used included pioneer songs and diaries, maps of Mormon and western migrations, films and filmstrips of the gold rush, newspaper headlines and stories about gold in California, an account of Sutter's mill, textbook and encyclopedia selections, and current news stories regarding migration and persecution. The teacher sustained inquiry through skillful questions related to student feelings, student values and student initiative in probing for and explaining evidence.

A Little-Known Declaration of Freedom: Another Puzzling Document

The document below—written by four black men three years before the Declaration of Independence—serves as another example of how a historical item can be used as a puzzling, emotion-charging episode in social inquiry. In its present form the document has been adapted for fifth-grade history students during an inquiry into the American Revolution and Declaration of Independence. With a few hypothesizing and position questions, a teacher has used this document as a springboard to stimulate student inquiry into such concepts as freedom, rights, slavery, revolution, and justice. The Boston declaration poses many questions that challenge students to think and value. Fortunately, for both students and teacher many other excellent sources of documents are available in which fascinating springboards can be located.[4]

A LITTLE-KNOWN DECLARATION FOR FREEDOM

Boston, April 20, 1773

Sir, the Government of Massachusetts tried to free itself from slavery under England in their last meeting. This gave us who are slaves much happiness. We expect great things from men who have done such a brave thing in standing up against their fellow man and the plans to make them slaves.

We cannot but wish and hope, Sir, that you will have the same ideas of freedom and religious liberty in your next meeting.

We know that it would be bad for our Masters, if we asked that all of what rightfully belongs to us for our past work be given to us; we do not want that.

We know that we owe you for what you have done, but the people of this colony are now fighting for equality and justice. We must hope that you will think again about our terrible life and will help us get our freedom, as men who have a right to do so.

We ask for God's help in our peaceful and legal steps to get our freedom.

We are willing to obey the laws until we can earn money and leave this colony.

[4] The teacher might find the following anthologies extremely useful: *Annals of America* (Chicago: William Benton, 1969); *March of America Facsimile Series* (Ann Arbor: University Microfilms, Inc., 1966); *The American Immigration Collection* (New York: Arno Press and *The New York Times*, 1969); *The Papers of Alexander Hamilton* (New York: Columbia University Press, 1961); *The American Negro: His History and Literature* (New York: Arno Press and *The New York Times*, 1968); *The Jewish Experience in America* (Waltham, Mass.: American Jewish Historical Society, KTAV Publishing House, Inc., 1969); Jeremiah Curtin, *Creation Myths of Primitive America* (New York: Benjamin Blom, 1969); Audrey Hawthorn, *Art of the Kwakiutl Indians* (Seattle: University of Washington Press, 1967); *Handbook of Middle American Indians*, ed. Robert Wauchope (Austin: University of Texas Press, 1966); and *The North American Indian* (New York: Johnson Reprint Corp., 1970).

This is written for our fellow slaves in this colony and was ordered by their committee.

> *Peter Bestes*
> *Sambo Freeman*
> *Felix Holbrook*
> *Chester Joie* [5]

Sample Questions

1. How is this letter similar to the Declaration of Independence? Explain.
2. Why was this letter written at this time?
3. What technique did the authors of this letter use to get what they wanted? Do you think they got what they wanted? What might they do next?
4. How should people try to get what they want?
5. What might be the difference in results when the two types of declarations are used? Why?

Music and Songs as Springboards

It was previously suggested in connection with the Mormons' westward trek that their folksongs could help students hypothesize about their migration. Other migrating groups, including the Forty-Niners, blacks, hunters, Indians, and frontiersmen, also had their songs. Students, then, might analyze pioneer songs—like the ones on pages 115 through 117—to obtain data about the ideas and feelings of people on the move.

Teachers and parents alike are aware of young people's interest and attachment to music, especially popular music. They are also aware that many popular songs have themes that are controversial and intriguing to students. Many popular songs in the sixties and seventies carry a message or provide words, ideas, and feelings that can serve as springboards into many social issues. Popular songs in the past two decades have had such issue-oriented themes as war, bigotry, drugs, cannibalism, interracial dating, corporate greed, government corruption, political assassinations, apathy, courtship, middle class values, controlled genetics, population, and birth control. All the teacher need do is play a song with a social message and have students listen carefully and study the words on an overhead or ditto master. In this manner students finally *hear* the words of their favorite songs and are willing to discuss related ideas and feelings. They are ready then to research the topics the songs take up.

---

[5] Herbert Aptheker, ed., *A Documentary History of the Negro People in the United States* (New York: The Citadel Press, 1951), I:7-8.

Sometimes teachers are surprised by the response. Students have been known during an inquiry to bring in new records as further sources of information. On the other hand, we have known teachers who include songwriting as a class project to get students into the social content under study and to have them think, explore, identify issues and share conclusions with one another. The songs that follow have been used successfully to introduce units of study and to promote social inquiry in social studies. Other verbal media can, of course, be used in the same way as songs. Speeches, poetry, stories, even commercials are always good sources of social matters.

A few years ago the popular song "1984" [6] captured the essence of the famous book, *1984*, written by George Orwell, when it asked several questions about the listener's future. The lyrics posed such questions as, "Will you let it run your life?," "Where will you be when your freedom is dead . . . ?," and "Will you let it come?."

The song further introduces such concepts as "plexy-plastic eyeballs," "Big Brother," "plexi-plastic copters," and "you're never out of his sight." This record has been used effectively to stimulate inquiry into topics related to dictatorship, totalitarianism and freedom. Much of its success with students came from the playing of the record and the careful study of the lyrics by the students.

The song below is a well-known selection that is an excellent introduction or motivating episode related to prejudice and human relations. In fact it would also serve as springboard and source of information for the sample activities related to "I Walked in his Moccasins" given on page 48.

EVERYDAY PEOPLE [7]

Sometimes I'm right and I can be wrong
My own beliefs are in my song
A butcher, a banker, a drummer and then
Makes no difference what group I'm in
I am everyday people, yeah, yeah.

There is a blue one who can't accept the green one
For living with a fat one tryin' to be a skinny one
And different strokes for different folks
And so on and so on,
And skoobedoobedoobe
Oo-sha sha
We got to live together.

[6] "1984" was written and sung by SPIRIT, c/o Hollenbeck Music Company, 1968.

[7] © 1969, Daly City Music (BMI). Composed by Sylvester Stewart.

I am no better and neither are you
We are the same whatever we do
You love me, you hate me, you know me
And then you can't figure out the bag I'm in
I am everyday people, yeah, yeah.

There is a long hair that doesn't like the short hair
For being such a rich one that will not help the poor one
And different strokes for different folks
And so on and so on
And skoobedoobe, oo sha sha
We got to live together

There is a yellow one that won't accept the black one
That won't accept the red one
That won't accept the white one
And different strokes for different folks
And so on and so on
And skoobedoobe, oo sha sha
We got to live together
I am everyday people

Historical Songs as Springboards

PIONEER DAY 1870 [8]

Dear friends, I pray just lend an ear
Whilst I relate a song,
I do not mean disloyalty
Or anything that's wrong.
But all of you will bear me out
In what I now relate,
That Uncle Sam has been unkind
In denying us a state.

Chorus:
Then shout and sing for Zion's sons,
Three cheers for Deseret,
Although they've tried to kill us all,
We're all alive as yet.

Just three and twenty years have passed,
If I do not mistake,
Since a noble band of pioneers
First gazed upon Salt Lake.
They built the bridges, made the roads
And left their homes behind;

[8] Thomas E. Cheney, *Mormon Songs from the Rocky Mountains*, pp. 105-108.
Reprinted by permission of the American Folklore Society.

Their tracks were marked by stains of blood
In fleeing from mankind. . . .

Judge Titus Cradlebaugh and company
With Pat Connor at their head
And a host of army contractors
All wished the Mormons dead
And urged the Government to send more troops,
More rogues and pimps;
We wished them all a good warm place
With Satan and his imps.

And lastly Poland and his crowd
Thought it was wondrous wise
To introduce in Washington
A bill to disenfranchise
The Mormon people of their rights
And send them all to jail
For marrying in Celestial law,
Oh, how we fear and quail! . . .

THE CAMP OF ISRAEL [9]

Altho' in woods and tents we dwell,
Shout, shout O Camp of Israel!
No Gentile mobs on earth can bind
Our thoughts, or steal our peace of mind.

Chorus:
Tho' oppression's waves roll o'er us,
    We will praise our God and King;
We've a better day before us—
    Of that day we proudly sing.

We'd better live in tents and smoke
Than wear the cursed Gentile yoke;
We'd better from our county fly
Than by religious mobs to die.

We've left the city of Nauvoo
And our beloved Temple too;
And to the wilderness we go
Amid the winter frosts and snow.

Our homes were dear, we lov'd them well;
Beneath our roof 'twas sweet to dwell,
And honour the great God's commands,
By mutual rights of Christian lands.

[9] Thomas E. Cheney, *Mormon Songs from the Rocky Mountains,* pp. 49-50. Reprinted by permission of the American Folklore Society.

Our persecutors will not cease
And for their hatred we must go
To the wilds where reeds and rushes grow.

The Camp—the camp—its numbers swell!
Shout, shout O Camp of Israel!
The King, the Lord of Hosts is near;
His armies guard our front and rear.

These Mormon folksongs have been used both as springboards into topics for further study, using, for example, such lines as ". . . denying us a state," "Then by religious mobs to die," and ". . . to disenfranchise/The Mormon people of their rights," and as sources of information to test student hypotheses about migration and about music as a reflection of the culture and experience of people. In one class, students generated a list of words and phrases that might be found in Mormon songs after their emigration from Nauvoo (p. 111). Teachers will find that both historical and contemporary song titles and lyrics can be employed as interesting documents for study—as springboards and as new sources of data.

ROLE PLAYING
AS A SPRINGBOARD

Many teachers have found that students at all levels rise to the occasion when putting on a class play or skit in the school follies. Many have said, after seeing one of their students give a thrilling performance or outstanding comedy sketch, "I never knew she could do that. She's so quiet in class." The Shaftels[10] and others have suggested that students be encouraged to role play, present skits, write their own plays and skits, and become involved in creative dramatics. It has been our experience that students in elementary and secondary schools are both excited and serious when it comes to acting in front of their peers. Often, social studies teachers can use a structured role play—one in which the roles and sometimes the speeches are well defined for the student—as an excellent springboard into a topic. Employers and employees, new parents, Supreme Court Justices, teen-agers on a date, participants in a trial, police demonstrators, parents of teen-agers, legislators, collective bargainers, are all social "roles" that lend themselves to a dramatic presentation. One asset

[10] See Fannie and George Shaftel, *Role Playing for Social Values: Decision Making in Social Studies* (New York: Prentice Hall, 1967), and Bruce Joyce, Marsha Weil, and Rhoada Wald, *Three Teaching Strategies for the Social Studies* (Chicago: Science Research Associates, 1972).

of dramatics, structured or unstructured, is the high degree of involvement and spontaneity it creates. Students can forget themselves and portray some of their own feelings and perceptions without inhibitions. Their impulsiveness does not detract from the play but adds a new twist for student inquiry and value clarification. Students and teacher can capitalize on a student's free characterization to compare his ideas and feelings with those of other students and with those the playwright outlined in the original role.

Several sources of plays and skits are available for use in social studies classrooms.[11] Teachers can also locate historical and contemporary scripts and dialogues of social import. Students usually find trials, such as the one below, rather fascinating, and they serve as excellent material for motivation and discovery. The Penn trial, which took place in 1670, has been used with great success in classrooms from the fifth to the eighth grade. In this trial dramatization, as in others, students were cast in the roles of jurors, defendants, and other participants. Frequently, there are not enough roles for each class member so others are added, such as visitors (family and friends), reporters, courtroom artists, and newsmen.

Was It Justice?

THE TRIAL OF WILLIAM PENN [12]

Those People at the Trial

Samuel Starling, mayor	Thomas Howel, recorder
Thomas Bloodworth, alderman	William Peak, alderman
John Robinson, alderman	John Smith, sheriff
Richard Ford, alderman	James Edwards, sheriff
Joseph Shelden, alderman	Richard Browne, sheriff

Jury

Thomas Veer, Edward Bushel, John Hammond, Charles Wilson, John Brightman, William Plumstead, John Bailey, Gregory Walklet, Thomas Damask, William Lever, Henry Michel, Henry Henley.

The Trial Begins

Cryer: You shall well and truly try the prisoners according to the evidence. So help you God. William Penn and William Mead with many other people not known to the jury with force in the Parish

---

[11] Mark Chesler and Robert Fox, *Roleplaying Methods in the Classroom* (Chicago: Science Research Associates, 1966); *The Can of Squirms* (Downers Grove, Ill.: Arthur Meriwether, Inc., 1971); and Charles N. Quigley and Richard P. Longaker, *Voices for Justice: Role Playing in Democratic Procedures* (Boston: Ginn and Co., 1970).

[12] Adapted from *The Tryal of William Penn and William Mead*, ed. Don C. Seitz (Boston: Marshall Jones Co., 1919).

of St. Bennet Grace Church did unlawfully and loudly gather together to the disturbance of the peace of the king. William Penn did also preach and speak to William Mead and the other people there in the open street. This did last a long time and did break the law of the king. This frightened and disturbed many citizens and set a bad example for other people who would disturb the peace of the king.

What say you, William Penn and William Mead? Are you guilty as you stand charged in the statement read before? Or not guilty?

Penn and Mead:	Not guilty!
Recorder:	Do you know where you are?
Penn:	Yes.
Recorder:	Do you know it is the king's court?
Penn:	I know it to be the king's court.
Recorder:	Do you not know there is respect due to the court?
Penn:	Yes.
Recorder:	Why do you not pay respect? Why do you not pull off your hat?
Penn:	Because I do not believe that to be any respect.
Recorder:	Well, the court sets forty marks upon each of you.
Clerk:	Cryer, call James Cook into the court, give him his oath. James Cook, put your hand on this book.
	The evidence you shall give to the court, between our king and the prisoners, shall be the truth, and the whole truth, and nothing but the truth. So help you God.
Cook:	I was told to go and break up a meeting in Gracechurch-street. There I saw Mr Penn speaking to many people in the streets. I could not hear what he said, because of the noise made by the crowd. I tried to get closer, but I couldn't get through the crowd of people. Then Mr. Mead came up to me and asked me to let Mr. Penn go on preaching. He said that he would bring Penn to me when he was done.
Court:	How many people do you think were there?
Cook:	About three or four hundred people.
Court:	Call Richard Read, give him his oath.
Cryer:	The evidence you shall give to the court, between our king and the prisoners, shall be the truth, and the whole truth, and nothing but the truth. So help you God.
Court:	What do you know about these two prisoners?
Read:	My Lord, I went to Gracechurch-Street, where I found a large crowd of people. I heard Mr. Penn preach to them; and I saw Captain Mead speaking to Lieutenant Cook. What he said, I could not hear.

Mead: What did William Penn say?

Read: There was such a great noise, that I could not hear.

Mead: Jury, here is your proof. He said he heard Penn preach, and does not know what he said.

       He now says that he saw me there, too. But, when he told the story to the mayor, when I was arrested, he said that he had not seen me! Is that not true, Mr. Mayor?

Mayor: (No answer.)

Court: How many people were there?

Read: About four or five hundred?

Recorder: What do you say, Mr. Mead, were you there?

Mead: It is part of English law, that no man must give evidence against himself. Why do you try to trap me with this question? Does not this show that you are against me?

Recorder: Sir, hold your tongue! I did not try to trap you.

Cryer: All people keep silence upon pain of going to jail! Silence in the court!

Penn: We agree that we gathered together to preach, to pray, and to worship our Holy, Just God. We believe that this is our right. No power upon earth will be able to stop us from worshipping our God.

Brown: You are not here for worshipping God, but for breaking the law.

Penn: I have broken no law, nor am I guilty of the charges against me.

Recorder: Upon the Common Law of England!

Penn: Where is the Common Law?

Recorder: Sir, which way do you plead, guilty or not guilty?

Penn: I shall not plead to charges that are not against the law! If I have broken a law of the Common English Law, show me which one. Let the jury see the law so they can decide on their verdict.

Recorder: You are a sassy fellow! Plead to the charges against you.

Penn: The court is trying me for breaking a law. It is hard to defend yourself without knowing what law you have broken. If you do not show me the law, then I will know the court is against me.

Recorder: The question is, how do you plead?

Penn: The question is, am I guilty of the charges under the law?

Recorder: You are a stubborn fellow! Will you teach the court what the law is?

Penn: The Common Law is an Englishman's Common Right. It is so written in our great charter.

Recorder: You are a troublesome person. It will not do any good for you to say any more. Take him away. If no one can keep him quiet, we shall never end this trial.

Mayor:	Take him from the court.
Penn:	I will not be quiet when my rights and freedom are to be taken away, and the rights and freedom of other Englishmen.

(Penn is taken from the court.)

Mead:	You did promise us a fair trial. Why don't we have the rights of Englishmen?
Recorder:	I look upon you as an enemy of the laws of England. You are not worthy of these rights.

(Then Mead was taken away.)

Recorder to the Jury:	You have heard the charges. It is for preaching to the people, and causing a crowd to come. Mr. Penn was speaking. There are three or four witnesses that have proved this. He did preach there! Mr. Mead did allow it to happen. You must now decide.

(The jury leaves.)

What Do You Think?

(HYPOTHESIS QUESTIONS)

1. How will this trial end? Write *your* verdict down. Why will the trial end that way?
2. What are rights? Where do they come from? Explain and give examples.
3. What rights do you think everyone should have? Make a list of rights for all Americans and for students in school. Why are these rights important?
4. Why would a group of people or a nation write down its laws?
5. Why might a person be called "an enemy of the law" or "government"? What might happen to him? Explain and give examples.
6. What questions do you have about the trial thus far?

The Trial Ends

The jury has heard the evidence and has gone to decide upon their verdict. After one and one-half hours, eight of the men come back with a decision. Four of the men do not return, because they do not agree. A policeman is sent to get the other four jurors. One of them is Edward Bushel. The recorder stares angrily at the men as they come into court.

Recorder to Bushel:	You are the reason for this trouble. I will make you pay for this.
Clerk:	Are you agreed on your verdict?
Jury:	Yes.
Clerk:	Look at the prisoners. How say you? Guilty or not guilty?
Foreman:	Guilty of speaking in Gracechurch-Street.
Judge:	Is that all?

Foreman: That is all I have.

Recorder: You might as well have said nothing!

Mayor: Was it not an unlawful meeting? You mean he is guilty of speaking to an unlawful crowd?

Foreman: This is our decision.

(The members of the court look angrily at the jury.)

Recorder: The Law of England will not allow you to leave until you have given your verdict.

Jury: We have given it.

Recorder: Gentlemen, you have not given it! Go back and think about it once more.

(Jury leaves. One-half hour later they return.)

Clerk: Are you agreed?

Jury: Yes

Clerk: Is William Penn guilty or not guilty?

Foreman: Here is our verdict.

(Gives a piece of paper to the clerk.)
We the jurors do find William Penn to be guilty of speaking or preaching to a group of people in Gracechurch-Street. And that William Mead is not guilty.

Recorder: Gentlemen, you shall not be dismissed till we have a verdict that the court will accept. And you shall be locked up without meat, drink, fire, and tobacco. You will not act this way in Court. We will have a verdict, by the help of God, or you will starve!

Penn: The Court should not treat the jury this way!

Recorder: Stop that fellow's mouth or put him out of Court!

Mayor: You have heard the witnesses. Penn did preach to a crowd. He broke the king's law and the people's law as well.

(The jury was kept over night without food, water, heat or other things to make them comfortable.)

Cryer: O yes, silence in the court, upon pain of going to prison.

(Calls the names of the jurors).

Clerk: Are you agreed on your verdict?

Jury: Yes, William Penn is guilty of speaking in Gracechurch-Street.

Mayor: To an unlawful crowd?

Bushel: No, my Lord, we give no other verdict than we did last night. We have no other verdict.

Mead: How is not guilty no verdict?

Recorder: No, 'tis no verdict.

Penn: The agreement of a jury is a verdict in law. If William Mead is not guilty, then I am not guilty.

Clerk: What say you, jury? Is he guilty or not guilty?

Foreman:	Guilty of speaking in Gracechurch-Street.
Recorder:	I will have a verdict!
Penn:	It is wrong that my jury should be treated this way. What hope do Englishmen have for justice, when juries are threatened and their verdicts not allowed?
Mayor:	Stop his mouth; Jailer, bring chains and chain him to the ground.
Recorder:	Your verdict is nothing. You insult the Court. Go and bring in another verdict or you will starve!
Cryer:	The court adjourns until tomorrow morning. (The jurors are kept all night again!)
Clerk:	Are you agreed on a verdict?
Jury:	Yes.
Clerk:	How say you? Is William Penn guilty or not guilty?
Foreman:	Not guilty!
Clerk:	Then you say William Penn and William Mead are both not guilty.
Jury:	Yes, we do.
Recorder:	I am sorry, gentlemen, you have kept to your own judgements and opinions rather than to my advice. You are fined Forty Marks each.
Penn:	I demand my freedom.
Mayor:	No, you are in for your fines.
Penn:	Fines, what fines?
Mayor:	For contempt of court.
Penn:	I ask, is this what we call English rights?
Recorder:	Take him away, take him away! Take him out of the court!

How Do You Feel?

(POSITION QUESTIONS)

1. Do you feel this was a fair trial? What is a fair trial? Explain.
2. Why do you think William Penn was really on trial? Explain.
3. How would you have felt if you had been William Penn? Why would you feel that way?
4. Is being fair important? Why or why not? Should people always be fair? Why or why not?
5. Why are people arrested and brought to trial for speaking publicly?
6. Do you believe people can always be fair? Explain. How should someone act to be fair? Explain and give examples.

The role-playing presentation of the William Penn trial usually takes two full periods, including discussions at the end of each session. Students should also be asked what they would like to find out next (page 126) so that materials and topics of interest can be identified, researched, developed, and brought to class. Generally, student questions based on the trial are extremely provocative and make for interesting inquiry. Some sample questions that invariably arise are: "What did the Quakers believe?" "Why was the court against them?" "What did William Penn do after the trial?" "Were there others persecuted in England?" "What was Penn's colony in Pennsylvania like?" Below are brief segments of one class's discussion of the trial following the role-playing activity.

Classroom Dialogue [13]

What Is the Problem?

(DATA QUESTIONS)

Teacher:	What was this trial really about?
Teresa:	About Penn preaching in Gracechurch-Street or whatever it is. It was about prejudice, too.
Teacher:	Why prejudice?
Several students:	It was an unfair trial!
Teresa:	They were against them because they were Quakers.
Joe:	There were two kinds of people, two kinds of religious groups here.
Teacher:	Anything else?
Cattrina:	I think the trial is about rights because all they [Quakers] wanted was freedom of religion. This is why they came to America, right?

How Would You Feel?

(FEELING QUESTIONS)

Teacher:	How would you have felt if you had been in Penn's or Mead's place?
Lynn:	I would be afraid I would be found guilty.
Lorrie:	I would be worried because all the people were against me because I was a Quaker.
Raymond:	I'd be afraid because the Englishmen would not give me a fair trial.
Chris:	I'd be worried because I had a wife and family.
Michelle:	I'd be worried because the court kept sending the jury back for another verdict and I'd be found guilty.

[13] Actual dialogue taken from a seventh-grade social studies class.

Cattrina:	I would have been angry and would not have been as calm as Penn was in the trial. They were treating him unfairly.
Ilene:	I would have been very mad!
Michelle:	I would have been scared.
Emily:	I agree with Cattrina and Ilene. I would have been so mad because I know about the rights in the Magna Carta; because I was getting an unfair trial.

What Do You Think?

(HYPOTHESIS QUESTIONS)

Teacher:	Why might a person be called an enemy of the law? Or of the government?
Michelle:	Well, if they broke the law or if they were arrested or if they were dangerous, they might be called enemies of the law. They're outlaws.
Teacher:	Ilene, what do you think?
Ilene:	They endanger your rights and your protection as another person.
Teacher:	Cattrina.
Cattrina:	It is someone who *tries* to do things against the law.
Emily:	I think an enemy of the law is a person who disagrees with the law.
Cattrina:	People who leave the army and stop fighting might be called enemies of the government because they are deserting.
Chris:	People who kill presidents or leaders and ones who kidnap leaders are enemies.

What Do You Value?

(POSITION QUESTIONS)

Teacher:	What are some of the other verdicts in the class?
Chris:	I said Penn was guilty and Mead was innocent because he just listened.
Teacher:	What about Mead?
Chris:	He was not really breaking the law. He was just letting Penn speak. Penn broke the law so he should be found guilty.
Teacher:	Which law?
Chris:	Disturbing the peace.
Michelle:	And preaching! It says right here he was being tried for preaching! He was guilty of that.
Susan:	Both of them were innocent because they should have had the *right* to worship in the church.

What Do You Think?

(DEFINING QUESTIONS)

Teacher: What are rights?

Emily: A right is like a privilege except a privilege can be taken away from you. A right is something you have and you are entitled to.

Winky: A right is something you deserve.

Teacher: What do you mean deserve? How do you deserve it?

Paul: Like if you're an American citizen you get the right to vote. You deserve it.

Teacher: Where do the first rights come from?

Teresa: They come from the Constitution and the people who make the laws.

Teacher: What Constitution are you talking about?

Teresa: About our Constitution.

Teacher: How shall we define a right?

Steven: It is something that everyone should have.

Amy: Privileges are given to you and can be taken away, but rights usually cannot be taken away.

What Reasons Can You Give?

(PROBING QUESTIONS)

Teacher: Can you think of other times when this [people treated unfairly by other persons] has happened? Does this happen often?

Emily: Just before the American Revolution people could not meet in large groups because the king was afraid they would revolt.

Ilene: We all get treated unfairly sometimes.

Steve: People get treated unfairly lots of times, because they're different.

Teacher: Can you give me an example?

Emily: I don't know what war it was, but Hitler killed the Jews. I don't remember why.

Chris: This happened to the American Indians, too. Remember the report on the Indians we gave?

Teacher: Any other examples from America?

Maria: I can't think of one, but it happens between black and white people.

Bryan: Students get treated unfairly in school sometimes. I was blamed for something I did not do!

Teacher: Do you think we need to find more evidence?

Students: Yes.

What Can We Conclude?

Teacher: What have we decided about people today?

Greg: People who are different in some way sometimes get treated unfairly by other people.

Joe: If people don't like you, they will treat you unfairly sometimes.

Cattrina: Some people who are dangerous to other people or are dangerous to the government will be called enemies.

Joe: If people don't like you, they may call you an enemy of the law.

Teacher: Write down some things that you would like to study further.

VISUAL MEDIA AS SPRINGBOARDS

Much of the data used in previous examples has emphasized reading materials and verbal communication. There is also a wealth of visual materials available to teachers and their students. For instance, historical and contemporary cartoons, art work, and photographs can be used effectively as both springboards and sources of evidence. Similarly, charts, graphs, tables, maps, diagrams, pictures, and advertisements can be used in ways similar to the documents, letters, and music presented earlier. Cartoons are usually easy to find and can, from time to time, serve as excellent springboards into social issues. The historical cartoon below, for example, can spark student thinking, feeling, valuing, and research about monopolies. Carefully developed inquiry questions can then stimulate student exploration into human behavior, thoughts, feelings, beliefs, and values regarding the social issue described. Some sample questions are:

What is the cartoonist trying to say? Why do you think so?

What is the central idea of the cartoon?

Why might a cartoonist draw such a cartoon? What do you know about the times that supports what you say?

How does the cartoon make you feel? Why?

How might other people feel about this cartoon?

Does the cartoonist offer any solutions to the problem? Why or why not? What do you think should be done? Why?

Why are the trusts drawn in this way? How would you draw them? What caption might you put under the cartoon?

What ideas and topics would you like to study after analyzing this and the other political cartoons of the times?

What resources will we need? How can we get them?

There are many excellent sources of contemporary cartoons, including magazines, newspapers, and anthologies of popular (and historical)

THE BOSSES OF THE SENATE.

Joseph Keppler's *The Bosses of the Senate*, 1889. (Courtesy Library of Congress.)

cartoons. The cartoons below are two of several that have been used with students of different ages to introduce the topics of autocracy, dictatorship, and absolute monarchy. *The Wizard of Id* and similar cartoons have been used by teachers to get students to state the defining attributes of absolute rulers and some of their characteristic behaviors.

Similarly historical and contemporary art work and pictures can stimulate student hypothesizing, value positions, and value clarification.

By permission of John Hart and Field Enterprises, Inc.

By permission of John Hart and Field Enterprises, Inc.

Massialas and Zevin have used pictures of political leaders, photographs of events and scenes, a Howard Johnson's menu, and other creative visuals to stimulate social inquiry.[14] Paintings, sculpture, and photographs can also be presented by teachers as springboards to inquiry. Like car-

The Boston Massacre by Paul Revere. (The Metropolitan Museum of Art, Gift of Mrs. Russell Sage, 1910.)

[14] Byron G. Massialas and Jack Zevin, *World History Through Inquiry* (Chicago: Rand McNally & Co., 1969).

toons, pictures and photographs are readily available in magazines and newspapers. With the aid of copying machines and opaque projectors teachers can display large-scale visuals on screens or on their classroom walls and use them as springboards and sources of evidence.

Teachers in elementary social studies classrooms already know that visuals are necessary for their students. For instance, ancient picture maps and pictures of deep-sea monsters have been used by one of us to stimulate elementary student inquiry about the discovery and exploration of the New World. Similarly, paintings by colonists and cartoons from England and the Colonies at the time of the Revolution have been used to initiate social inquiry in fifth and sixth grade social studies about rebellion and conflict. Students were asked to interpret the visuals and make hypotheses from their content and to speculate about the feelings of the colonists and artists at the time. The visuals introduced students to many events in the Revolution in a more interesting way than by lecture, traditional film, or textbook paragraph because the visuals depicted such events as the first shot fired at Concord, the arrival of troops in Boston, the tarring and feathering of tax collectors, the ride of Paul Revere, the Boston Massacre, and the Boston Tea Party. Combined with other materials, these visuals served as first-rate springboards and data sources.

Often, visual springboards are powerful in their simplicity. The drawing below by a teacher has been used to introduce the concepts of selective perception, stereotyping, and cultural differences in perception. Most students tend to see the situation as an arrest or conflict situation.

FIGURE 8:1
A Teacher's Visual Springboard

When other hypotheses are requested, students begin to see that many other situations are possible: asking for directions, buying tickets to the Policemen's Ball, passing out handbills. Thus, inquiry begins here with student perceptions of a situation, of biases, and of misunderstandings that were prompted by a very simple teacher-made visual. Many high-school and junior-high-school materials contain a wide assortment of visuals.[15] Some of these materials use the visuals to inspire thought and valuing rather than as mere colorful illustrations.[15]

SUMMARY

We have tried in this chapter to show through examples that teachers can develop and adapt materials available to them to serve as springboards and sources of evidence for inquiry in social studies classrooms. Alternative strategies and materials that may motivate students and promote thinking, feeling, and valuing have been suggested. Teachers should be aware that their roles as questioners and value investigators are extremely important to the success of any inquiry into social issues, and that to initiate and maintain social inquiry they must integrate different types of questions—data, hypothesis, position—with a variety of springboards and learning activities.

Many of the examples given here emphasize teachers' roles as planners. They are primarily responsible for developing activities and materials for inquiry. However, many teachers have found that if they exhibit searching and challenging behavior themselves, then students will begin to challenge them and their fellow students and will bring in new data sources and springboards themselves. Students may also be encouraged to create or collect cartoons, open-ended stories, cases, songs, poems, letters, charts, and so forth as projects that will increase their role in class planning and in initiating inquiry.

[15] See M. W. Sandler, E. C. Rozwenc, and E. C. Martin *The People Make a Nation* (Boston: Allyn & Bacon, 1971); Lawrence Cuban and Phillip Roden, *Promise of America Series* (Glenview, Ill.: Scott, Foresman and Co., 1971).

7

evaluating social inquiry in the classroom

The field of education has entered into an exciting new era. It is an era characterized by faith in the ability of young people to develop their own explanations about the world and to make their own judgments about the worthiness of certain social institutions and actions.

The new direction in education can be traced back to the fifties or even earlier, but the movement began to gain momentum in the mid-sixties with the emphasis on social inquiry as a basis for both teaching and learning. As we stated before, contrary to commonly held views, inquiry is not simply a technique but it is based on a style of life that includes, among other things, specific world perceptions, the individual's role in society, a theory of learning and what constitutes knowledge, and man's relation to this knowledge. This intellectually affective style, which we call "inquiry" and which we have already described in many of its manifestations, can be translated into classroom practice.

Given this movement in education, what is the emerging role of educational evaluation? Generally speaking, the whole field of examinations and evaluation procedures has not kept pace with changes in education. For example, the evaluation of inquiry is still not a major component of available tests and standardized instruments. Memorization of information rather than interpretation and analysis of data is still emphasized. The prevailing philosophy of evaluation is still one that looks upon the pupil as a recipient of ready-made conclusions rather than a producer of ideas. What Bloom calls the "destructive effects of evaluation" —the traumatic experiences for students that arise from our highly competitive educational system—still seem to predominate in American schools, as well as schools all over the world.[1] Some new and promising developments, however, may in time bring about the needed revolution in educational evaluation. To these developments we now turn our attention.

AN INQUIRY-ORIENTED PHILOSOPHY OF EVALUATION

One provocative new idea in the field is the distinction between summative or terminal and formative or feedback evaluation. The distinguishing characteristics of the two have to do with their intended uses. The College Entrance and Graduate Record Examinations, for example, can be thought of as a form of summative evaluation on the basis of which students gain admission into or are rejected by a university. Summative evaluation is often used for promotion purposes, for grading students, and for judging the effectiveness of teachers and school curricula. When a summative evaluation is applied at the end of a course or program of studies, the students affected by it do not have the opportunity to do anything about modifying their performance. Bloom, J. Thomas Hastings, and George Madaus point to the most important usage of summative evaluation:

> Perhaps the essential characteristic of summative evaluation is that a judgment is made about the student, teacher or curriculum with regard to the effectiveness of learning or instruction, after the learning or instruction has taken place. It is this act of judgment which produces so much anxiety and defensiveness in students, teachers and curriculum makers.[2]

Summative evaluation helps the system make decisions after the fact, but does not provide any assistance about ongoing teaching and learning.

Formative evaluation, on the other hand, is the type of evaluation administered at various phases of the learning process and provides the opportunity for feedback to both students and teachers.[3] Formative evaluation has two objectives: (1) to find out where certain instructional difficulties—student, teacher, or curricular—lie in each aspect of learning

---

[1] Benjamin Bloom, "Some Theoretical Issues Relating to Educational Evaluation," in *Educational Evaluation: New Roles, New Means*, ed. Ralph W. Tyler, the sixty-eighth yearbook of the National Society for the Study of Education, Part 2 (Chicago: The University of Chicago Press, 1969), pp. 26-50.

[2] Benjamin S. Bloom, J. Thomas Hastings, and George F. Madaus, *Handbook on Formative and Summative Evaluation of Student Learning* (New York: McGraw-Hill Book Co., 1971).

[3] See Bloom, "Some Theoretical Issues," and Michael Scriven, "The Methodology of Evaluation," in *Perspectives of Curriculum Evaluation*, ed. R. W. Tyler, R. M. Gagne, and Michael Scriven (Chicago: Rand McNally & Co., 1967).

and teaching, and (2) to suggest, on the basis of what has been determined, possible new directions. Formative evaluation is a systematic use of instruments, feedback data, and revision processes for the purpose of improving learning in the classroom. It is meant to be a motivational and guiding device that reinforces the climate for learning.

Formative evaluation is compatible with the goals of inquiry, goals that underscore how important it is for one to understand and judge one's world through one's own efforts and at one's own pace. When examination procedures used in schools conform to the purposes of formative evaluation, then a major obstacle that has slowed down the introduction of inquiry teaching and learning will have been eliminated. At that point we can invest energies in removing obsolete curricula, promotion policies, grouping procedures, and certain administrative-bureaucratic arrangements that hinder the conditions for inquiry learning.

Another important idea in the assessment of inquiry is the learning objective. Educators often employ vague terms as statements of instructional intent. "To develop good citizens" is a popular objective of social education. "To provide an understanding of government" is another. The essence of these objectives is certainly worthwhile, but their vagueness makes them virtually useless. There is no way in which such global goals can be measured; thus the teacher has no way in which to determine the effectiveness of the instructional process. Educational objectives for inquiry teaching that rely on broad terms like "to understand,' "to see," "to develop an appreciation of," seriously hamper the effective evaluation of inquiry behavior.

Considerable argument has taken place over the degree of specificity to which statements of instructional objectives should conform. Specificity, of course, should depend upon the purposes of the objectives and the types of behaviors being described. Generally, long-term or course objectives will be less specific than the instructional objectives used to achieve them. Or, as in the case of social scientific inquiry, if the content and process of a field of study are expanding rapidly, the objectives may need to stress transferable skills more than pure knowledge and comprehension. Ultimately, the objectives for inquiry learning must be stated in clear operational statements so that they can be used for formative evaluation of student competencies.

Inquiry objectives, therefore, can be broad statements of learning intent that include terms like "hypothesizing," "generalizing," and "taking value positions." Useful instructional objectives, on the other hand, should be specific statements including such phrases as "stating a hypothesis," "making predictions," and "supporting positions with evidence." Statements like these describe what the student does and under what conditions.

In view of our philosophy that evaluation should be used for motivational and remedial purposes rather than for grading and invidious comparisons, what types of relevant objectives and instruments can we develop? Elsewhere we have provided several examples of test items that would form the basis for evaluating both the cognitive and affective aspects of inquiry.[4] In this chapter we will concentrate on two ideas: (1) the development of clearly stated objectives and relevant evaluation items and (2) the use of tables of specifications.

DEVELOPING CLEAR OBJECTIVES

Various formulas can be employed for developing operational objectives based upon the level of specificity involved. A simple rule to keep in mind is whether or not the objective clearly answers the following questions:

1. What will each student do?
2. Under what circumstances will he do it?
3. How can we tell when he has done it?

Here is an example of a clear, operational objective that includes these three elements taken from a class which is dealing with political processes:

> Given a value position about the political community of a political system, the student will choose from a list of five statements of evidence the two statements that support the position, the two that attack the position, and the one that has no bearing on the position.

For the specific performance objectives included as examples here, the following five criteria have served as the guide for developing clear statements of intent: (1) *the situation confronting the learner* ("Given a value position about the political community of a political system"); (2) *the action required* ("student must choose"); (3) *the object of the action* ("the statements that support, attack, or are irrelevant to the position"); (4) *the particular limits of the activity* ("from a list of five statements of evidence"); and (5) *the degree to which the task must be done* (without error is implied).

An appropriate test item can then be constructed or collected to meet the specific objective of grounding positions about a political system. Here is one sample test item:

---

[4] Byron G. Massialas and C. Benjamin Cox, *Inquiry in Social Studies* (New York: McGraw-Hill Book Co., 1966), pp. 236-278.

Sample Test Item

Read the position and statements below. Mark an:

S   if you feel that the statement could be used to support the position.
A   if you feel that the statement could be used to attack the position.
X   if you feel that the statement has nothing to do with the position.

Position: "The political community of a nation should have the following characteristics: loyalty, unity, and common goals."

STATEMENTS:

_____ 1.   No political system can work well for a long time unless its members work together to make important decisions.
_____ 2.   "Too much agreement in political affairs leads to a stale government and a lack of progress."
_____ 3.   The nationalistic spirit, "My country right or wrong," has led to many unfortunate events in world history.
_____ 4.   The function of political parties in the United States is to select leaders and maintain an active system in government.
_____ 5.   Violent conflicts between French-speaking people and English-speaking people in Canada have occurred because they have different beliefs and goals.

Below is another clear objective stated in behavioral form that refers to the ability of exploring consequences with regard to the functioning of a political system:

Objective: Given a table about citizens' feelings concerning their ability to make changes in the inputs and outputs of their political system, the student will select from a list of four (4) possible consequences, the one (1) that is *most likely* to happen.

Sample Test Item

EXPLORING CONSEQUENCES:

Feelings about Government in Country X by City

	City A (small village)	City B (town)	City C (large city)
Officials would listen to my opinions and take them seriously.	75%	45%	30%
Local government actions are usually helpful to the community.	90%	75%	50%
It is almost impossible to change an unfair local law by my own efforts.	30%	40%	65%
I am not likely to try to change an unfair local law.	38%	45%	61%

A local election is about to take place in each of the three cities described in the above chart. Which of the following is *most likely* to happen because of the feelings expressed by the citizens in the chart. Place a check (V) beside the action *most likely* to happen in the election.

_____ 1.   Fewer people in City A will try to change local decisions they think are wrong than will people in City B.

_____ 2.   People in City A will say that local government is not helpful and will refuse to support their decision.

_____ 3.   More people in City A will vote than in City C because they think they can change local policies.

_____ 4.   A large percentage of people in City C will try to get other citizens to vote because their wishes will be listened to and taken seriously.

As indicated in both the objectives and the accompanying test items, there is an attempt to state as clearly as possible the task for the learner and the conditions under which the task should be performed. Naturally, teachers and their students will have to make their own decisions as to what objectives and materials are appropriate for their purposes.

DEVELOPING TABLES OF SPECIFICATION

One of the reasons why our evaluation instruments have not developed as rapidly as our instructional methodology is that we have not sought to bring sufficient specificity to our educational objectives. We have talked constantly about producing the informed and critically minded citizen who has high expectations for political participation as being desirable objectives of civic education, but rarely have we tried to express these objectives in behavioral and measurable terms. The fourteen goals developed some years back by a Committee on Concepts and Values of the National Council for the Social Studies demonstrate the global way by which the profession has been tackling the problem of defining its operational goals. Even though many objectives, especially in the social and personal realms, are difficult to define and express concretely, we should still be able to do better than we have done in the past. A first step toward making objectives operational is the development of tables of specifications. A table of specifications, as used in our example of a study unit on political systems in Table 7:1, is a two-dimensional matrix that includes substantive-procedural concerns on one dimension and behavioral specifications on the other. Tables of specifications can be developed for small segments of instruction, perhaps daily lessons, or for larger segments, such as six-week units or entire courses. In developing these tables, one's philosophy of education, ideas about the nature of learning, the role of students and teachers in classroom discussion, and other similar considerations are inescapably taken into account. In this chapter we are including a set of materials that we have used with teachers to explain how the system outlined here works. The materials include "How to Use a Table of Specifications," "Behavioral Definitions," and "Behavioral Objectives: A Political System."

The vertical axis in Table 7:1 is based on the concepts and methods of politics, which can be drawn from formal political science readings or from direct political experience of the class. The prime concern here is to have the members of the class understand how governments in different political settings function and to develop defensible reasons to support their hypotheses as well as their evaluation of these governments. The first two categories on the substantive-experiential dimension (1.0 and 2.0) deal with the concept of a political system and its major elements, functions, and processes. The subcategories (2.1–2.4) deal with such ideas as who rules, how the government establishes its right to rule, the way in which leaders of the political system are selected, and the degree of citizen involvement with the system's political processes. These criteria for determining the kind of political system prevailing in a nation suggest some of the bases for making hypotheses and judgments about the system. The third category, Comparative Political Systems (3.0–3.4), focuses on some standards for cross-national comparisons.

The horizontal axis represents the behavioral dimension of evaluation. It includes student behaviors grouped under three categories: cognitive, affective, and evaluative. The cognitive category includes such important behaviors as Identifying Problems (C) and Forming Hypotheses (E). The affective component deals with attitude formation, especially those attitudes that are essential to inquiry: Being Objective (L), Showing Interest (M), and Showing Involvement (N). The evaluative category focuses on the ability to develop a defensible position

Political Systems		Behavioral (Student)																		
Substantive—Procedural—Experiential		Cognitive												Affective				Evaluative		
		A	B	C	D	E	F	G	H	I	J	K	L	M	N	O	P	Q	R
		Making Distinctions	Demonstrating Conceptual Understanding	Identifying a Problem	Stating a Problem	Forming a Hypothesis	Exploring Consequences	Collecting Relevant Data	Analyzing Data	Testing Ideas	Making a Generalization	Applying a Generalization	Being Objective	Showing Interest	Showing Involvement	Demonstrating Value Consistencies	Identifying an Issue	Taking a Defensible Position	Grounding a Position
1.0 The Concept of a Political System																			
2.0 A Political System																			
2.1 Locus of Power																			
2.2 Legitimacy of Government																			
2.3 Selection of Leaders																			
2.4 Citizen Participation																			
3.0 Comparative Political Systems																			
3.1 System Maintenance																			
3.2 Enforcing Societies' Rules																			
3.3 Subsystem Autonomy																			
3.4 Justice																			

TABLE 7:1

Table of Specifications

Unit Evaluation: Senior High—Political Systems

concerning an issue, a political object, or a political process (Q) and on the ability to base value positions on supportable grounds or evidence (R).[5]

One way in which to use tables of specifications is to construct operational objectives and paper-and-pencil items to be employed in the spirit of formative evaluation. Depending on what concepts and behaviors the class finds to be important in studying politics, the teachers may collect or write their own test items. The performance of students on these items may provide additional motivation to explore other aspects of political life or provide the basis for identifying gaps in a student's experience and competencies. Certainly it should not be expected that all 198 cells in the matrix (11 x 18) should be used to form objectives and evaluation items. Teachers should judge carefully the appropriateness of the objectives suggested by the merging of the two dimensions in each cell in the matrix. It is expected that they will exclude some of the cells as irrelevant to the concerns of the class. Certain cells—for example, 1.0 L, will always remain empty because the two dimensions do not logically yield a meaningful objective.

For illustrative purposes, let us assume that political systems is the subject for inquiry in the classroom and that the teacher wants to develop relevant objectives and evaluation items. His first task is to identify those cells that he wants to serve as the basis for evaluation. The second task is to construct operational objectives and appropriate test items (or draw from those already available) that would be anchored in the cells identified as important or relevant to classroom activities. Suppose he wants to see how students are doing behaviorally in testing ideas as they relate to the first two major substantive-experiential categories (1.0–2.4). Here is an example of a sequence of his operations that will yield the evidence sought after:

GENERAL OBJECTIVES (2.4)—Testing Ideas on Citizen Participation:

The student will test ideas in the form of hypotheses about citizen participation in a political system.

SAMPLE OPERATIONAL OBJECTIVE:

Given a hypothesis about the relationship between voter interest, concern for the results, and familiarity with the issues in a Presidential election, the student will identify, from a list of five statements of evidence, the two that support, the two that attack. and the one that is irrelevant to the hypothesis.

---

[5] The reader should keep in mind that Table 7:1 is not a definitive table of specifications dealing with all inquiry behaviors or aspects of political systems. It is presented here only as an example that needs further refinement.

Sample Test Item:

Read the hypothesis below carefully. Next read the statements that may or may not relate to the hypothesis. Place an:

S   if the statement supports the hypothesis.
A   if the statement attacks the hypothesis.
X   if the statement has nothing to do with the hypothesis.

Hypothesis: If a person is very familiar with the issues in an election, very interested in the campaigning of candidates, and very concerned about who wins the election, then he is very likely to be an active participant in the election.

———— 1.   In a Southwestern county many students actively working in a political election were not interested in the campaign and were not familiar with the issues of the campaign, but they did care who won.

———— 2.   In Rose Wall County the following happened in the last national election:

      "Highly interested" citizens: 90% voted in the election
      "Somewhat interested" citizens: 73% voted in the election
      "Not much interested" citizens: 55% voted in the election

———— 3.   Approximately 65% of the eligible voters in the United States voted in a given election.

———— 4.   In Jackson City 100% of its eligible voters voted in the last election.

      Percent of voters very familiar with issues: 20%
      Percent of voters somewhat familiar with issues: 40%
      Percent of voters not familiar with issues: 40%

———— 5.   Most of the highly active workers in the campaign in the city of Rose Wall were very much informed about the issues involved in the election.

Here is an example dealing with aspects of the concept, citizen participation:

SAMPLE OPERATIONAL OBJECTIVE:

Given a generalization about citizen interest and party differences on issues and an incomplete bar graph showing party differences and voter interest on two major issues, the student is to use the generalization to predict voter behavior and to complete the chart to conform with the given rule in the generalization.

Sample Test Item

Study the incomplete graph below. Make your own prediction based on the generalization by completing the bar graph. Draw a bar in the blanks and label its percentage based upon what you know from the generalization.

Generalization: The more interest voters have in a major issue "A," the greater the difference will be in the percentage of the two party's members voting for that issue.

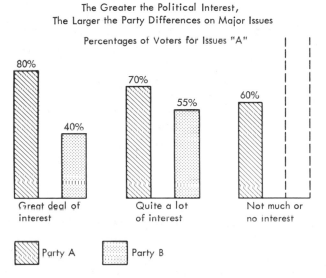

The Greater the Political Interest,
The Larger the Party Differences on Major Issues

These two test examples demonstrate how general ideas can be operationalized into an instructional objective and an appropriate evaluation item. Generally, questions that deal with stating problems, hypothesizing, generalizing, and position-taking seem to be better suited to a short answer or an essay format. Such questions allow the student to both state an answer in his own words and explain his reasoning. Such formats do demand more from teachers in stating their criteria for acceptable answers to the questions.

The teacher has now identified the cells in the table that pertain to the content and behaviors to be learned. By going to lists of objectives, he can find the ones he wants to examine listed by number and letter—for example, 2.0 A Making Distinctions—A Political System. The objectives are written to define what students will do and give suggestions for what they will be given to use, and how learning can be evaluated.

Suppose the teacher decides to use the objectives 2.0 A, 2.1 A, 2.1 B, 2.3 D, and 2.4 B to begin to develop a unit. Along with each of these objectives, at least two sample test items are included to measure how students perform, and how effectively the materials and teaching strategies are working. These items have many uses. The teacher can use some of them (1) for pre-tests to see what the students already know and to identify learner weaknesses, (2) for quizzes or weekly tests to see how well students are learning (using this information to make changes or help students who are having trouble), and (3) for post-tests to measure the learning for the whole unit. If the teacher wants, he can use only the items he deems appropriate for his students or he can use the items listed only as samples for guiding him to write his own test items, projects, or assignments.

Similarly, the objectives may be used as guides for the teacher to write his own objectives and the table suggests a way to identify important goals and systematically measure how well they are being met. A teacher could construct tables to organize content and behaviors in his own class if he likes, and then use the tables to develop or collect appropriate objectives, evaluation instruments, learning materials and teaching strategies.

The usefulness of this table lies in the teacher's own flexible selection of learning objectives and appropriate test items (or other methods) to measure these objectives. A teacher may skip around the table and select only those cells and appropriate objectives that fit his class. What is suggested is that the teacher feel free to use the materials here as he chooses, create other objectives and measures appropriate to his own class, and use them to help students and teacher create a better learning environment in the classroom.

A Subscript for the Teacher

The table does not impose any given order on the teacher who uses it. Objectives and measures should be selected that assist the teacher and students to improve learning in the classroom. A teacher need not be teaching a course on political systems, technology, or environment to use the table. For instance, many of these objectives could be used in history, world geography, world cultures, civics, and problems courses as well as in elementary social studies units. The table is for a teacher's reference, not to tell her what to do.

For instance, one group of students may be seniors in an advanced problems course who have had a rich background in social studies.

Many of the objectives may be ignored because students already have achieved them. Another group may be students in freshman civics who need to start at 1.0 A and go from there. Finally, another group may be weak in a particular skill (for instance, forming hypotheses) and may find all or some portion of the objectives and items in column E useful. Still another teacher may use all or part of the objectives and items from a given row (like 2.3—Selecting Leaders), while another teacher may want to deal with a value problem and select a block of objectives P, Q, and R for 2.0, 2.1, 3.1, and 3.4.

How to Use
a Table of Specifications

A table of specifications shows how subject matter or experience can be matched with desirable student behaviors. The column along the left side of each table is a list of important ideas from social science that define a content area (for example, political system, technology, environment). Some of these areas are new, others are old ideas with new names. To describe these content areas, a short definition and a set of clarifying statements for each idea should be included with each table.

The column along the top of the table is a list of student behaviors in three areas: (1) cognitive-thinking skills; (2) affective-attitudes; and (3) evaluative-issues and value positions. These behaviors are briefly defined below for the teacher.

Tables are easy to use. A teacher who has a topic and some general ideas about creating a unit can find objectives and test items or other ways to measure her desirable goals for the unit. How? Look at the section of the table on Political Systems below. Suppose the teacher wanted to teach a section about American government. In the table under 2.0, 2.1, 2.2, 2.3, and 2.4, cells can be found that concern a political system, locus of power, selection of leaders, and so forth.

By looking at the behaviors along the top of the table, a teacher could find student skills and attitudes that would pertain to plans for student learning. Suppose that, to begin with, A (making distinctions), B (demonstrating conceptual understanding), and D (stating problems) are important learning objectives of the unit. Given all these considerations, the teacher may proceed to test items shown or develop her own, which would correspond to the cells marked with X's. The instructional sequence and the materials used should also be appropriately organized and should issue from these cells.

In summary, a table of specifications is one way to organize what goes on in a classroom so that important content, thinking skills, attitudes, and evaluative abilities can be combined in a meaningful way. Once a

	Making Distinctions	Demonstrating Conceptual Understanding	Identifying a Problem	Stating a Problem
1.0 Concept of Political System				
2.0 A Political System	x	x		x
2.1 Locus of Power	x	x		x
2.2 Legitimacy	x	x		x
2.3 Selection of Leaders	x	x		x
2.4 Class Participation	x	x		x

table has been designed or is available, other useful tools can be developed or collected to provide necessary assistance for building a powerful learning environment. Tables can be used for selecting and developing worthwhile curriculum materials, audiovisuals, and teaching strategies as well as for selecting and developing worthwhile objectives, assignments, test items, and other instruments for evaluation.

BEHAVIORAL DEFINITIONS

The behavioral definitions below, taken from the table of specifications in Table 7:1, explain in more detail the dimensions of each of the behaviors that are sought:

A. *Making Distinctions*

   Making distinctions refers to the students being able to differentiate between dissimilar objects, ideas, values, and behaviors. For example, the student can examine three types of behavior and identify two which are similar to each other and one which is not related to the other two behaviors. Or more simply, making distinctions involves identifying simple similarities and differences.

B. *Demonstrating Conceptual Understanding*

   Conceptual understanding can be demonstrated at three levels: (1) the identification of examples and non-examples of concept groups, (2) the identification of attributes, functions, or processes of a given system or concept from a list of examples and non-examples, and (3) the classification of individual ideas, objects, actions, values, beliefs, into a group based on similar characteristics defined explicitly. In grouping or classifying objects, students are going beyond a simple definition of a word by showing they can identify similar characteristics of a concept. In showing conceptual understanding, students must also be able to identify examples that do not belong to a specific group (non-examples). Thus, students are able to go beyond the simple observation of differing phenomena. They are able to place observed phenomena into conceptual categories that they can define in their own words and to create their own original examples.

C. *Identifying a Problem*

A problem is usually defined as a situation in which there is a conflict between or a discrepancy in data or knowledge about a given topic the learner is experiencing. Because problems most often concern knowledge processes, information, and beliefs about what is true, no obvious answer to the discrepancy exists. In studying a problem, some questions arise as to what is meant, what is true, what might happen next, what can be done to terminate the discrepancy, or all of these. Problems can be personal, local, national, or international in scope.

D. *Stating a Problem*

This operation differs slightly from identifying a problem. Students are given greater flexibility in interpreting the data presented. When students are asked to state a problem, they are given a few guidelines to direct their thinking, yet the question is open-ended. Student responses should follow logically from the information.

E. *Forming a Hypothesis*

A hypothesis is a declarative general statement of explanation or solution or both that states a relationship between two or more factors or events. Hypotheses are usually posed in such a way that if they are true, they will provide a solution to the problem. Hypotheses are also general in that they do not relate to one instance or one time, but are stated in the present tense and include more than one case. One example of a hypothesis from social science will demonstrate this point:

If people are kept from obtaining important goals, then they will become frustrated and demonstrate withdrawal, aggression, rationalization, or other frustration-related behaviors.

In forming a hypothesis, students are presented with data and a question asking them to explain a relationship. The statement (hypothesis) should be in the students' own words and reflect that they understand the relationship shown in the data.

F. *Exploring Consequences*

In exploring consequences, students are looking for the logical deductions and implications of a statement, hypothesis, or position. One assumes that if a position or hypothesis is true, then the logical implications of the position or hypothesis will also be true. This task opens new means for finding additional information to test ideas.

G. *Collecting Relevant Data*

An important skill in testing a hypothesis or position is the collection of relevant data. This operation measures the ability of the students to (1) discern whether specific data would be useful in studying a subject, (2) know where to locate relevant data, and (3) decide whether further information is needed for the analysis of the hypothesis or position.

H. *Analyzing Data*

In analyzing data students are expected to break down a set of information into its component parts and determine the relationship among the parts. In analyzing data students use critical thinking skills to discover the underlying assumptions, to distinguish fact from opinion, to determine the relevance of facts, to detect fallacies in arguments, and to discover the major ideas of a statement.

I. *Testing Ideas*

On the basis of a given case study, hypothesis, or statement, students would be asked to test an idea in the material. In this operation, they are using relevant data to test whether the hypothesis is supported, needs to be changed, or is unsupported by data. Students should be able to demonstrate their ability to discern whether data support, attack, or are irrelevant to the idea being tested and to suggest their own data to support or attack a given hypothesis.

J. *Making a Generalization*

A generalization is an expression of an explanatory, causal, correlative, or practical relationship between two or more factors or events. The generalization differs from a hypothesis only in the degree of tentativeness of the hypothesis. A generalization is the best possible solution based upon all available evidence. It is a statement of a relationship that is applicable to all similar cases at all times and places. A generalization is always subject to revision as new data are introduced.

K. *Applying a Generalization*

In this operation students are demonstrating their ability to derive meaning from a statement (generalization) and to use this information to predict what might happen if the generalization were applied to a novel situation or to explain events that have already taken place.

L. *Being Objective*

Objectivity refers to the process of approaching a problem, issue, or situation without having a closed or biased position concerning the solution. Biases can be identified and minimized in the scientific and rational analysis of information, problems, and issues. In general, objectivity refers to an open mind and a willingness to analyze and accept or reject alternatives rationally without predetermined conclusions. It also includes the process of identifying accurate sources of information. The following criteria may be used to measure the objectivity and reliability of a source.[6]

1. The observer's familiarity with the event being described.

2. The extent to which the observer had a vested interest in the event.

[6] Based on Massialas and Zevin, "Looking into History, in *World History Through Inquiry*, p. 9.

3. The extent to which the observation was direct or indirect.
4. The amount of time that has passed between the observation and the writing of the account.
5. The extent to which the author (or observer) of the source was limited by cultural, ethnic, religious, social, or other biases.
6. The extent to which the author was influenced by a special interest, such as financial reward or personal hatred.
7. The extent to which the ideas and information are consistent or noncontradictory.
8. The extent to which other documents and research support the content of the source in question.

M. *Showing Interest*
Showing interest in a particular subject indicates that students are willing to give it their attention or that their attitudes are positive when confronted with a specific subject or stimulus. Their attitudes indicate that students are sensitive to certain phenomena, and that they do not consciously try to avoid contact with the stimulus. Students' interest may be observed in some of the following ways: listening, being excited about something, coming up after class to talk more about the topic.

N. *Showing Involvement*
Showing involvement in a particular subject indicates that students have gone beyond the level of just showing interest and are willing to participate in it. Students show involvement when they are willing to commit themselves to a subject or activity by using their own initiative to participate in it.

O. *Demonstrating Value Consistencies*
Actions often conflict because of differences in values. This is normal. If one has formed values on a given topic, then one's actions should be consistent with these values in similar situations where the same values are involved.

P. *Identifying Issues*
An issue is much like a problem in that a conflict or discrepancy exists between positions and many solutions to the conflict are possible. The basis of the conflict is one of values, beliefs, and attitudes that lead to controversy over what should or ought to be done. As is true of a problem, there is no obvious right answer. In issues, the discrepancy is based on values, emotions, beliefs, and attitudes, rather than on knowledge and information. Like problems, issues can be at different levels—international, societal, personal, or all three. In this operation students are given data and are asked to find one or more value conflicts in the data.

Q. *Taking a Defensible Position*
A position approximates the idea of a value judgment where one states a degree of worth, evaluates an action, or places a value on something or someone. Value judgments come from people's conception of how things ought to be. Value positions stem from value judgments made by the in-

dividual. The relationship between the two is close. Value positions refer to what should or should not be; value judgments place a worth on what is, was, or might be. In this operation students are asked to take a position about "what should be." At times students are asked to choose among alternatives (Do you feel eighteen-year-olds should vote? Yes or no). At other times, they are given open-ended questions. Students are asked to provide at least one defensible reason for their choice. If the reason given is supportive of the position and follows logically from the data, then the student has demonstrated the skill of taking a defensible position by stating his position and defending his choice.

R. *Grounding a Position*
    Grounds refer to the evidence upon which a value position or judgment is based. This evidence can include factual data, conclusions of authorities and experiments, positive and negative consequences, personal experience, the experiences of others, appeals to general knowledge, and other positions or value principles. Positions and judgments are not considered to be right or wrong, but supported or unsupported by valid evidence. In this operation, students are being measured on their ability to provide valid, reliable, and defensible evidence to support a position. Often this skill is measured by providing students with a position statement and several statements concerning the position. Students demonstrate their ability to identify evidence that supports, attacks, or is irrelevant to the position. In other cases, they are asked to supply their own supportive or nonsupportive evidence.

BEHAVIORAL OBJECTIVES:
A POLITICAL SYSTEM

The sample behavioral objectives below demonstrate how the substantive and the behavioral domains can be integrated.

2.0 A Making Distinctions—A Political System

From a list of eight (8) examples defining elements of the American political system, students will identify the two (2) examples of each of the following elements of the American political system: leadership, organization, and community.

2.0 B Demonstrating Conceptual Understanding—A Political System

Given a set of five (5) one-line statements describing events that are examples of political input, output, feedback and processes, students will correctly identify and label at least one (1) example of each.

2.0 C   Identifying a Problem—A Political System

After reading a table describing the feelings of citizens regarding their ability to affect the inputs and outputs of a specific political system, students will select from a list of four (4) problems, the one (1) that is suggested by the data.

2.0 D   Stating a Problem—A Political System

Given a table about the attitudes of citizens regarding their ability to make a change in the inputs and outputs of a specific political system, students will state, in their own words, a specific problem reflected in the data.

2.0 E   Forming a Hypothesis—A Political System

Given a table on the feelings of citizens about their ability to affect the political inputs and outputs of a political system, students will form a hypothesis regarding which group is more likely (or less likely) to feel able to influence political decisions.

2.0 F   Exploring Consequences—A Political System

Given a table on citizens' feelings about their ability to make changes in the inputs and outputs of their political system, students will select from a list of four (4) possible consequences, the one (1) that is *most likely* to happen based upon information in the table.

2.0 G   Collecting Relevant Data—A Political System

Given a hypothesis about the probable public response to political decisions and one-sentence statements defining the central themes of each of four (4) published articles, three (3) of which support or attack the hypothesis, and one (1) of which has no bearing on the hypothesis, students will select the articles that are relevant to (that is, defend or attack) the hypothesis.

2.0 H   Analyzing Data—A Political System

Given a summary paragraph that describes citizens' reaction (feedback) to proposed legislation (output), students will select from a list of five (5) statements, the one (1) statement that best expresses the logical conclusion of the citizens' argument.

2.0 I   Testing Ideas—A Political System

Given a hypothesis about the type of governmental political response to a continuing situation of social unrest, and a list of four

(4) statements that either support or do not support the hypothesis, students will identify those statements which do and those which do not support the given hypothesis.

2.0 J   Making a Generalization—A Political System

Given a table describing the feelings of citizens toward different types of legislation, students will write in their own words a generalization that could serve as the title for the table.

2.0 K   Applying a Generalization—A Political System

Given a generalization about the possible responses to government control in a society and a case study about a political decision, students will use the generalization to predict what might happen in the case study by writing their own ending to the story.

2.0–2.4 L   Being Objective—American Political System

Given a list of thirty (30) statements, fifteen (15) objective and fifteen (15) subjective statements, about the American political system, students will show their objectivity by agreeing with at least twelve (12) of the fifteen (15) objective statements or by disagreeing with at least twelve (12) of the subjective statements.

2.0–2.4 M   Showing Interest—American Political System

Given seventeen (17) statements reflecting political activities with which students could become involved, students will demonstrate their interest in these activities, given three (3) alternatives (like, neutral, and dislike), by responding "like" to at least six (6) of the statements.

2.0–2.4 N   Showing Involvement—American Political System

Given seventeen (17) statements reflecting political activities with which students could become involved, students will demonstrate their involvement in these activities, given four (4) alternatives (very often, frequently, seldom, and never), by indicating the "very often" or the "frequently" level for not less than six (6) of the statements.

2.0–2.4 O   Demonstrating Value Consistencies— American Political System

Given five (5) general value principles of the American political system and five (5) specific statements of hypothetical examples of each principle, students will demonstrate their value consistency by agreeing with at least three (3) of the five (5) statements for each principle.

2.0 P   Identifying an Issue—A Political System

Given a newspaper article about citizens attempting to influence the outputs of the United States political system, students will select from a list of four (4) issues the one (1) that best describes the general public issue involved in the article.

2.0 Q   Taking a Defensible Position—A Political System

Given a summary paragraph that describes citizens' reactions (feedback) to proposed legislation, students will state, in their own words, their position on passing of the proposed legislation and will state at least one positive consequence that could possibly follow from the legislation to be used to defend their position.

2.0 R   Grounding a Position—A Political System

Given a value position about the political community of a political system, students will choose from a list of five (5) statements of evidence the two (2) that support the position, the two (2) that attack the position, and the one (1) that has no bearing on the position.

SUMMARY

As in our case study of political systems, which is only a six-week unit, other units or subunits may provide the teacher with the basis to form tables of specifications. Constructing such tables helps teachers:

1. To understand and organize better the ideas constituting a unit of study that may include content from specified material and life experience of the classroom participants.
2. To suggest gaps in the ideas that purport to explain a social phenomenon.
3. To identify and list the inquiry behaviors developed in class discussion.
4. To focus on the substantive and behavioral items that are important.
5. To translate certain items on both dimensions (substantive and behavioral) into objectives and questions for evaluation.
6. To examine continuously their instructional goals and to assess their own performance in meeting these goals.

In sum, tables of specifications provide conceptual clarity and sharpen one's own instructional objectives.

While we advocate a systematic approach to instruction using concrete objectives and accompanying test items, we do not subscribe to the tenets of behavioralism. We believe that there is flexibility in matters dealing with human affairs and that, accordingly, flexibility should be reflected in the instructional programs in the schools. We recommend that flexibility should be observed in (1) whether or not teachers choose to use these types of materials, (2) whether or not a particular objective is used, teachers should be able to develop their own objectives with their own language and instructional mode, (3) developing specific objectives and test items because, given the nature of society, there is an inherent danger in pressing for a neat set of categories and relations (as in science and mathematics) of reducing important matters to trivial ones. In short, the quest for specificity should not bring about triviality but increased understanding. If triviality results from specificity, then teachers should strive for more global but seriously meaningful objectives.

Inquiry teaching and learning should be evaluated by instruments that directly pertain to desirable student behaviors. Formative evaluation, that is, evaluation that performs a motivational function and points to certain weaknesses in teaching and learning, is most compatible with the theory and practice of inquiry. Evaluation that is used as a system of external rewards and punishments is not consistent with the goals of inquiry.

The field is in great need of making its objectives operational so that they can be measured. Tables of specifications and clearly stated objectives are two means teachers have to refine their instructional goals and provide the basis for systematic formative evaluation. By using these instruments, and the conceptual framework under which they are subsumed, teachers can begin to evaluate their performance and see in what areas additional work is needed. It is hoped the profession will soon make the means consistent with the ends of inquiry. Evaluation is one of the means that is being discussed. The organizational structure of the schools is another means, which presently is not even remotely related to the goals of inquiry. It is to this area that we need to turn many of our efforts so that inquiry as an inspiring and realistic way of looking at the world is reinforced and continuously promoted.

8

the assessment of teaching:
checklists
and category systems

There are two instruments that teachers can use for purposes of self-evaluation. Both instruments have been designed to help teachers learn about themselves—their attitudes toward the instructional process as well as their classroom performance. The instruments are the checklist and the category system. Both are based on the concept of inquiry as we define it in this volume, and both are the concern of this chapter.

PERFORMANCE IN THE CLASSROOM:
A TEACHER CHECKLIST

The checklist presented here is constructed on the basis of our definition of inquiry as the process of exploring and testing alternatives. The questions on the checklist are grouped under seven general categories, each category reflecting a dimension in teacher classroom performance. The reader will notice that the categories on the checklist parallel the teacher roles as planner, introducer, questioner, and so forth—task functions that were discussed in several parts of this book.

The main purpose of the checklist is to give classroom practitioners a way in which to organize and evaluate their performance. Though the instrument may elicit some subjective judgments, it does provide the opportunity for teachers to reflect upon their teaching and to score themselves. If teachers value the various dimensions and processes of inquiry, they should be able to look at themselves objectively and identify areas of strength as well as weakness.

The checklist may be used at the beginning of a school year and then used intermittently throughout the year to see if any noticeable change has occurred. When appropriate, the teacher may team up with a colleague and after several exchange classroom visits perform an evaluation on each other. While scoring, in itself, is not important, the teacher, for purposes of measuring change, may assign certain scores to the type of behavior actually performed. It is recommended that four points be given for behaviors performed "regularly," three points for "frequently," two for "sometimes," and one for "seldom." No one is expected to achieve the perfect sum of 156 points. Nonetheless, the total of the individual scores given for the various inquiry behaviors will give the teacher a broad self-profile. The summing up of scores under each of the seven categories will provide the teacher with a separate profile for each cluster of behaviors.

Am I an Inquiry Teacher? [1]

	Regularly	Frequently	Sometimes	Seldom

As Planner

I focus on lessons involving exploration of significant ideas, concepts, or problem areas that can be investigated at many levels of sophistication.

I prepare for a broad range of alternative ideas. and values that the students may raise related to a central topic.

I select materials and learning experiences to stimulate student curiosity and support student investigation.

I make available a wide variety of resources and material for student use.

Skill-building exercises are tied directly to on-going learnings where they can be utilized and applied.

As Introducer

My introductory lessons present some problem, question, contradiction, or unknown element that will maximize student thinking.

My aim is for students to react freely to the introductory springboards with little direction from me.

I encourage many different responses to a given springboard and am prepared to deal with alternative patterns of exploration.

As Questioner and Inquiry Sustainer

The students talk more than I do.

Students are free to discuss and interchange their ideas.

When I talk, I "question," not "tell".

I consciously use the ideas students have raised and base my statements and questions on their ideas.

	Regularly	Frequently	Sometimes	Seldom

As Questioner and Inquiry Sustainer (cont.)

I redirect student questions in such a way that students are encouraged to arrive at their own answers.

My questions are intended to invite the pupils to explore, explain, support, and evaluate their ideas.

I encourage the students to evaluate the adequacy of grounds provided for statements made by them or by others.

Students gain understanding and practice in logical and scientific processes of acquiring, validating, and using knowledge.

My questions encourage the students to test the validity of their ideas in a broad context of experience.

I encourage students to move from examination of particular cases to more generalized concepts and understandings.

As Manager

I emphasize learning and the use of ideas rather than managerial functions, such as discipline and record keeping.

I opt for flexible seating, student movement, and maximum student use of materials and resources.

Class dialogue is conducted in a fashion that emphasizes courtesy and willingness to listen to each person's ideas.

Students are actively involved in the planning and maintenance of the total classroom environment.

I foster balanced participation by encouraging the more reticent students to take an active role in classroom activities.

As Rewarder

I encourage and reward the free exchange and testing of ideas.

I emphasize the internal rewards that spring from the successful pursuit of one's own ideas.

I avoid criticizing or judging ideas offered by students

Each student's contribution is considered legitimate and important

I evaluate students on growth in many aspects of the learning experience, rather than simply on the basis of facts acquired.

As Value Investigator

I emphasize that concepts, social issues, policy decisions, attitudes, and values are legitimate areas for discussion.

All topics are critically examined, not "taught" as closed issues with a single "right" solution.

Use of unfounded, emotionally charged language is minimized in discussing attitudes and values.

As Value Investigator (cont.)

	Regularly	Frequently	Sometimes	Seldom
I encourage the students to explore the implications of holding alternative value and policy positions.	____	____	____	____
I make the students aware of personal and social bases for diversity in attitudes, values, policies.	____	____	____	____
I encourage the students to arrive at value and policy positions of their own that they understand and can defend.	____	____	____	____

As Formative Evaluator

I state my objectives clearly so that I can see whether I have accomplished them.	____	____	____	____
I use evaluation measures that relate directly to my objectives.	____	____	____	____
The results of evaluation help me make appropriate adjustments to increase understanding and interest.	____	____	____	____
I share the results of evaluation with the student identifying strengths as well as areas where we both need to improve.	____	____	____	____
Evaluation is a means to improve instruction and not to judge people.	____	____	____	____

In using a checklist one should not overestimate its importance and the contributions it can make to effective teaching and learning. Checklists provide only partial feedback to the teacher, and there is an inherent tendency, when one evaluates oneself, to be subjective. Along with checklists, category systems that are objectively administered and apply to classroom discourse should be employed. Such a category system, again developed from the perspective of inquiry teaching, is presented and discussed in the next section of this chapter. In addition to these two instruments, we have also discussed in Chapter 7 the use of criterion referenced instruments designed to tap inquiry behaviors in certain substantive areas.

PERFORMANCE IN THE CLASSROOM: A CATEGORY SYSTEM

The Problem of Teaching Issues

Concern for studying classroom dialogue on social issues stems from the following general observations:

1. It is perhaps a rare occasion when teachers plan for and include in their formal classroom activity an issue that elicits a range of conflicting views

[1] This checklist is an expanded version of the one prepared by Mary Sugrue Murphy and Jo A. Sweeney for a special feature of *Today's Education*, 58 (May, 1969), 44, under the direction of Byron Massialas. Reprinted with permission.

and creates considerable emotional involvement on the part of students. Real controversial issues are excluded. For example, topics such as the legality of abortion, forms of sterilization, birth-control advice, referral system for sanitary abortions, use of contraceptives, are rarely dealt with.

2. It is not unusual to find a civics or humanities course explicitly aimed at indoctrinating the student into accepting on faith alone the prevailing social norms and standards of behavior. The orientation of these courses contradicts the aim of the President's Commission on National Goals and several civic and educational agencies, which is to develop responsible citizens who would be, in the true Periclean spirit, "sound judges of policy" and would participate actively in public affairs.

3. It is not unusual to see textbook authors, teachers, and students commit the "naturalistic fallacy"—that is, the fallacy of converting, without warrant, an "ought to" judgment into an "is" statement, a value judgment into a statement of fact. Also, in the resolution of a value conflict, there is a tendency to emphasize merely the collection of facts, as if facts alone point to a right decision or a just policy. Though the identification of the factual and evidential roots of a social problem is a necessary operation in the conduct of inquiry, facts alone do not provide sufficient warrant for the acceptance or rejection of a value position. Often facts neither prove nor disprove—they are irrelevant. Moreover, selective perception might be operating. Many individuals have problems because they refuse to take a position. There is also the difficulty of communication.

4. It is not infrequent to encounter teachers whose only strategy in dealing with controversial issues is "to present all possible sides to a problem." It is generally assumed that when all sides are presented, teachers have attained the highest state of morality in the adjudication of values. It is important to present and study issue alternatives and issue consequences in an objective manner, but it is equally important for teachers to encourage students to take a value position that can be publicly communicated.

5. Issues that involve students emotionally provide excellent springboards for discussion; yet in many instances, the students are either discouraged or they are not given any clues as to how they should proceed to examine issues reflectively. In other instances the loudest or most "knowledgeable" voice prevails in a way that inhibits free discourse.

6. Very little material is available in the way of tapes or stenographic reproduction of classroom discourse when controversial issues are studied. Consequently, many judgments about the treatment of controversial issues in class lack authoritative documentation or are based on indirect sources, like textbooks and curriculum guides. Often these judgments fail to reflect classroom conditions.

All these observations prompted us to develop the Michigan Social Issues Cognitive Category System described below.

The Development of a Category System

In developing our category system we were guided by: (1) an inquiry model, (2) a social issues model, (3) a consideration for an open classroom climate. Let us elaborate:

An *inquiry model* assumes that certain cognitive operations—orientation, definition, hypothesis or position, explanation, evidencing, generalization—can be used productively in the classroom to help the discourse on the examination of social issues. Let us point out, however, that the model of the scientific method (or its variants as proposed by Dewey, Joseph Schwab, Bruner, and others, which work in the new curriculum projects) does not apply to the analysis of social issues without important adjustments. Furthermore, many of the cognitive operations in our model are discrete, and the employment of one does not necessarily imply the employment of another.

A *social issues model* presumes that when teachers deal with value-laden topics they take the position of "defensible partisanship." This position implies that the teacher is *partisan* to: (1) the rational processes of inquiry, (2) democratic classroom participation, and (3) defensible and explicit choices rather than impulsive or uncritical choices. The acceptance of the model of defensible partisanship automatically implies rejection of such teaching positions as deliberate exclusion of controversy, ethical neutrality, indoctrination, and the uncritical perpetuation of the status quo.

By *deliberate exclusion* of social issues we refer to teachers who, for various reasons, consider issues to be inappropriate for classroom discussion and thus systematically avoid them. *Ethical neutrality* means that whatever the nature of the controversy being discussed, the teachers' position is one that consciously avoids taking a stand. In such instances, teachers may provide the opportunity for an open discussion of issues, but refuse to take a position themselves. *To indoctrinate* is to purposefully pass on to other individuals a set of beliefs without submitting them to critical examination. As we have seen previously, teachers do, in many respects, indoctrinate students into accepting on faith their own point of view. *Uncritical perpetuation of the status quo* resembles indoctrination, but it is unplanned. For various reasons teachers continue to transmit to younger generations beliefs and values from the past without any attempt to examine them. In many instances, this uncritical transmission is a matter of habit.

An *open classroom climate* encourages wide student participation and the expression of diverse viewpoints that may be in conflict with one another. Each student is given the opportunity to express a position on an issue and is encouraged to offer defensible grounds for it. A value position is accepted by the class to the extent that it rests on explicit and valid grounds.[2]

In sum, we have assumed that a classroom that provides a defensible model for analyzing controversy is one in which there is a climate supportive of both the presentation of conflicting value alternatives and the taking of explicit positions (for example, hypothesis formation) that are accompanied by grounding (for example, tracing logical consequences). These have been the general considerations that guided us in developing the Michigan Social Issues Category System. The actual system, however, evolved from our observations in the classroom.

The Use of a Category System

The main goals in constructing the category system described here are to provide an instrument that permits teachers to classify meaningfully spontaneous classroom discourse focused on social issues and, on that basis, to analyze the sequence and distribution of patterns of interaction between members of a class. As with other category systems, the Michigan Category System can be used to (1) get a better understanding of the dynamics of instruction, which may help individuals learn how to teach; (2) provide objective feedback to teachers for assessing their classroom performance, which may provide them with the rational grounds for changing their instructional program; and (3) give researchers a system of logical categories and a set of procedures for determining the interactive communication patterns in the classroom. As is true of almost all other cognitive category systems that are fairly complex, the Michigan System was not used originally to categorize directly communication in live classrooms; rather, we relied initially on transcribed tapes taken in the classroom. Recently, however, we were able to adapt the system to live classroom situations.

Unlike the other category systems, our system focuses on classroom dialogue related to contemporary controversial issues.[3] As used in this context, controversial issues are components of larger societal problems in which classroom participants are emotionally involved. These social issues

[2] For an elaboration of the theoretical dimensions upon which the category system is built, see Byron G. Massialas and C. Benjamin Cox, *Inquiry in Social Studies* (New York: McGraw-Hill Book Co., 1966), chapters 4 and 7.

[3] Of the two dozen-plus category systems (both cognitive and affective) reported by Simon and Boyer, only one purports to deal with controversial issues. However, its direction and focus is significantly different from the Michigan Social Issues Cognitive Category System. See Anita Simon and E. Gil Boyer, *Mirrors for Behavior: An Anthology of Classroom Observation Instruments* (Philadelphia: Research for Better Schools, Inc., and the Center for the Study of Teaching, Temple University, 1967).

are presented as alternatives. The issues provide the springboards for inquiry. Though issues are drawn from the larger society, they are given shape and are interpreted by the actors in the classroom who form their own social system.

An Explanation of the Categories

In this section we are presenting the Michigan System primarily from the point of view of teachers who are interested in improving their instruction. The system is given below.

FIGURE 8:1

The Michigan Social Issues Cognitive Category System

A. *Request for Cognitive Operation*
  1. *Exposition:* The speaker requests statements that provide general information or summarize the discussion.
  2. *Definition and Clarification:* The speaker requests statements that
    (a) tell how the meaning of words are related to one another, or
    (b) clarify a previous statement.
  3. *Positions and Hypotheses:* The speaker requests statements that include or imply the phrases, "I believe," "I think," "I hold," "I feel," and so forth, followed by *his* or *her* hypotheses, preferences, evaluations, or judgments regarding a given issue.
  4. *Grounding:* The speaker requests reasons supporting a position or hypothesis. Requests for grounding must be clearly linked to a position-statement, hypothesis, or proposed definition.
B. *Noncognitive Operations*
  5. *Noncognitive*
    5.0 Request for Noncognitive Operation.
    5.1 Directions and Classroom Maintenance.
    5.2 Restatement of Speaker's Ideas.
    5.3 Acceptance or Encouragement.
    5.4 Nonproductive Responses.
    5.5 Negative Responses.
    5.6 Fragmented Discussion.
C. *Performance of Cognitive Operation*
  6. *Exposition:* The speaker makes statements that provide general information or summarize the discussion.
    6.1 Background.
    6.2 Summarizing.
  7. *Definition and Clarification:* The speaker makes a statement that
    (a) tells how the meanings of words are related to one another, or

(b) clarifies a previous statement.

7.1 General-Stipulative.

7.2 Quality-Value.

7.3 Clarification.

8. *Positions and Hypotheses:* The speaker makes statements that include or imply the phrases, "I believe," "I think," "I hold," "I feel," and so forth, followed by *his* or *her* hypotheses, preferences, evaluations, or judgments regarding a given issue.

8.1 Nonprescriptive.

8.2 Prescriptive.

8.3 Reassessment.

9. *Grounding:* The speaker gives reasons supporting a position or hypothesis. Grounding statements must be clearly linked to a position-statement, hypothesis, or proposed definition.

9.1 General Knowledge.

9.2 Authority.

9.3 Personal Experience.

9.4 Experience of Others.

9.5 Consequences.

9.6 Position-taking.

9.7 No Public Grounds.

The Michigan Social Issues Cognitive Category System consists of nine basic categories, eight of which are cognitive (categories 1–4 and 6–9) and one of which is identified as noncognitive (category 5). Categories 5 through 9 are further subdivided into more specific categories to make a total of twenty-six. All twenty-six categories are defined in terms of a classroom speaker; no single category is restricted to teacher statements or student statements. Figure 8:1 summarizes the categories.

Categories 1–4 are "request" categories. In these categories the speaker—either the teacher or the student—makes statements requesting that another speaker perform a particular cognitive operation. Category 1, Exposition, includes all statements in which the speaker requests that another individual provide general information or summarize the discussion. "What does your textbook say about the causes of World War II?" is an example of a request for general information. In category 2, Definition and Clarification, the speaker asks another individual to explain the meaning of a word or words or to clarify the meaning of a previous statement. For example, the teacher might ask a student, "Define what you mean by democracy."

In contrast with categories 1 and 2, wherein the speaker is simply asking questions requiring knowledge or comprehension, in categories 3 and 4 the speaker is requesting that more complex cognitive operations be performed.[4] In category 3, Positions and Hypotheses, the speaker requests that another individual indicate his hypotheses, preferences, evaluations, or judgments regarding a given issue. For example, when a student asks a teacher if she "thinks burning draft cards is wrong," she is making a category 3 request. If the teacher does take a position on the issue of burning draft cards, the student might then ask the teacher to state the reasons for her position. This constitutes a category 4 request: Grounding. Here the speaker asks another individual to support positions or hypotheses. Requests for grounding must be clearly linked to a position-statement or hypothesis.

Categories 1 through 4, then, focus on questions raised in the classroom. These categories are defined in such a way that they include all the cognitively oriented questions that might occur. In addition, the questions are grouped into four distinct categories involving different levels of cognitive complexity.

Category 5 in the system is what we have called Noncognitive and consists of seven subcategories. The operations in this category do not involve explicit contributions to the cognitive discourse. In category 5.0, Request for Noncognitive Operation, the speaker requests (1) information concerning students, classroom procedure, or operation, or (2) that an individual repeat a previous statement. Examples include questions such as, "Where is Joanne?" "Did we talk about this yesterday?" or "Would you repeat that?" Category 5.1, Directions and Classroom Maintenance, refers to statements on classroom procedure or operation. Statements calling for recognition of students are included here—for example, "Sue, you had your hand up." When speakers paraphrase or restate a statement made by a previous speaker or by themselves, it is coded as 5.2, Restatement of Speaker's Ideas. "As John noted, the balance in the Senate changed"—is an example of restatement. Category 5.3 refers to statements of acceptance or encouragement, implying that the individual should continue his or her behavior: "You've brought up a good point." Nonproductive Responses, category 5.4, indicates the inability or unwillingness of the speaker to respond to a request or perform a task: "I don't know the answer to your question." Negative Responses, category 5.5, refers to a speaker making irrelevant or disruptive statements or to a speaker correcting or stating the inappropriateness of another speaker's statement. "Sue, I don't think you were listening" is a category 5.5 response. Finally, Fragmented Discussion, category 5.6, refers to a period

---

[4] Benjamin S. Bloom, ed. *Taxonomy of Educational Objectives; Handbook 1: Cognitive Domain* (New York: David McKay Co., Inc, 1956). This taxonomy identifies knowledge and comprehension as less complex cognitive operations than application, analysis, synthesis, and evaluation.

that cannot be categorized because the statement or statements cannot be understood: "Ah, well . . ."

Categories 6 through 9 are cognitive categories paralleling categories 1 through 4. Whereas in the first four categories the speaker is *requesting* that a cognitive operation be performed, in categories 6, 7, 8, and 9 the speaker (the teacher or the student) is *performing* a cognitive operation. In addition, the last four categories are subdivided into more specific categories.

Category 6, Exposition, is one in which the speaker makes statements providing background or summary information. Using some of the terminology of earlier category systems, many of the operations in this category can be properly referred to as lecturing or imparting information on a topic. When a statement is coded as 6.1, Background, the speaker makes statements that provide general information by explaining or elaborating upon the material. For example, "Citizens of the United States may vote after their eighteenth birthday," is a statement that is coded as Background. In Summarizing, 6.2, the speaker makes statements reviewing the progress of discourse. The speaker does more than paraphrase another; she or he also integrates previous discussions. The following excerpt provides an example; "Let's see if I can tie this discussion together. Two major points have been mentioned—first, that worldwide birth control may be necessary if we are to control the population explosion, and secondly, that when developing family planning programs, we must consider the religious orientations of the community or country involved."

The seventh category deals with Definition and Clarification, and here the teacher or the student tries to provide the meaning of words or statements. This category is considered important in the conduct of inquiry into social issues for the reason that many contemporary issues cannot be understood or resolved because of ambiguity and confusion over meaning of key concepts. This category includes three subcategories. The General Stipulative category, 7.1, refers to generally accepted or contextual definitions of words for class use. Users of a term either accept a general definition as provided—for instance, in a dictionary—or they specify how they propose to use the term in the present context. Here is an example of a definition in this category: "A slave is a person who is held in servitude as the property of another person." Category 7.2 is labeled "Quality-Value and it refers to word definitions that have judgmental or prescriptive connotations. This judgmental aspect is illustrated in the following exchange: "What is a good citizen?" "A good citizen is a person who exercises his voting responsibilities." Category 7.3, Clarification, refers to statements made to remove ambiguities in the meaning of previous statements, as, for instance, in the statement, "When I said 'that treaty,' I was referring to the Treaty of Versailles."

The eighth category focuses on position-taking and the formation of hypotheses regarding social issues. This is a very important classroom operation. Its incidence determines the extent to which participants are willing not only to take positions, some of which may be in conflict with one another, but to reveal their biases. Statements of this sort are usually prefaced with "I believe" or "I think" or "I hold" or their equivalent, Although sometimes these prefatory remarks remain implicit. The kind of position one may take can be nonprescriptive (8.1), prescriptive (8.2), or it can be a reassessment (8.3) of a previous position or hypothesis. In the nonprescriptive category are statements that, once their key concepts are defined, are subject to validation by reference to factual evidence or to observations in the real world. "I think that the medical treatment given blacks in the United States is not equal to that given whites" is an example of a position statement that does not prescribe what ought to be done but can be validated by reference to evidence, provided the concept of equality is defined. "All men should be treated equally under the law" is a prescriptive statement that clearly expresses a preferential position on how men ought to be treated. "Taking into account John's comments, I tend to think that socialism is not always evil," is a re-evaluation of a position in light of new evidence.

The last basic category in the cognitive area is Grounding. As mentioned before, grounding is a category with strong qualitative implications and the operations included in it constitute, in the judgment of the authors, the heart of the process of examining and analyzing social problems. In grounding operations the speaker is giving reasons for taking a position or offering a hypothesis. The authors assume that what separates a classroom where social issues are productively discussed from one where they are not is a regular 8-9 sequence—that is, position statements invariably followed by grounding.

Category 9 includes seven subcategories as follows: The General Knowledge category, 9.1, refers to grounds based on general knowledge without revealing the source of that knowledge. For example, to support the position that eighteen-year-olds should have all the rights of an adult a speaker might state, "eighteen-year-olds can vote." Category 9.2, Authority, refers to a speaker defending a position by citing an expert or a particular source. Here is an example of 9.2: "I'm against the riots and I think they can be stopped. I was reading a *Newsweek* article, and it seems that tear gas works pretty well" (position statement followed by expert citation). Category 9.3 pertains to a Personal Experience that one cites to defend a position: "I don't think that blacks are discriminated against . . ."

(position) ". . . because up at the shop where I work some of them have better rates on their machines than the whites do" (grounding). In category 9.4 one can cite "Experience of Others" to defend a position, as, for instance, "I think that the publicity given LSD has encouraged kids to take it" (position). "This girl was saying that the reason she took LSD was because they gave such a write-up in the papers about what it does for you" (grounding). In Consequences, 9.5, the speaker supports a statement or position by pointing to its logical or pragmatic results: "We should not have used nuclear bombs on North Vietnam . . ." (position) ". . . because if we had, Russia would probably have entered the war" (grounding). One may also ground a position by referring to another position, category 9.6: "I think the riots at Columbia University were necessary . . ." (position) ". . . because the president of Columbia was incompetent" (grounding). Finally, category 9.7, No Public Grounds, refers to a statement in which the speaker fails to provide any explicit grounds for a position; the speaker expects that mere affirmation of belief provides adequate justification for the position. A statement coded under this category occurs in the following exchange: "I think we should try to prevent other nations from exploding nuclear devices" (position statement). "Why?" (request for grounding). "I just think we should" (grounding by no public grounds).

Obviously, categories 9.6, position-taking, and 9.7, No Public Grounds, contain statements that do not involve explicit logical grounding. Although one might question the validity of including these sub-categories, the fact remains that individuals do attempt to support a position with these types of statements.

SUMMARY

In the spirit of formative or feedback evaluation teachers may use to advantage such instruments as checklists and category systems. They are not difficult to administer and provide teachers with the necessary information to assess strengths and weaknesses in learning and instruction.

Both tools are built on our model of social issues inquiry. Checklists elicit information on how teachers view their classroom role—their feelings and attitudes toward students and the general conditions for learning. Category systems, such as the one described here, furnish teachers with a mirror image of themselves as they interact with students. The information gathered through this system is based on actual classroom events and happenings—on real, not imagined, discussions and other verbal activities.

If checklists and category systems are used together with the criterion referenced tests described in Chapter 7 teachers may gain a rather comprehensive picture of their class and their personal performance. When behaviors and concepts exist that are not included in the materials presented here, teachers should make appropriate modifications to reflect their particular situation and instructional goals.

9

analyzing
social issues dialogue:
using the
Michigan category system

This chapter discusses the dialogue patterns found in a sample of social issues classes and suggests ways in which data obtained from applying the Michigan Social Issues Cognitive Category System to classroom dialogue can be analyzed. Sixteen social studies classes in fifteen different Michigan secondary schools were studied. The teachers of these social studies classes were unique in that they said that social issues instruction was important and expressed attitudes that supported the reflective examination of these issues in the classroom. The classes in the sample regularly devoted at least 25 percent of their time to the discussion of social issues.

Because the intent of the study was to examine social issues discussions that exist in normal practice in the classroom, the teachers and classes were encouraged not to change their course of study or class routine when we visited the classes for taping. Special topics were not selected by our research staff; instead, the teacher outlined what social issues were coming up for discussion and with the staff selected a day for recording the discussions. Each of the classes was taped while social issues were being discussed and the tapes were transcribed and coded using the Michigan Cognitive Category System. The coded data for each class were then tabulated into interaction matrices that were used to analyze the verbal interaction patterns.

The first part of this chapter describes how the Michigan Category System is used to formulate classroom interaction records. These records are then used to produce a number of *interaction matrices* that can give us insight into many aspects of the class discussion.

The remainder of this chapter concentrates on conceptually relevant *dimensions of classroom discourse* such as student participation, teacher influence, cognitive interaction, and the context of inquiry. Some of the questions that may be answered by examining these dimensions are: How much and what type of student participation occurs in the discussion? In what manner does the teacher influence the interaction? Do students respond to questions raised by the teachers? Does the teacher lecture? Is the style of the class discussion opining or inquiry? What is happening in an "inquiry" class?

INTERACTION MATRICES

Interaction matrices record a sequence of coded verbal dialogue in a classroom in such a way that the interaction between the classroom participants can be summarized and examined meaningfully. To illustrate how matrices are developed from coded dialogue, let us look at the dialogue in Figure 9:1, which has been coded using the Michigan Cognitive Category System.

The three columns, R, P, and NC at the left of the dialogue are the three major divisions of intellectual operations used in the Michigan Social Issues Cognitive Category System as outlined in the previous

R	P	NC	Time		
T3			8	T:	What about these draft-card burners? She claims they're unpatriotic. Is there anyone who thinks they're not?/
		T5.1	1		Janet?/
	S8.1		7	G:	I think they're just against the draft and they're not really unpatriotic. They just don't want to be drafted./
		T5.1	1	T:	Faye?/
	S8.1		3	G:	No, I don't think that they're not being patriotic./
S2			3	B:	Would you define what you mean by patriotic?/

FIGURE 9:1
Coded Classroom Dialogue

chapter. In other words, R represents request operations; P performance operations; and NC noncognitive operations. The letters T and S merely refer to teacher and student. The request operations, in accordance with the category system, include categories T1 through T4 and S1 through S4. Categories T6 through T9 and S6 through S9 encompass the performance operations while categories T5 and S5 comprise the noncognitive operations. All the performance and noncognitive categories have more specific subcategories as indicated by the number following the decimal. The column next to the dialogue labeled Time allows the coder to record in seconds the duration of a coded operation.

The first intellectual operation in Figure 9:1 is a request by the teacher and is entered as T3 in the R column. The letter T indicates that the teacher is speaking, whereas the number 3 means that the teacher is asking that a position be taken or a hypothesis be formed. The eight seconds the teacher took to make the request is entered in the Time column. The second operation is coded T5.1 and is entered in the NC column. The T5 means that it is a noncognitive operation by the teacher and the 1 after the decimal indicates that the teacher called on a student. The 1 in the Time column parallel to the T5.1 indicates that the operation lasted one second. The first entry under P is S8.1. The S8 signifies that a student is taking a position or offering a hypothesis; the 1 after the decimal indicates that the position or hypothesis is nonprescriptive. The operation took three seconds, which is recorded in the Time column. In general, then, each coded intellectual operation has four components: the *speaker* (indicated by S or T), the *main category*, the *subcategory*, and the *time* associated with the intellectual operation.

If only the main categories in the Michigan Category System are used (ignoring subcategories for the moment), the coded dialogue in Figure 9:1 becomes this *interaction record:* T3(8), T5(1), S8(7), T5(1), S8(3), S2(3). T3(8) is the first entry in Figure 9:1 and in the interaction record; again, T3 represents the speaker and the intellectual operation and the 8 indicates in seconds the duration of the operation.

A given interaction record may, then, be used to produce a number of interaction matrices. In our analyses of the data we employed three types of matrices: *intellectual operations, timed,* and *cognitive operations.* An intellectual operations matrix shows the distribution and interrelationship of the intellectual operations that occur in the class dialogue, a timed matrix reveals how classroom time is distributed among the various operations, and the cognitive operations matrix reveals the distribution and relationship among the cognitive operations that occur in the class dialogue.

Intellectual Operations Matrix

Table 9:1 shows the distribution and relationship among all the intellectual operations that occurred in class H's discussion of the draft. The sequence of interaction codes for this class are tallied in the matrix, one pair at a time, with the pairs overlapping; the duration of each operation is not taken into account. The cell in which a particular pair is tabulated is determined by using the first operation in the pair to indicate the row and the second operation the column. For example, this series of interaction codes—T3, T5, S8, T5, S8, S2—would be entered in the matrix as follows: The first pair of codes is T3-T5 and is tallied in the cell formed by the matrix row T3 and the column T5. The number 7 in this cell means that the pair of codes, T3-T5, occurred seven times in the dialogue. The second pair is T5-S8 and is entered into the cell formed by row T5, column S8. The third pair, S8-T5, the fourth pair, T5-S8, and the fifth pair, S8-S2 are tallied in a similar fashion. Each pair of operations overlaps with the previous pair, and each operation, except the first and last, is used twice.

The Totals column to the right of the matrix shows the number of times a particular operation was the first operation in a pair while the Totals row at the bottom of the matrix shows the number of times a particular operation was the second operation in a pair. In class H there were 412 separate intellectual operations. The teacher performed 94 noncognitive operations, T5, and requested 43 hypotheses, T3. The students gave 82 hypotheses, S8, and provided 48 separate grounding operations, S9. Let's see what happened after the teacher requested a hypothesis. Looking at the T3 row under the NC column, we discover that seven times the teacher followed his request with a noncognitive operation, T5—probably he called on a student. Continuing across the T3 row we find that once the teacher followed his request for a hypothesis with his own hypothesis, T8, once a student requested a hypothesis, S3, but the majority of the time, 27 times, after the teacher requested hypotheses the students provided hypotheses, S8.

Timed Matrix

Table 9:2 shows how the class time was distributed among the intellectual operations. In this matrix the duration of each intellectual operation is taken into account and the interaction codes are tallied at one-second intervals. The two total columns in this matrix show the amount of time in seconds devoted to a particular operation. For example, class H students spent 318 seconds providing exposition, S6; 376 seconds

TABLE 9:1
Intellectual Operations for 18 Main Categories
Discussion of the Draft by Class H

CATEGORY		TEACHER									STUDENT									TOTALS
		REQUESTS				NC	PERFORMS				REQUESTS				NC	PERFORMS				
		T1	T2	T3	T4	T5	T7	T8	T9		S1	S2	S3	S4	S5	S6	S7	S8	S9	
TEACHER Requests	T1														2	5				8
	T2														6		6			12
	T3					7		1							5		1	27	1	43
	T4														4			1	6	12
Noncognitive	T5	4	1	6	2	22	3	2			5	2			3	5	2	28	5	94
	T6			2		7	1				1	2			1	1		1	1	16
Performs	T7		1	2		1									4			1		9
	T8		1		1	2													2	9
	T9		1	1			1													1
STUDENT Requests	S1			1		1	1								1					7
	S2					3	1	1							1					7
	S3			2		1		1												4
	S4					1		1												2
Noncognitive	S5	2	3	3	2	9	2						1	1	3			4		34
	S6	2		2	1	5									1	3				14
	S7			2		6	1											1	1	10
Performs	S8		3	11	3	18		3				2	2					8	31	82
	S9		3	11	3	10	1					2			4		1	9	2	48
TOTALS		8	12	43	2	94	16	9	9	1	7	7	4	2	34	14	10	82	48	412

TABLE 9:2
Timed Matrix for 18 Main Categories
Discussion of the Draft by Class H

CATEGORY		TEACHER									STUDENT									TOTAL NUMBER OF SECONDS
		REQUESTS				NC		PERFORMS			REQUESTS				NC		PERFORMS			
		T1	T2	T3	T4	T5	T6	T7	T8	T9	S1	S2	S3	S4	S5	S6	S7	S8	S9	
TEACHER Requests	T1	17				1									2	5				25
	T2		32												6		6			44
	T3			180		7			1				1		5		1	27	1	223
	T4				28									1	4			1	6	40
Noncognitive Performs	T5	4	1	6	2	102	4	3	2		5	2			3	5	2	28	5	174
	T6			2		7	97				1	2			1	1		1	1	113
	T7		1	2		1	1	51		1		1						1	1	60
	T8		1	1	1	2			41						4					50
	T9									11									1	12
STUDENT Requests	S1					1	4	1	1		65									72
	S2			2		3	2	1	1			25			1			1		32
	S3					1							9	3						13
	S4					1			1											5
Noncognitive Performs	S5	2	3	2	2	9	2	2	4		1	1	1	1	70					101
	S6	2		2	1	5									1	307				318
	S7					6											51			61
	S8		3	11	3	18	3		3			2	2					302	31	376
	S9		3	11	3	10	2	1							4		1	9	365	411
TOTAL NUMBER OF SECONDS		25	44	223	40	174	113	60	50	12	72	32	13	5	101	318	61	376	411	2130

offering hypotheses, S8; and 411 seconds grounding S9. The diagonal cells in the matrix (T3–T3 for instance) are steady-state cells; they represent the duration of time spent performing a given operation. The other cells are transitional cells. The number of operations in these transitional cells is identical to the number of operations in the corresponding cells in the matrix in Table 9:1.

Cognitive Operations Matrix

Table 9:3 shows the distribution and relationship among the cognitive operations that occurred in class H. All of the noncognitive categories, T5s and S5s, were ignored when this matrix was tabulated. This matrix is helpful if one is interested in answering a question like, What cognitive operations followed the teacher's request for a hypothesis? Frequently the presence of the noncognitive categories masks the flow of cognitive operations. For example, in the matrix in Table 9:1 we saw that the teacher followed a T3 request seven times with a noncognitive operation, T5; if the teacher was simply recognizing a student, did the student then provide the requested hypothesis? By ignoring the noncognitive operations and looking at the T3 row in the matrix in Table 9:3, we can find our answer. Thirty-four times (out of a possible 43) the students responded with hypotheses. This is seven more times than was apparent in the first matrix. Evidently, then, those seven teacher noncognitive operations were followed by the students providing hypotheses. To discover what other cognitive operations, besides a T3 question on the part of the teacher, preceded a student hypothesis or position, we can simply refer to the vertical S8 column. By doing so, we discover that a student hypothesis or position was preceded eighteen times by another student hypothesis or position (cell S8-S8) and fourteen times by grounding (S9-S8).

Looking at the totals at the bottom of Table 9:3, we discover that this discussion was comprised of 284 separate cognitive operations, 110 by the teacher and 174 by the students. The teacher made 75 requests for cognitive operations and performed these operations 35 times, whereas the students made only 20 requests and performed 154 times. It is evident from these figures that the teacher did not dominate the discussion by lecturing to the students, but concentrated on asking questions and evoking student performance. The totals for each of the categories reveal that the most popular categories are T3, S8, and S9, with 43, 82, and 48 entries respectively. The concentration of operations in these three categories (173 of the 284 total cognitive operations) means that more than half of the cognitive interaction consisted of the teacher requesting a

| CATEGORY | TEACHER | | | | | | | | STUDENT | | | | | | | | TOTALS |
| | REQUESTS | | | | PERFORMS | | | | REQUESTS | | | | PERFORMS | | | | |
	T1	T2	T3	T4	T6	T7	T8	T9	S1	S2	S3	S4	S6	S7	S8	S9	
TEACHER Requests — T1	1												6			1	8
T2		3											1	6	1	1	12
T3			1	2						1	1	1		1	34	2	43
T4			2				1					1			2	6	12
Performs — T6			1	2	2				2	2		1	2		3	1	16
T7			3						1		1				4		9
T8						3		1		1					4		9
T9			1														1
STUDENT Requests — S1		1	1		1								1		2	1	7
S2			1				1							1	1	3	7
S3			1				1								2		4
S4			1				1										2
Performs — S6	4	1	3	1			1						4				14
S7		1	3		1	2								1	1	1	10
S8	1	3	14	4	3		3		2		2			1	18	31	82
S9	2	3	12	3	4		1		1	3					14	5	48
TOTALS	8	12	43	12	16	9	9	1	6	7	4	3	14	10	82	48	284

TABLE 9:3

Cognitive Operations for 16 Main Cognitive Categories
Discussion of the Draft by Class H

hypothesis or position (T3) and the students giving a hypothesis or position (S8) and then grounding it (S9).

How does the distribution of intellectual operations in class H compare with the other fifteen classes in the study? To answer this question, data from class matrices are synthesized, compared, and discussed in the sections that follow.

DIMENSIONS OF CLASSROOM DISCOURSE

In order to understand and study a major aspect of the instructional process, classroom discourse, it is necessary to identify conceptually important dimensions of classroom interaction and examine their interrelationships. By following this procedure we will be able to contrast dialogue occurring in different classrooms and maintain a basis for comparison in our investigations. Too many studies to date have focused on only one dimension of interaction—student participation—or they have developed global descriptions of teaching styles. One of the goals of our study was to delineate several important dimensions of classroom dialogue, to quantify related interaction variables, and to study their interrelationships. We were particularly interested in developing a way to classify objectively discussions as expository, opining, or inquiry. The differences between the three types of discussions could then be compared on several important dimensions: (1) student participation, (2) teacher questions, (3) teacher influence, and (4) probing of hypotheses.

Classifying the Discussions
as Expository, Opining, or Inquiry

The Michigan Cognitive Category System not only discriminates between different levels of critical thinking, it highlights verbal cognitive behaviors that are inquiry-oriented and go beyond the traditional classroom skills of simple exposition and recall. Using the categories in the Michigan System, we characterized as inquiry classes those that spent a major portion of their *time* presenting, clarifying, and supporting hypotheses, positions, or opinions. Classes that spent considerable time presenting hypotheses or positions but that did not devote much time to probing their positions were characterized as opining. In classes where most of the time was devoted to exposition and very little to either presenting or probing hypotheses, the discussion was categorized as expository. Classifying the discussions was a two-step process. An i/e ratio was first used to distinguish between inquiry oriented and expository discussions and then a p/i ratio was used to distinguish between opining and inquiry discussions.

The categories used to calculate a class's i/e ratio are summarized in Figure 9:2. The ratio of time devoted to inquiry performance operations to the time devoted to exposition indicates whether the class concentrated

---

Inquiry Performance Operations

T7	Teacher definition and clarification
T8	Teacher positions or hypotheses
T9	Teacher grounding
S7	Student definition and clarification
S8	Student positions or hypotheses
S9	Student grounding

Exposition

T6	Teacher exposition
S6	Student exposition

FIGURE 9:2
Categories Used to Calculate a Class i/e Ratio

on exposition or inquiry. An i/e ratio *above 1.0* means that the class spent more time presenting hypotheses, definitions, evidence, and clarification than providing exposition: an i/e ratio below 1.0 means that the class spent more time providing exposition. Thus, classes with i/e ratios *below 1.0* were classified as expository, not inquiry.

Looking at the i/e ratios in Table 9:4, we find that 11 of the 16 social issues classes focused on inquiry interaction. These results are en-

TABLE 9:4
Inquiry/Exposition Ratios

Indirect Influence

T1	Request for exposition
T2	Request for definition and clarification
T3	Request for positions or hypotheses
T4	Request for grounding
T5.0	Request for noncognitive operation
T5.2	Restatement of speaker ideas
T5.3	Acceptance or encouragement

Direct Influence

T5.1	Directions and classroom maintenance
T5.5	Negative responses
T6.1–T6.2	Exposition
T7.1–T7.3	Definition and clarification
T8.1–T8.3	Positions and hypotheses
T9.1–T9.6	Grounding

couraging but not totally unexpected. Social issues by their very nature involve conflicting values, and it would be surprising if every person in a given classroom agreed on the policy we ought to follow in the Mideast, that abortion should be legalized, or that our tax laws are equitable. Thus, it is logical to assume that discussion of these issues would evoke a variety of positions and hypotheses and that the classroom participants would make some effort to support their views. When this does not happen, the issues are usually discussed in a very loose, descriptive manner without any attempt by the class to come to grips with underlying values or conflicting views. The five classes (C, E, F, J, M) that discussed social issues in an expository fashion should be the exception rather than the rule.

Just because a class has a high i/e ratio does not necessarily mean, however, that social issues are being dealt with in a probing fashion. It is quite possible that only a cathartic session is taking place; that is, everyone is throwing out positions and hypotheses, but not attempt is being made to examine the merits of any particular position. Certainly it is important to get all views out in the open, but it is equally important for students and teachers to defend their points of view on grounds that can be publicly communicated.

The p/i ratio helps us distinguish between the opining classes where probing does not take place and the inquiry classes where the participants test and defend their hypotheses and positions. The p/i *ratio* is defined as the proportion of inquiry time spent performing the operations of definition, clarification, and grounding. The p/i ratio in our study was computed by totaling the time spent in categories T7, T9, S7, and S9 and dividing by the time spent in categories T7, T8, T9, S7, S8, and S9. Classes with p/i ratios of .50 or above concentrated on probing; classes with p/i ratios below .50 devoted more time to generating hypotheses and positions than to probing them.

In Table 9:5 the sixteen classes are listed in their respective groups

TABLE 9:5

Classifying the Discussions

EXPOSITORY		OPINING			INQUIRY		
Class	I/E Ratio	Class	I/E Ratio	P/I Ratio	Class	I/E Ratio	P/I Ratio
C	.14	A	2.47	.29	H	2.25	.56
E	.16	B	6.08	.31	K	8.03	.52
F	.12	D	2.95	.32	L	5.14	.51
J	.73	G	1.89	.33	N	5.63	.50
M	.50	I	3.63	.40	O	1.74	.54
					P	1.69	.68
AVG.	.33	AVG.	3.40	.33	AVG.	4.08	.55
AVG. i/e ratio = 3.77							

along with their i/e and p/i ratios. Five class discussions were expository; that is, hypotheses were infrequently generated or tested. The i/e ratios ranged from .14 to .73, with an average of .33—indicating thereby that a large proportion of time was devoted to exposition. In contrast to the expository classes, the eleven opining and inquiry classes had an average i/e ratio of 3.77; thus, the time they spent in inquiry operations was triple the time they devoted to exposition.

Five of the discussions, in classes A, B, D, G, and I, were characterized as opining. In these classes the participants spent most of their time hypothesizing and did not clarify or defend many of their positions. The average p/i ratio for the opining classes, .33, indicates that only a third of the inquiry time was devoted to probing operations. The six inquiry classes, on the other hand, had an average p/i ratio of .55. These classes emphasized all three components of reflective thought—recognizing a problem, generating hypotheses, and probing hypotheses by testing their defensibility.

Having classified the discussions into three main groups, we are now ready to inquire into specific aspects of the interaction in expository, opining, and inquiry classes. Do teachers in inquiry and opining classes use more indirect influence than teachers in expository discussions? How much impact do teacher questions have on the nature of the discussion? In which classes do students participate most frequently?

Student Participation

Go into a classroom and what do you usually hear? According to Flanders, "If someone is talking, the chances are that it will be the teacher more than 70 percent of the time." [1] Of course, this figure varies from class to class, but it does help one evaluate the amount of student participation that took place in the classes in this study.

Overall student participation in classroom discourse may be quantified by stating the amount of time students participated as a percentage of the total time of the discussion. Using this approach, we are then able to compare two different discussions and conclude that students in one discussion spent more or less time talking than students in the other discussion.

Another important aspect of student participation is the amount of sustained student-student interaction. When the noncognitive categories are deleted from the interaction record, student-student interaction in-

[1] Ned A. Flanders, *Teacher Influence, Pupil Attitudes, and Achievement* (Washington, D.C.: U.S. Department of Health, Education, and Welfare, Office of Education, 1965), p. 1.

cludes a sequence of cognitive operations performed by one student or by a series of students without substantial teacher interruption. For example, the coded dialogue in Figure 9:3 consists of five student-student cognitive interactions. The first interaction (S8.1-S8.1) is an exchange between two different students, whereas the second (S8.1-S9.2) consists

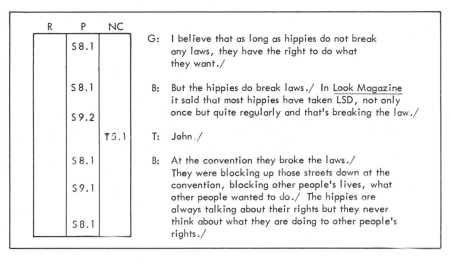

R	P	NC		
	S8.1		G:	I believe that as long as hippies do not break any laws, they have the right to do what they want./
	S8.1		B:	But the hippies do break laws./ In Look Magazine it said that most hippies have taken LSD, not only once but quite regularly and that's breaking the law./
	S9.2			
		T5.1	T:	John./
	S8.1		B:	At the convention they broke the laws./ They were blocking up those streets down at the convention, blocking other people's lives, what other people wanted to do./ The hippies are always talking about their rights but they never think about what they are doing to other people's rights./
	S9.1			
	S8.1			

FIGURE 9:3
Student-Student Cognitive Interactions

of two cognitive operations performed by the same student. The third student-student interaction (S9.2-S8.1) consists of two students talking without substantial teacher interruption. Although the teacher has intervened between the two student operations by calling on a student (T5.1), this is a noncognitive operation and therefore is not defined as substantial teacher interruption. The T5.1 is deleted when the noncognitive categories are edited from the interaction record.

The amount of sustained student-student interaction may be seen graphically by referring to the shaded areas in the matrix in Table 9:6. Area A represents student participation that follows teacher cognitive operations while area B stands for cognitive student-student interactions. Areas A and B are used to form the SS/TS ratio, which measures the amount of sustained student cognitive interaction. The SS/TS ratio is calculated by first deleting the noncognitive categories (T5 and S5) from the interaction record, and then dividing the number of cognitive operations in Area B, student-student interaction, by the number of cognitive operations in Area A, student operations following teacher operations. An SS/TS ratio below 1.0 shows that more than one-half of the student cogni-

CATEGORY		TEACHER									STUDENT									TOTAL
		REQUESTS				PERFORMS					REQUESTS				PERFORMS					
		T1	T2	T3	T4	T6	T7	T8	T9		S1	S2	S3	S4	S6	S7	S8	S9		
TEACHER Performs	T1																			
	T2																			
	T3																			
	T4																			
	T6																			
	T7																			
	T8																			
	T9																			
STUDENT Performs	S1																			
	S2																			
	S3																			
	S4																			
	S6																			
	S7																			
	S8																			
	S9																			
TOTALS																				

TABLE 9:6

Student Participation: Michigan Social Issues Cognitive Category System
Cognitive Operations for 16 Main Cognitive Categories

tive operations followed teacher cognitive operations, whereas an SS/TS ratio above 1.0 shows that more than one-half of the student operations are in response to student comments.

The student participation for the sixteen classes in our study is summarized in Table 9:7.

TABLE 9:7

Student Participation

CLASSES		Student Participation as a Percent of Total Time	SS/TS
Expository	C	07	.06
	E	65	.70
	F	15	.16
	J	48	1.40
	M	16	.50
	AVG	30.2	.56
Opining	A	60	.80
	B	75	3.80
	D	48	1.60
	G	74	3.97
	I	70	3.93
	AVG	65.4	2.82
Inquiry	H	64	1.02
	K	60	2.47
	L	32	.76
	N	61	2.05
	O	28	.44
	P	36	.40
	AVG	46.8	1.19

Looking at the average amount of time students participated, we find that the student participation in the five expository classes was close to the figure quoted by Flanders—the students talked only 30.2 percent of the time. Student participation in these classes, even so, differs tremendously. For example, in class C the teacher completely dominated the discourse. He lectured on Malthus's ideas about the population crisis and only rarely interrupted his lecture to question students on selected points. The teachers in classes F and M dominated the discussion in a similar fashion. These two teachers tended to raise exposition-type questions and then provided their own exposition-type answer. On the other hand, the students in class E participated 65 percent of the time. In this class the students read and summarized passages from the text—not the most challenging intellectual activity, but the students did participate.

Students in the opining and inquiry classes were more deeply involved in the class discussion than those in the expository classes. In the five opining classes the students talked an average of 65.4 percent of the time, and in the inquiry classes students talked almost 47 percent of the time, an even balance between teacher and students that would please most educators. Although the amount of student participation varied from class to class, the variance in the inquiry and opining classes was not so great as that in the expository group. In only one inquiry class, O, did the teacher talk more than 70 percent of the time; in this class the teacher's participation consisted primarily of presenting four case studies to the students for their reaction.

An interesting aspect of the data presented in Table 9:7 is the fact that students in the opining discussions talked more than students in the inquiry classes. Although the difference between these groups is not dramatic, it does provide some food for thought. A number of the opining discussions were characterized by the taping teams as "rambling" or "bull sessions," whereas the inquiry discussions generally evidenced a clear focus. Perhaps it was to discourage rambling and encourage students to probe and test their hypotheses and positions that teachers in the inquiry classes intervened more frequently in the discussion than teachers in the opining classes. The students in the inquiry classes with relatively high student participation, classes H, K, and N, may have spontaneously grounded their positions, whereas the students in the three inquiry classes with relatively low student participation may have depended upon the teacher to get them to probe positions.

There is also some evidence in Table 9:7 that supports the notion that inquiry teachers L, O, and P, intervened more frequently in the discussion than any of the other opining or inquiry teachers. If we look at the SS/TS ratios, we find that in these three inquiry classes the amount of sustained student interaction that was relatively free of teacher intervention was lower than in any of the opining classes.

One of the striking findings in this table is that the average SS/TS ratio for the opining classes is 2.82, the average for the inquiry classes is 1.19, and the average for the expository classes is only .56. Sustained student development of ideas and positions is particularly important when one considers that the topics under discussion were controversial social issues. It is also interesting to note that the classes where the SS/TS ratio was more than 3.00 were also the three opining classes (B, G, and I), which had the highest overall student participation. In the expository classes C, F, and M, where the students participated less than 20 percent of the time, the SS/TS ratio was only .06, .16, and .50 respectively. Very high total student participation thus tends to indicate a considerable amount of sustained student interaction, whereas very low student participation points to low student-student interaction.

When student participation is measured in terms of time or the SS/TS ratio, opining classes B, G, and I, clearly emerge with the highest percentage. In these classes students rather than teachers were the dominant actors and account for over two-thirds of all classroom operations. The question is, though, how did the students spend their time? Were the performed operations inquiry-oriented (for example, did they emphasize categories S7, S8, and S9) or were they simply providing background information (did they emphasize category S6 responses)? A closer examination of these three classes in the distribution of relevant categories suggests some answers to the above questions (Table 9:8). First, it is quite obvious that students with a high level of freedom of participation

TABLE 9:8

Three Opining Classes

	Class D		Class G		Class I	
Cat.	Time	Frequency	Time	Frequency	Time	Frequency
S6	3.7%	2.0%	21.6%	11.1%	8.6%	2.4%
S7	1.4	1.5	0.9	0.4	3.7	2.5
S8	37.6	27.0	29.1	27.3	30.2	26.4
S9	15.8	6.9	12.1	10.3	16.0	11.9

spent little time defending terms and clarifying propositions (S7). The percentage of the distribution given to definition and clarification is negligible. This pattern would certainly disappoint some educational theorists who contend that clarification of meaning is the single most important operation in critical thinking.[2] Educators who believe that hypothesis formation constitutes the heart of the inquiry process will most likely be pleased with the performance of the students in these three opining classes. In class B students spent 37.6 percent of the total classroom time in hypothesis formation and position taking (S8). Students in classes C and I did almost as well in the performance of these operations as students in class B. Class G, however, spent comparatively more time in exposition (S6)—that is, giving background and summarizing statements.[3] It is clear, though, in these three opining classes that students did not spend much time grounding or defending their statements. These classes point to the importance of going beyond the student participation index to the specific nature of the discourse. As we shall see when we examine addi-

[2] Maurice P. Hunt and Lawrence E. Metcalf, *Teaching High School Social Studies: Problems in Reflective Thinking and Social Understanding*, rev. ed. (New York: Harper & Row, 1968). Also, see B. Othanel Smith and Robert Ennis, eds., *Language and Concepts in Education*. (Chicago: Rand McNally & Co., 1964).

[3] The higher incidence of student exposition in this class is explained by the existence of a student panel that provided background information on the topic before the general class discussion began.

tional data, participatory climate constitutes a necessary but not sufficient condition for inquiry.

Teacher Questions

Some educators contend that the nature of a teacher's questions is the key to the type of intellectual climate that will prevail in the classroom. One educator puts the proposition this way: "An excellent way to attack this problem of over-emphasis on memory is for teachers to use one of the taxonomies of questions. . . . Bloom and his associates devised a classification system that defines seven kinds of thinking. A teacher can lead students to practice each of these forms of thought by asking specified kinds of questions in recitation, projects, homework, and examinations."[4] In a similar vein, another educator states: "The types of questions a teacher asks as he leads a student to look at the logical implications of his position holds the key to success."[5] Gallagher and Aschner. in their analysis of classroom interaction, found that the number of divergent questions asked by teachers was directly related to the amount of divergent thinking exhibited in the classroom by students.[6] Two other educators studying the impact of teacher verbal behavior on the thinking of students in the clasroom also found that the type of teacher questions had an enormous influence on the cognitive nature of the class discussion.[7]

The questions a teacher asks in the classroom are of utmost importance because they determine the cognitive processes of students. This assumption is based on the idea that there is a high correspondence between questions raised by teachers and answers given by students. If the teacher asks a question, there must be an answer by a student. Furthermore, it is assumed that there is also a correspondence in the nature of the question and answer exchange. If the question calls for an interpretation, in other words, the answer will be an interpretation.[8] These are certainly plausible claims but there is very little in previous

[4] Norris Sanders, "Changing Strategies of Instruction: Three Case Examples," in *Social Studies Curriculum Development*, ed. D. M. Fraser, 39th Yearbook of the National Council for the Social Studies (Washington, D.C.: The National Council for the Social Studies, 1969), pp. 151-152.

[5] Edwin Fenton, *The New Social Studies*, (New York: Holt, Rinehart and Winston, 1967), p. 44.

[6] James J. Gallagher and Mary Jane Aschner, "A Preliminary Report on Analyses of Classroom Interaction," *Merrill-Palmer Quarterly of Behavior and Development*, IX (July 1963), 186.

[7] Hilda Taba and Freeman F. Elzey, "Teaching Strategies and Thought Processes," *Teachers College Record* (March, 1964): 524-534.

[8] Sanders, "Changing Strategies of Instruction," pp. 151-152.

research literature to indicate whether there is indeed any direct correspondence between the type of teacher questions, on the one hand, and student response, on the other.

Table 9:9 provides data on the question-response patterns found in the sixteen classrooms under study. The main concern here is to simply see what happens when the teacher asks a question. In order to determine the relationship between the cognitive operations, the noncognitive categories for both teacher (T5) and student (S5) have been deleted from the interaction record. The vertical axis represents the types of questions asked, beginning with T1, which asks for exposition, and ending with T4, which asks for grounding. On the horizontal axis, the responses of both teachers and students are given in two sets of figures. The first number in each cell represents the actual number of tallies in that category, whereas the number in the parentheses ( ) is the percent of the responses to the question in that category.

Let us look at the performance of teacher B as an illustration. This teacher asked only two questions dealing with exposition (the T1 row). Both questions were answered in an expository mode, one by the teacher himself (T6) and one by a student (S6). Teacher B also asked twelve questions dealing with clarification and definition (T2). These questions seem to have elicited corresponding types of answers from the students: six, or 50 percent of the total response, was of the S7 variety, definition and clarification. With T3 questions (asking for hypotheses and positions), teacher B elicited 74 percent of the total in the corresponding student performance category (S8). With T4 questions (asking for grounding), he evoked 63 percent of the total in the corresponding student response category (S9). Obviously, the degree of correspondence between teacher questions and student responses varied from class to class, but on the average there seemed to be general congruence between teachers' questions and the students' responses.

Let us turn to Table 9:10 to obtain the overall class averages. Of the four general types of questions that the teacher asked, T1, or request for exposition, elicited the highest student response of the same intellectual mode. That is, 78.2 percent of what follows a teacher request for exposition (T1) is a student background or summarizing statement (S6). Request for grounding (T4) and hypothesis (T3) are followed by relatively high performance in the corresponding student categories, with 77.3 percent and 68.7 percent respectively of the total for each question. The figures in Tables 9:9 and 9:10 suggest that not only is there a high level of accommodative interaction between teacher and student, but that the interaction exhibits a relatively high degree of community because most of the questions and answers occur within the same cognitive category. Indeed, our data show that there is validity to the proposition that

NUMBER (AND %) OF RESPONSES IN EACH CATEGORY

Class	Question	T1	T2	T3	T4	T6	T7	T8	T9	S1	S2	S3	S4	S6	S7	S8	S9	Total
A	T1	5 (13)	–	1 (3)	–	3 (8)	–	–	–	–	–	–	–	29 (74)	–	1 (3)	–	39 (100)
	T2	1 (7)	1 (7)	2 (13)	–	–	–	–	–	1 (7)	–	–	–	2 (13)	5 (33)	2 (13)	1 (7)	15 (100)
	T3	4 (8)	–	4 (8)	–	2 (4)	–	–	–	–	1 (2)	2 (4)	–	5 (10)	–	30 (61)	1 (2)	49 (100)
	T4	–	–	1 (20)	–	–	–	–	–	–	1 (20)	–	–	–	–	1 (20)	2 (40)	5 (100)
B	T1	–	–	–	–	1 (50)	–	–	–	–	–	–	–	1 (50)	–	–	–	2 (100)
	T2	–	–	5 (42)	–	1 (8)	–	–	–	–	–	–	–	–	6 (50)	–	–	12 (100)
	T3	–	–	3 (8)	2 (5)	–	–	–	–	–	–	–	–	2 (5)	2 (5)	28 (74)	1 (3)	38 (100)
	T4	–	–	1 (13)	–	–	–	–	–	–	–	–	–	–	–	2 (25)	5 (63)	8 (100)
C	T1	3 (9)	–	2 (6)	–	2 (6)	–	–	–	–	2 (6)	–	–	24 (73)	–	–	–	33 (100)
	T2	–	–	–	–	1 (14)	2 (29)	–	–	–	1 (14)	–	–	–	1 (14)	2 (29)	–	7 (100)
	T3	1 (3)	2 (6)	2 (6)	–	4 (11)	–	2 (6)	–	–	1 (3)	–	–	–	–	24 (67)	–	36 (100)
	T4	1 (25)	–	–	–	–	–	–	–	–	–	–	–	–	–	–	3 (75)	4 (100)
D	T1	–	–	1 (33)	–	–	–	–	–	–	–	–	–	2 (67)	–	–	–	3 (100)
	T2	–	1 (10)	1 (10)	–	–	1 (10)	–	–	–	–	–	–	1 (10)	2 (20)	3 (30)	1 (10)	10 (100)
	T3	–	–	1 (2)	–	4 (9)	–	1 (2)	–	–	–	–	–	–	–	36 (84)	1 (2)	43 (100)
	T4	–	–	–	–	–	–	–	–	–	–	–	–	–	–	–	4 (100)	4 (100)

TABLE 9:9

Question-Response Pattern for 16 Classes

		1	2	3	4	5	6	7	8	9	10	11	12	13	14	15	16	Total
E	T1	—	—	—	—	—	—	—	—	—	—	—	—	10 (90)	1 (9)	—	—	11 (100)
	T2	—	—	—	—	—	—	—	1 (25)	—	—	—	—	—	3 (75)	—	—	4 (100)
	T3	—	1 (25)	—	—	—	—	—	—	—	—	—	—	—	—	3 (75)	—	4 (100)
	T4	—	—	—	—	—	—	—	—	—	—	—	—	—	—	—	—	—
F	T1	8 (13)	2 (3)	1 (2)	—	8 (13)	—	—	—	3 (5)	—	—	—	38 (63)	—	—	—	60 (100)
	T2	1 (17)	—	—	—	—	—	—	—	1 (17)	—	—	—	—	4 (66)	—	—	6 (100)
	T3	1 (33)	—	—	—	—	—	—	—	—	—	—	1 (33)	—	—	1 (33)	—	3 (100)
	T4	—	—	—	—	—	—	—	—	—	—	—	—	—	—	—	—	—
G	T1	—	—	—	—	—	—	—	—	—	—	—	—	6 (100)	—	—	—	6 (100)
	T2	—	—	—	—	—	—	—	1 (4)	—	1 (4)	—	—	—	—	—	—	—
	T3	1 (4)	—	3 (13)	—	—	—	—	—	—	—	—	—	2 (8)	—	16 (64)	2 (8)	25 (100)
	T4	—	—	—	—	—	—	—	—	—	—	—	—	—	—	—	—	—
H	T1	1 (13)	—	—	—	—	—	—	—	—	—	—	—	6 (75)	—	—	1 (13)	8 (100)
	T2	—	3 (25)	1 (2)	—	1 (2)	1 (8)	1 (2)	1 (2)	1 (2)	1 (2)	—	—	1 (8)	6 (50)	1 (8)	—	12 (100)
	T3	—	—	1 (8)	—	—	—	—	—	—	—	1 (2)	—	—	1 (2)	34 (79)	2 (5)	43 (100)
	T4	—	—	—	2 (17)	—	—	—	—	—	—	—	1 (8)	—	—	2 (17)	6 (50)	12 (100)

TABLE 9:9 Continued

																		Total
I	T1	—	—	—	—	—	—	—	—	—	—	—	—	1 (50)	—	1 (50)	—	2 (100)
	T2	—	—	—	—	—	—	—	—	—	—	—	—	1 (13)	4 (50)	2 (25)	1 (13)	8 (100)
	T3	—	1 (4)	—	—	—	—	1 (4)	—	—	2 (8)	1 (4)	—	—	1 (4)	18 (72)	1 (4)	25 (100)
	T4	—	—	—	—	—	—	—	—	—	—	—	—	—	—	—	1 (100)	1 (100)
J	T1	—	—	—	—	—	—	—	—	—	—	—	—	13 (93)	1 (7)	—	—	14 (100)
	T2	—	—	—	—	—	—	—	—	—	—	—	—	—	—	—	—	—
	T3	—	—	—	—	—	—	—	—	—	—	—	—	1 (8)	—	12 (92)	—	13 (100)
	T4	—	—	—	—	—	—	—	—	—	—	—	—	—	—	—	3 (100)	3 (100)
K	T1	—	—	—	—	—	—	—	—	—	—	—	—	1 (100)	—	—	—	1 (100)
	T2	—	—	1 (20)	—	1 (20)	—	—	—	—	—	—	—	1 (20)	1 (20)	1 (20)	—	5 (100)
	T3	1 (3)	—	2 (6)	—	1 (3)	—	3 (8)	—	—	1 (3)	—	—	—	1 (3)	25 (69)	2 (6)	36 (100)
	T4	—	—	1 (25)	—	—	—	—	—	—	—	—	—	—	—	—	3 (75)	4 (100)
L	T1	—	—	—	—	—	—	—	—	—	—	—	—	1 (100)	—	—	—	1 (100)
	T2	—	—	4 (25)	—	1 (6)	—	—	—	—	1 (6)	—	—	—	4 (25)	4 (25)	2 (13)	16 (100)
	T3	—	3 (7)	2 (5)	—	—	—	1 (2)	—	—	2 (5)	—	—	—	—	34 (81)	—	42 (100)
	T4	—	—	—	—	—	—	—	—	—	—	—	—	—	—	1 (17)	5 (83)	6 (100)

TABLE 9:9 Continued

M	T1	—	—	—	—	—	—	—	—	—	—	—	—	—	—	—	—	—
	T2	—	—	—	—	—	—	1 (50)	—	—	—	—	—	—	1 (50)	—	—	2 (100)
	T3	—	—	2 (12)	—	1 (6)	—	—	—	1 (6)	—	1 (6)	—	—	—	12 (71)	—	17 (100)
	T4	—	—	1 (25)	1 (25)	—	—	—	—	—	—	—	—	—	—	—	2 (50)	4 (100)
N	T1	—	—	—	—	—	—	—	—	—	—	—	—	1 (100)	—	—	—	1 (100)
	T2	1 (7)	3 (21)	—	—	—	—	—	—	—	—	—	—	—	8 (57)	2 (14)	—	14 (100)
	T3	—	2 (6)	4 (12)	—	3 (9)	2 (6)	—	—	—	1 (3)	—	—	3 (9)	—	16 (48)	2 (6)	33 (100)
	T4	—	—	—	—	—	—	—	—	—	—	—	—	—	—	—	—	—
O	T1	2 (13)	—	—	—	3 (20)	—	—	—	1 (7)	—	—	—	8 (53)	—	1 (7)	—	15 (100)
	T2	—	—	—	—	—	—	—	—	—	—	—	—	—	2 (100)	—	—	2 (100)
	T3	—	—	3 (9)	—	2 (6)	—	1 (3)	1 (3)	—	1 (3)	—	—	—	—	22 (67)	2 (6)	33 (100)
	T4	—	—	—	—	—	—	—	—	—	—	—	—	—	—	—	3 (100)	3 (100)
P	T1	—	—	3 (7)	—	—	—	—	—	—	3 (7)	—	—	38 (84)	—	—	—	45 (100)
	T2	—	3 (18)	1 (6)	—	—	—	—	—	—	—	—	—	—	11 (65)	2 (12)	—	17 (100)
	T3	4 (8)	1 (2)	6 (11)	1 (2)	1 (2)	—	—	—	—	—	—	—	4 (8)	—	33 (62)	3 (6)	53 (100)
	T4	—	—	—	—	—	—	—	—	—	—	—	—	—	—	1 (8)	11 (92)	12 (100)

TABLE 9:9 Continued

| | AVERAGE PERCENT OF RESPONSES IN EACH CATEGORY | | | | | | | | | | | | | | | | |
Question	T1	T2	T3	T4	T6	T7	T8	T9	S1	S2	S3	S4	S6	S7	S8	S9	Total
T1	4.2	0.2	3.4	—	6.5	—	—	—	0.8	0.9	—	—	78.2	1.1	4.0	0.9	100
T2	2.2	5.8	8.3	—	3.4	3.4	3.6	—	2.2	3.2	—	—	4.6	48.2	12.6	3.1	100
T3	3.8	3.1	5.9	0.4	3.3	0.4	1.7	0.2	0.5	2.1	1.0	2.1	3.0	0.9	68.7	3.1	100
T4	2.1	—	7.6	3.5	—	—	—	—	—	1.7	—	0.7	—	—	7.3	77.3	100

TABLE 9:10
Average Class Question-Response Pattern for 16 Classes

certain types of questions raised by the teacher will elicit corresponding kinds of responses from the students. For example, if the question calls for hypothesis, exposition, or grounding, chances are that a corresponding answer in the respective category will be forthcoming.

With regard to questions calling for definition or clarification (T2), however, the response pattern in the respective categories is relatively low. That is, on the average only 48.2 percent of the responses to T2 questions are in the corresponding student category (S7). Of the other responses to question T2, 12.6 percent are in the form of student hypotheses (S8) and 8.3 percent consist of a teacher request for a hypothesis (T3). It is difficult to explain the relatively low response pattern to T2 questions. Perhaps the manner of questioning is ambiguous to the students and they are not sure how to respond to the question. Also, 26.7 percent of the response is preempted by the teacher who either raises new questions (16.3 percent) or responds to his own questions (10.4 percent). Perhaps, since the overall occurrence of operations that we call definition and clarification is so low (1.3 percent for the teacher and 1.6 percent of the total for the students), we are constrained in producing meaningful analyses and interpretations.

In general, then, we find that the correspondence between teacher question and student response is quite high. These findings confirm the belief mentioned earlier that the question pattern is extremely important because it greatly influences the chain of verbal interactions in the classroom. Questions raised by the teacher will normally bring about cognitively related responses by the students. Therefore, if the questions deal with a topic in a *significant* manner, the responses are apt to be *significant*.

If teachers' questions do have a major impact on the character of classroom discourse, then one would expect teachers in the inquiry and opining classes in this study to ask significantly more higher level inquiry questions than teachers in the expository classes. Teacher requests for inquiry include teacher questions that call for definition, clarification, hypotheses, or grounding. The total number of operations in the categories T2, T3, and T4 over the total number of teacher operations represents the percentage of teacher operations devoted to inquiry questions.

The proportion of inquiry questions asked by each of the sixteen teachers is summarized in Table 9:11. A striking characteristic of the data in this table is that every teacher in the inquiry and opining classes asked more inquiry questions than any one of the expository teachers. Not a single expository teacher devoted more than 17 percent of his influence to inquiry questions, whereas no opining or inquiry teacher apportioned less than 23 percent of his operations to inquiry questions. In the expository classes the percent of inquiry requests ranged from 5 to 17; in the opining classes the percent ranged from 24 to 31; in the

TABLE 9:11

Teacher Inquiry Questions

EXPOSITORY CLASSES		OPINING CLASSES		INQUIRY CLASSES	
Class	Inquiry Questions	Class	Inquiry Questions	Class	Inquiry Questions
C	17%	A	27%	H	33%
E	7	B	31	K	32
F	5	D	26	L	30
J	12	G	28	N	29
M	13	I	24	O	23
				P	30
Mean = 10.8%		Mean = 27.2%		Mean = 29.5%	
		Mean = 28.5%			

inquiry classes the range spread from 23 to 33. The average for the inquiry and opining classes is almost triple the average for the expository classes.

It can be safely concluded from the data that teacher inquiry questions are instrumental in promoting and sustaining opining and inquiry discourse. The teacher sets the stage by the type of question she asks, and the students perform accordingly. A teacher who desires to promote student inquiry into social issues would do well to evaluate the questions she poses during class discussions.

Teacher Influence: Direct and Indirect

Besides asking questions, teachers also affect the discourse through other actions. If they choose, they can easily dominate the interaction by lecturing for an entire period or through frequent interjection of their own hypotheses, positions, or supporting evidence into the discussion. Other influence techniques include giving directions, reinforcing the comments of students, or providing criticism of student actions. In his studies of classroom interactions, Flanders classified various teacher actions in the classroom as having either a direct or an indirect influence on the course of the classroom interaction. Teacher behaviors that he identifies as "direct" include lecturing, giving directions, and criticizing students; he terms "indirect" those behaviors that include asking questions, reinforcing students, and using student ideas. Flanders argues (and his findings substantiate his position) that teacher behaviors classified under indirect influence tend to promote student participation and give students the opportunity to become more influential whereas the behaviors subsumed under direct influence are ones that "tend to increase teacher participation and to establish restraints on student behavior." [9]

In the current study we have followed Flanders' example of classifying teacher behaviors as direct or indirect and calculating an I/D ratio of indirect/direct influence on the part of the teacher. Although our teacher categories are not the same as those used by Flanders, they can easily be divided into direct and indirect groups parallel to his. The division of the teacher categories in the Michigan Social Issues Cognitive Category System into direct and indirect teacher influence is shown in Figure 9:4. The I/D ratio consists of dividing the time spent in the

Class	I/E Ratio	Class	I/E Ratio
A	2.47	I	3.63
B	6.08	J	.73
C	.14	K	8.03
D	2.95	L	5.14
E	.16	M	.50
F	.12	N	5.63
G	1.89	O	1.74
H	2.25	P	1.69
	Average 2.70		

FIGURE 9:4
Teacher Influence

indirect influence categories by the time spent in the direct influence categories. A high I/D ratio indicates that the teacher concentrated on asking questions and using student ideas, and a low I/D ratio indicates that a teacher concentrated on lecturing, giving directions, and stating her own opinions and ideas.

The I/D ratios of the sixteen teachers in our study are summarized in Table 9:12. Teachers with I/D ratios above 1.0 use more indirect than direct influence; teachers with I/D ratios below 1.0 employ more direct than indirect influence. It can be seen from this table that in inquiry and opining discussion, teachers do use more indirect influence than teachers in expository discussion. The average I/D ratios for the opining teachers, 1.13, and inquiry teachers, 1.09, is almost twice as great

[9] Flanders, *Teacher Influence*, pp. 20-21.

TABLE 9:12

Influence Styles of Teachers

EXPOSITORY CLASSES		OPINING CLASSES		INQUIRY CLASSES	
Class	Teacher I/D Ratio	Class	Teacher I/D Ratio	Class	Teacher I/D Ratio
C	.39	A	1.40	H	1.33
E	.24	B	.98	K	.63
F	1.11	D	.49	L	.74
J	.76	G	2.11	N	1.05
M	.32	I	.68	O	.46
				P	2.33
Mean = .56		Mean = 1.13		Mean = 1.09	

as the average I/D ratios for the expository teachers, .56. Apparently in most expository discussions, the teacher provides a majority of the exposition and primarily asks questions when she would like students to recall and summarize what has been previously said or fill in information that she, as the teacher, wishes to develop in class. On the other hand, opining and inquiry sequences depend more heavily on indirect teacher influence. The teacher promotes student inquiry by asking questions that encourage students to present, probe and test ideas. Although it is possible for the teacher to use direct influence in opining and inquiry discussion (for example, she could be an active participant in the inquiry process by stating and defending her own ideas and opinions), in most instances one would not expect direct influence to be the dominant teacher style in opining and inquiry discussions.

In examining the I/D ratios for the individual classes in the table, though, it is also apparent that the teachers' I/D ratio in the expository classes ranges from .24 to 1.11 while in the opining classes it fluctuates from .49 to 2.11 and in the inquiry classes from .46 to 2.33. That this large variance within each of the discussion groups is clearly evident should temper our idea that indirect influence automatically leads to opining or inquiry class discussions. How can this large variance in teacher I/D ratios be explained? Why are the I/D ratios for the teachers in expository classes F and J comparatively high and the I/D ratios for the teachers in the opining class D, and the inquiry class O, comparatively low? In examining the discussions in classes F and J, we find that these two teachers consistently chose *not* to provide background information themselves, but instead chose to ask questions that required the students to recall or summarize information they had previously read. In class F the teacher presented ten situations regarding actions of state governments and then asked the students to tell what a state could or could not do. The following excerpt is typical of much of the discussion that took place in this class.

Codes	Dialogue
T1	T: Michigan has decided to levy a tax on all vegetables going out of the state by truck.
T5.1	Is that legal or illegal?/Janet./
S6.1	S: Illegal. The book says it is illegal./
T1	T: Why is it illegal?
S6.1	S: Because the Constitution gives the federal government the power to regulate interstate commerce.

Class J discussed the history of immigration and immigration quotas in the United States and the teacher depended heavily on student recitation. For example,

Codes	Dialogue
T6.2	T: Now a couple of days ago we said that basically there were three reasons why immigrants came to this country. We said three main reasons./
T1	What might those reasons be?/
T5.1	Carol?/
S6.1	S: Freedom of religion./
T.52	T: Freedom of religion./ What else?/
T1	
S6.1	S: Political and economic freedom.
T5.1	T: Let's go through our book and see if we
T1	can't find some examples./1607. What about
T5.1	that one./Gary?/
S6.1	S: "Founding of Virginia by English colonists to fetch treasures, to enjoy religious freedom, and a happy government."

Turning to the opining and inquiry classes with relatively low I/D ratios, we find that the opining teacher in class D read case studies to the class. In this class, the teacher first read four actual situations where two individuals were planning to get married, and then asked the students whether they thought the marriage would work. The case studies were very extensive and a great portion of the teacher's participation consisted of reading them. Inasmuch as reading is considered direct influence, teacher D had a low I/D ratio. Inquiry class O is interesting. In this discussion the teacher did two things: he frequently gave his own opinions and ideas *and* he spent more time than any other teacher in the study recapping the status of the discussion. Because both these operations are categorized as direct influence, he also had a low I/D ratio.

It does not appear from the data, therefore, that one can conclude with any great assurance that indirect teacher influence leads consistently to inquiry or opining discussions. Although teachers in the opining and inquiry classes tended to use somewhat more indirect influence than teachers in expository classes, their styles of influence varied tremendously. Also, a teacher may ask many questions, but if the questions call for student exposition, then the discussion is likely to be expository no matter how much indirect influence the teacher uses.

It was stated at the beginning of this section that Flanders had found that the greater a teacher's indirect influence the greater the student participation in a class discussion. Does this generalization hold for the social issues classes in our study?

Table 9:13 provides some insight into the relationship between

TABLE 9:13

Student Participation Under Indirect and Direct Teaching

INDIRECT TEACHERS				
Class	Discussion Style	I/D Ratio	Student Participation (Time)	SS/TS Ratio
A	Opining	1.40	60%	.80
F	Expository	1.11	15	.16
G	Opining	2.11	74	3.95
H	Inquiry	1.33	64	1.02
N	Inquiry	1.05	61	2.05
P	Inquiry	2.33	36	.40
AVERAGE		1.56	52%	1.40

DIRECT TEACHERS				
Class	Discussion Style	I/D Ratio	Student Participation (Time)	SS/TS Ratio
B	Opining	.98	75%	3.03
C	Expository	.39	07	.06
D	Opining	.49	48	1.06
E	Expository	.24	65	.70
I	Opining	.68	70	3.95
J	Expository	.76	48	1.40
K	Inquiry	.63	60	2.47
L	Inquiry	.74	32	.76
M	Expository	.32	16	.50
O	Inquiry	.46	28	.44
AVERAGE		.57	45%	1.44

student participation and the influence styles of the sixteen teachers. Although the average student participation in the indirect teacher's class is higher than the average in the direct teacher's classes—52 percent versus 45 percent—it will be observed that student participation in the classes of these six indirect teachers is not uniformly high. Not only do the students of two of the indirect teachers, F and P, participate only 15 and 36 percent of the time in the class discussion, but the students of four of the ten direct teachers, B, E, I, K, participate more than 60 percent of the time. Why doesn't the generalization stated by Flanders that indirect influence tends to increase teacher participation hold for six of the sixteen teachers in our study? The explanation may be found by looking at the SS/TS ratio. The two *indirect influence* teachers, F and P, who have relatively little total student participation in their classes, also have very low SS/TS ratios, .16 and .40 respectively. Although these two teachers are indirect in that they ask many questions and reinforce students, they do not allow sustained student development of ideas. Evidently what is occurring in these two classes is that after a student responds to a teacher question, the teacher does not wait for a second student to comment but again takes control and asks another question. On the other hand, the three indirect teachers (G, H, N) who have the highest total student participation in their classes also have SS/TS ratios above 1.0. These teachers allow considerable student-student interaction before they, again, step in to influence the discussion by asking another question. As for the *direct influence* teachers, we can also see from the table the importance of sustained student interaction in increasing student participation. The classes of three of the direct influence teachers with relatively high total student participation (B, I, K) also have very high SS/TS ratios (above 2.0). Although these three direct influence teachers tend to participate in the discussion by offering their own observations and comments instead of primarily asking questions, they do demonstrate the capacity to withhold their intervention and allow considerable student-student dialogue.

Classes A and K present an interesting contrast and show the cumulative effect of indirect influence on the part of the teacher and high student-student interaction on student participation. The teacher in class A uses indirect influence but allows relatively little student-student interaction (SS/TS ratio of .80); the teacher in class K uses direct influence but allows relatively high student-student interaction (SS/TS ratio of 2.47). The end result is that in both classes students participate 60 percent of the time. Thus, it is apparent from our data that not only is indirect influence on the part of the teacher an important factor in increasing student participation, but the willingness of the teacher *not to influence* the dialogue—either directly or indirectly—by letting the students interact with one another for sustained periods is also crucial in promoting student participation.

Taking That Crucial Step Toward Inquiry

For a class discussion to be truly inquiry in nature, the participants must clarify and defend their positions and hypotheses by grounding. In what ways do students and teachers defend their positions? Table 9:14, which combines teacher and student operations, shows that, overall, the most popular type of grounding is by taking a position (9.6). Almost one-half (44.7 percent) of the total class grounding operations are of this kind. The next most popular grounding operation, with 39.3 percent of the total distribution is 9.1, grounding by citing general knowledge. At this point there is quite a drop in the distribution of frequencies—from the 39.3 percent for category 9.1 to the 4.8 percent for category 9.5, grounding by pointing to the logical consequences of a position. The experience of others (9.4), personal experience (9.3), and appeal to authority (9.2) do not seem to be popular grounding operations.

How do our distributions compare with the proposals for logical discourse advanced by educational theorists? The most often used category, grounding by citing other positions (9.5), is one that most theorists would not promote because it involves some circularity—one defends a position by pointing to another position, which, in itself, may or may not be defensible. It is the general knowledge (9.1) category that is accepted by most theorists as the one that has a place in the inquiry classroom. Most educational theorists would be pleased with the relatively low performance of the classes in category 9.7—no public grounds. It appears that most students and their teachers have accepted the value of providing reasons for their claims to knowledge or positions on social affairs. No public grounds reduces the position or hypothesis to a matter of taste, which by definition is not subject to any kind of validation or negotiation. It is quite revealing to see that very few classes, indeed, engage in this type of operation. In view of our preliminary finding, educational theorists may want to stress the advantages of certain kinds of grounding in logical communication. For example, category 9.5 grounding by tracing logical consequences, is one that could apply well to confirming the validity of positions on issues. "If we provide federal legislation for open housing we will probably reduce the pattern of racial segregation existing in all of our cities" is an example of a statement that provides its justification by tracing one of the possible consequences of the proposed action. The consequences can be false or illogical, but these can be

TABLE 9.14
Distribution of Grounding

TEACHER AND STUDENT GROUNDING CATEGORIES

Class	T91 + S91		T92 + S92		T93 + S93		T94 + S94		T95 + S95		T96 + S96		T97 + S97		Total	
	Number	%	Number	%	Number	%	Number	%	Number	%	Number	%	Number	%	Number	%
A	7	29	–	0	1	4	–	0	1	4	14	58	1	4	24	100
B	12	28	1	2	11	25	1	2	1	2	15	35	2	5	43	100
C	2	40	–	0	–	0	–	0	1	20	2	40	–	0	5	100
D	1	3	1	3	3	9	3	9	2	6	23	70	–	0	33	100
E	2	100	–	0	–	0	–	0	–	0	–	0	–	0	2	100
F*	–	–	–	–	–	–	–	–	–	–	–	–	–	–	–	–
G	7	23	2	7	–	0	1	3	3	10	17	57	–	0	30	100
H	25	51	–	0	1	2	–	0	5	10	16	33	2	4	49	100
I	23	40	6	11	2	3	1	2	2	3	21	37	2	3	57	100
J	8	35	3	13	–	0	–	0	–	0	12	52	–	0	23	100
K	24	36	3	4	3	4	1	2	–	0	36	54	–	0	67	100
L	7	22	–	0	–	0	–	0	1	3	24	75	–	0	32	100
M	9	56	1	6	–	0	–	0	–	0	6	38	–	0	16	100
N	12	33	–	0	1	3	–	0	1	3	22	61	–	0	36	100
O	13	48	1	4	1	4	3	11	3	11	6	22	–	0	27	100
P	11	46	–	0	1	4	2	8	–	0	9	38	1	4	24	100
AVG		39.3		3.3		3.9		2.5		4.8		44.7		1.3		100

* In class F, there were no instances of student or teacher grounding operations. Since it is the distribution of grounding operations that is being presented in this table, class F has been eliminated from the calculations of percentages.

pointed out in the discussion. Other consequences, some of them possibly undersirable, may also be pointed out.[10]

What happens after a student presents a hypothesis or states a position? We expected to find in our study that the answer to this question would differ in opining and inquiry classes.[11] We know, by definition, that participants in inquiry classes spend significantly more time than the teacher and students in opining classes giving reasons for their positions and clarifying and defining concepts and terms. But exactly when and how does this probing occur? It was felt that by looking at the cognitive interaction following a student hypothesis we could begin to answer this question.

Tables 9:15 and 9:16 offer information concerning the cognitive operations that occur after a student presents a hypothesis or position, S.8. The classes are listed at the left of the table and the total number of student hypotheses in each class is indicated in the far right column. The operations immediately following the hypotheses are given in two sets of figures. The first number in each cell represents the number of times a student hypothesis was followed by the operation in that category; the number in parentheses is the percent of all cognitive operations following hypotheses that were in that particular category. The average distribution of responses for all the classes is at the bottom of the tables.

If we look at the average distribution for the opining classes in Table 9:15, we find that the cognitive operation that most frequently followed a student hypothesis was another student hypothesis (S.8), an operation that accounts for 32 percent of the distribution. This figure indicates that the same student is stating an uninterrupted series of hypotheses or another student is reacting to the first student by presenting his own hypothesis. In 18 percent of the operations the teacher and students asked for additional hypotheses (T3 and S3), whereas 4 percent of the time the teacher stated a hypothesis himself (T8). Thus, in more than half the cases, teachers and students in opining classes reacted to a student hypothesis by giving or requesting additional hypotheses. Neither teachers nor students in these opining classes have yet internalized a concept in inquiry—namely, public defensibility of claims to knowledge or value judgments. Perhaps what we are observing here is a recurrence of a pattern detected in an earlier section, that students prefer to ground ideas by referring to other ideas. We attribute to this pattern of discourse

---

[10] For an elaboration on grounding positions on social issues by tracing logical consequences, see Byron G. Massialas and C. Benjamin Cox, *Inquiry in Social Studies* (New York: McGraw-Hill Book Co., 1966). pp. 160-174.

[11] The expository classes are not included in this discussion; in four of these classes so few hypotheses were generated that any analyis would be meaningless.

TABLE 9:15

Opining Classes: Cognitive Interaction Following Student Hypotheses *

CLASS	NUMBER (AND %) OF RESPONSES IN EACH CATEGORY																TOTAL Student Hypotheses
	T1	T2	T3	T4	T6	T7	T8	T9	S1	S2	S3	S4	S6	S7	S8	S9	
A	4 (5)	7 (9)	17 (21)	3 (4)	1 (1)	—	5 (6)	—	—	2 (3)	—	—	6 (7)	1 (1)	22 (27)	13 (16)	81 (100)
B	1 (1)	6 (4)	15 (9)	5 (3)	4 (2)	2 (1)	5 (3)	—	—	2 (1)	7 (4)	—	4 (2)	—	84 (51)	30 (18)	165 (100)
D	2 (2)	5 (5)	20 (22)	3 (3)	8 (9)	—	8 (9)	—	—	—	—	—	1 (1)	1 (1)	21 (23)	23 (25)	92 (100)
G	1 (1)	—	11 (15)	—	3 (4)	—	—	—	—	2 (3)	6 (8)	—	6 (8)	—	22 (30)	23 (31)	74 (100)
I	1 (1)	4 (4)	7 (6)	1 (1)	8 (7)	1 (1)	4 (4)	1 (1)	—	2 (2)	10 (9)	5 (4)	1 (1)	3 (3)	32 (28)	33 (29)	113 (100)
Avg. Percent	(2)	(4)	(14)	(2)	(5)	(1)	(4)	(0)	(0)	(2)	(4)	(1)	(4)	(1)	(32)	(24)	(100)

* Taken from a 16-by-16 cognitive category matrix.

TABLE 9:16

Inquiry Classes: Cognitive Interaction Following Student Hypotheses *

CLASS	NUMBER (AND %) OF RESPONSES IN EACH CATEGORY																TOTAL Student Hypotheses
	T1	T2	T3	T4	T6	T7	T8	T9	S1	S2	S3	S4	S6	S7	S8	S9	
H	1 (1)	3 (4)	14 (17)	4 (5)	4 (5)	—	3 (4)	—	2 (2)	—	2 (2)	—	—	—	18 (22)	31 (38)	82 (100)
K	—	1 (1)	11 (14)	1 (1)	2 (3)	—	—	—	—	—	—	—	—	—	13 (16)	51 (65)	79 (100)
L	1 (1)	9 (13)	14 (21)	6 (9)	3 (5)	—	3 (5)	—	—	—	—	—	3 (5)	—	7 (10)	21 (31)	67 (100)
N	—	1 (2)	11 (19)	—	3 (5)	—	1 (2)	—	—	—	—	—	1 (2)	—	8 (14)	32 (56)	57 (100)
O	—	1 (3)	9 (26)	2 (6)	4 (11)	5 (14)	2 (6)	1 (3)	—	—	—	—	—	—	—	11 (31)	35 (100)
P	10 (21)	4 (8)	11 (23)	8 (17)	1 (2)	1 (2)	2 (4)	—	—	2 (4)	—	—	—	—	5 (10)	4 (8)	48 (100)
Avg. Percent	(4)	(5)	(20)	(6)	(5)	(3)	(4)	(1)	(0)	(1)	(0)	(0)	(1)	(0)	(12)	(38)	(100)

* Taken from a 16-by-16 cognitive category matrix.

some circularity that is not desirable in the inquiry process. As we look at Table 9:15, with its average of one-half the operations following a student hypothesis given to hypothesis-type requests or responses, the same kind of circularity we observed when we studied the subcategories within grounding seems to emerge. Although our analysis at this point is not exhaustive, it does suggest that a key to understanding the conduct of inquiry in the classroom is to look into the degree of correspondence between logical discourse and the verbal conduct of the participants.

What about giving or asking for probing operations, such as definition, clarification, and grounding? In the opining classes 24 percent of the entries consisted of spontaneous student grounding (S.9). That is, the students moved naturally from hypothesis to grounding without intervention on the part of the teacher or other students. If the student did not spontaneously defend her position, though, there was only a 3 percent chance that another member of the class would ask for grounding (T4 and S4). Six percent of the hypotheses were followed by teacher or student requests for definition or clarification (T2 and S2), and in 2 percent of the cases the students or teacher clarified or defined positions, concepts, or terms (T7 and S7). Combining all the probing operations (T2, T4, T7, T9, S2, S4, S7, S9), we find that approximately one-third of the student hypotheses were followed by the class participants providing or requesting probing.

The reverse pattern exists in the inquiry classes as shown in Table 9:16. Fifty-four percent of the student hypotheses were followed by individuals giving or asking for probing operations such as definition, clarification and grounding, and in 36 percent of the cases the teacher and students responded to a student hypothesis by offering or requesting additional hypotheses (T3, T8, S3, S8). The cognitive operation that most frequently followed student hypotheses was spontaneous grounding. Evidently, the members of these classes have made considerable progress toward internalizing a central concept in reflective inquiry—that is, defending or clarifying ideas and opinions.

In the previous section it was suggested that those inquiry discussions that evidenced relatively high student participation (classes H, K, and N) would also contain considerable student spontaneous grounding, and that those inquiry classes with relatively low student participation (classes L, O, and P) would be characterized by more frequent teacher requests for probing. Looking again at Table 9:16 we find that, in fact, those classes with relatively high student participation did exhibit higher levels of student spontaneous grounding (38, 65, and 56 percent, respectively) than the other three inquiry classes (31, 31 and 8 percent). In one of these latter classes (P), teacher requests for probing accounted for 17 percent of the operations following student hypotheses. In class P the students evidently depended on teacher questions to evoke further probing of positions.

That grounding, especially student grounding, follows naturally from hypothesis without intervention is, in itself, desirable in the inquiry classroom. However, if grounding occurs spontaneously only one-third of the time and if most of the grounding operations involve circular reasoning, then more teacher intervention would be appropriate. Teacher intervention, of course, would be appropriate only if the teacher asks for grounding and, in doing so, recognizes the logical distinctions among the subcategories of grounding (9.1-9.7) and sees that emphasis on certain of these subcategories will enhance the reflective enterprise in the classroom.

SUMMARY

This chapter seeks to find ways in which data collected through the use of the Michigan Social Issues Cognitive Category System can be presented and interpreted. The findings presented are both methodological and substantive.

From the methodological viewpoint, the use of interaction matrices allows the researcher to look at the operations of the main actors in the classroom—teachers and students—and to analyze them. The interaction matrices provide the investigator with the necessary data to answer important educational questions such as whether it is the teacher or student who usually dominates classroom discussion, which verbal operations elicit inquiry responses from students, the nature and quality of the inquiry response, and to what extent a participatory classroom climate influences inquiry operations. The interaction matrices are based on the Michigan Social Issues Cognitive Category System and thus reflect all the basic assumptions in that system about classroom interaction.

The second important methodological contribution is the use of the interaction matrices to identify rather distinct discussion styles centering on social issues. Discussions are categorized as expository, opining, and inquiry. Expository classes concentrate on sharing information about the social issues in question. Opining classes devote most of their time to giving opinions, hypotheses, and positions on issues but do not devote much time to grounding, clarifying, or testing their ideas. The members of inquiry classes stress both giving and probing their ideas and hypotheses.

Substantively, many interesting patterns of interaction emerged. Since our sample is not statistically representative, our findings here should be considered as tentative, subject to additional empirical testing.

Considerable attention has been paid to an examination of the climate of student participation and its relation to inquiry activity. Many educational theorists have maintained that a high-level participatory classroom milieu will inevitably increase both the intellectual and affective components of the classroom dialogue. Our data from the sixteen classes in our study indicates that the amount of student participation varied greatly and that interpretations regarding the relation between student participation and inquiry are not simple. Although we find that the level of student participation was greater in opining and inquiry classes than in expository classes, the direction and quality of the interaction are not always clear. Inquiry teaching has both cognitive and affective components. The existence of openness in discussion may provide the necessary affective component, but openness and high levels of student participation alone will not suffice to bring about sophisticated logical discourse. As a matter of fact, the evidence in this chapter indicates that teacher intervention may be necessary to get students to define and defend their hypotheses and positions and thus move the discussion from opining to inquiry. This supports ideas discussed in Chapter 2.

Educational leaders have long maintained that the questions teachers raise in the classroom determine to a considerable extent the type of student response. If the questions are of a high cognitive level the answers will also be of the same high level. Our data indicate that there is a definite relationship between teacher questions and student responses. If teachers ask for exposition, the chances are that they will get exposition type answers. The same teacher-student interactive pattern applies to hypothesis and grounding operations. The congruence we find between teacher-student, question-answer patterns is quite clear and suggests that the questions teachers ask may, indeed, affect the classroom discourse and determine to a large extent whether or not a given classroom is inquiry centered. The main factor distinguishing expository discussions from opining and inquiry discussions is the type of questions the teachers ask during the discussions. Opining and inquiry teachers ask students to present hypotheses, define or clarify their terms and ideas, and ground their positions whereas expository teachers tend to ask questions that require the students to recall and summarize information.

Turning to the influence styles of the teachers, we investigated Flanders' concept of direct versus indirect teacher influence. Our findings indicate that the use of an I/D ratio to explain teacher influence may be too simplistic. For example, in his studies, Flanders has found that students in classes of indirect influence teachers tend to participate more than students in classes of direct influence teachers. Overall, our data tend to support this generalization, but we also discovered that the relationship between indirect/direct influence and student participation is not consistent. Flanders' concept of teacher influence focuses only upon the mode of the teacher's verbal intervention (that is, the indirect teacher asks questions whereas the direct teacher provides his own opinions and comments) and ignores the frequency of the teacher's intervention. Our data indicate that an important aspect of indirect teacher influence may be teachers' ability to withhold their intervention and let the students interact with one another. A teacher who asks a question, obtains a response from a single student, then immediately asks another question, and so on, is certainly not as indirect as the teacher who asks a question and steps back and lets students discuss the question among themselves for a sustained period of time.

When the opining and inquiry discussions were contrasted, it was found that they differed considerably in the type of interaction that followed a student hypothesis. In the inquiry discussions, student hypotheses are more frequently followed by members of the class giving or asking for probing operations such as definition, clarification and grounding, whereas in opining classes, student hypotheses are more frequently followed by the teacher or students giving or requesting additional hypotheses.

When the six inquiry classes were examined more closely, it was discovered that in three of the classes the students spontaneously grounded their positions; in the other three classes the students probed and tested their ideas primarily as a result of teacher questions. In the three inquiry classes with relatively high spontaneous grounding, the students had evidently internalized the value of public defensibility of positions, and it was not necessary for the teacher to intervene as frequently in the discussion. Thus, the amount of student participation in these classes was as great as the amount of student participation in the opining classes. In the three inquiry classes with relatively low student spontaneous grounding, the teacher intervened more frequently in the discussion to ask students to probe their ideas and the total student participation was also much lower.

It appears from the findings presented in this chapter that if teachers are interested in promoting the reflective examination of social issues by their students, they should (1) ask questions and use student ideas, rather than lecture, (2) concentrate on questions that encourage students to present and support their ideas, and (3) be very aware of what happens after a student presents a position; if he does not spontaneously defend his ideas or if other students do not challenge him to do so, then the teacher should ask for further clarification, evidence, or grounding. It is to be hoped that, after enough encouragement, the students will begin to probe their own hypotheses naturally and challenge other students to do likewise.

10

student outcomes
of social issues instruction

What are students' attitudes toward social issues instruction? Do students' evaluation of their teacher and class vary depending on the discussion style present in the class? How well do students who are involved in inquiry discussions centering on social issues perform on a test designed to measure their ability to think critically about social issues? The answers to these questions are important to teachers who are interested in social issues instruction.

The research reported in this chapter was part of an intensive examination of the teaching of social issues in Michigan secondary classrooms carried out by the staff of the "Social Issues Project" at the University of Michigan.[1] In this study it was found that social studies teachers are hesitant to deal systematically with social issues in the classroom. In a random sample of 150 secondary social studies teachers surveyed by the Project, only 26 teachers held discussions of social issues on a regular basis.[2] Perhaps one reason that so few of the teachers regu-

[1] Byron G. Massialas, director and principal investigator, with Nancy Freitag Sprague and Jo Ann Cutler Sweeney, associate directors, *Structure and Process of Inquiry Into Social Issues In Secondary Schools*, 3 vols. (project performed pursuant to contract OEC3-7061678-2942 with the United States Department of Health, Education and Welfare, Office of Education, 1970). The research reported in this chapter is included in the volumes authored by Mary A. Shea Sugrue, *A Study of Teacher/Student Attitude-Congruence Patterns and Evaluation of Controversial Social-Issues Classes and Teachers*, vol. 2, and Nancy Freitag Sprague, *Social Issues Classroom Discourse: A Study of Expository, Inquiry-Nonprobing, and Inquiry-Probing Classes*, vol. 3.

[2] Sprague, *Social Issues Classroom Discourse*, 3:54.

larly discussed social issues is that many of them questioned the value
of social issues instruction and students' attitudes toward it.

Both Mary Sugrue and Nancy Sprague, members of the Michigan
Social Issues Project staff studied students' attitudes toward their social
issues classes. Sugrue was concerned with the students' general evaluation of social issues classes, whereas Sprague focused upon the relation
of instructional styles to student attitudes and critical thinking skills. The
teachers and students selected for the Sugrue and Sprague studies were
drawn from the twenty-six teachers in the Social Issues Project who took
up social issues on a regular basis. Seventeen of the teachers, along with
one of their classes, were randomly chosen for the Sugrue study and
Sprague taped the dialogue and examined the interaction in sixteen of
the seventeen classes used by Sugrue.

STUDENT ATTITUDES
TOWARD SOCIAL ISSUES CLASSES

Although a positive attitude on the part of students toward their teacher
and class is not the sole criterion that should be used to judge the value
of a given type of classroom instruction, student attitudes are important.
Research indicates that task achievement is frequently related to positive
feelings toward the group, its norms, its activities, and its leader. Students
tend to learn better when they have positive feelings toward their environment and are actively committed to the group and its task than
when they feel negative or indifferent toward their learning environment.[3] If one assumes that student attitudes are important, what is it
about social issues that might cause teachers to be concerned regarding
the students' reaction to such instruction?

The first possibility suggested by Sugrue is that social issues classes
are concerned with subject matter that is emotionally charged for the
student. Depending on how a class and teacher approach a given social
issue, students' beliefs or values may be threatened. If that occurs, a student who disagrees with others in the class may develop negative attitudes.

Because social issues classes do not deal with traditional subject
matter, Sugrue also suggested that students may react negatively to social
issues classes if the instruction does not fit their concept of what they
should be learning. Students may feel, in other words, that the class lacks
meaning or purpose or that they are "not learning anything." Sugrue attempted to determine under what circumstances, if any, students react

---

[3] Bernard Berelson and Gary Steiner, *Human Behavior* (New York: Harcourt,
Brace, and World, 1964), pp. 181-182.

negatively to social issues classes. The instrument used to assess students' attitudes toward their teacher and class was the Minnesota Student Attitude Inventory. The inventory was developed by Ned Flanders and his associates at Minnesota in 1961.[4] It is a widely used paper-and-pencil instrument specifically designed to measure students' attitudes toward the teacher and the class. The inventory requires the student to respond on a five-point scale to 59 items. The items are statements describing teacher attractiveness, classroom climate, rewards, and punishments. The student is asked to respond to each statement with "strongly agree," "agree," "undecided," "disagree," or "strongly disagree." Estimates of the reliability of this instrument vary from sample to sample, but the median reliability is 0.85. Selected items from the Minnesota Student Attitude Inventory formed the basis of a student attitudinal scale that was used by Sugrue to determine the extent to which students liked their teacher and classes.

The items from the inventory that measure a student's general attitude toward the teacher and class are summarized in Figure 10:1. The attitudes reflected in these statements indicate whether or not the student likes the teacher and class. Many of the positive statements in this appreciation scale picture the teacher as a person who makes it fun to study, who understands students, who is stimulating and helps students get the most out of every hour. A student who strongly agrees that "this teacher is one of the best I ever had" thinks highly of his teacher. Many of the negative statements indicate that the student does not like the teacher or is bored with the class. The students' responses to these items were scored on a scale that ranged from 0 to 48. The higher the score, the more students liked their teacher and class.

If the students on the average had mixed feelings toward their social issues classes, then one would expect the students to group around a mean score of 24 to 25. Sugrue, however, found that mean score of the total samples was 30, indicating that on the whole the students tended to like their teacher and class. Only 15 percent of the students indicated that they did not appreciate their teacher and class.

Sugrue also explored which types of students tended to like the teacher and class and which ones were most negative. She found several student characteristics that were significantly related to an individual student's score on the Appreciation of Teacher and Class Scale.

Three demographic characteristics were important: sex, grade-point average, and parents' profession. The 163 girls in the sample were significantly more positive in their evaluations of the classes than were the

[4] Ned A. Flanders, *Teacher Influence, Pupil Attitudes, and Achievement* (Washington, D.C.: U.S. Department of Health, Education, and Welfare, Office of Education, 1965), pp. 45-46.

Student Statements
I really like this class.
This teacher is one of the best I ever had.
Sometimes just thinking about this class makes me sick.
This is the best teacher I have ever had.
This teacher makes everything seem interesting and important.
I wish I could have this teacher next year.
This teacher makes it fun to study things.
I just don't trust this teacher.
This teacher really understands boys and girls my age.
Most of us get pretty bored in this class.
This teacher helps us get the most out of each hour.
I find it easy to talk to this teacher.

FIGURE 10:1

Appreciation of Teacher and Class Scale

146 boys. Students who had A averages were split; some gave high evaluations of their social issues teachers and some were very negative toward their teachers; few of these students were in the undecided range. The students who identified themselves as B students on the whole tended to like their social issues teachers; C or less students distributed themselves over the entire scale. Students whose parents were engaged in professional or semiprofessional occupations had the least liking for their social issues teachers and classes. Children of skilled-service and skilled-trade levels were more positive in their evaluation, and the students of parents who were laborers were the most positive in their appreciation of social issues classes.

These demographic findings are interesting. According to Sugrue the fact that girls tend to like these classes more than boys is consistent with other literature. Several social scientists have suggested that the norms of the school culture are more in line with girls' socialization patterns than with boys' and therefore girls tend to like school better.[5]

Why should A students split so dramatically in their evaluations?

[5] Dorothy Westby Gibson, *Social Perspectives in Education* (New York: John Wiley & Sons, 1965), pp. 307-308.

Perhaps some A students, particularly those whose parents are professionals, feel that social issues instruction is not meaningful and that they are not learning enough traditional social studies. The group of A students who are positive in their evaluations may be highly interested in current events and intellectually challenged by the discussion of issues. Sugrue points out that "average" students, in terms of both social background and educational success, react positively to their social issues classes. It may be that they are less motivated to learn traditional, factual material and react positively to the issues approach to instruction.

Sugrue found that students who believed strongly in student participation in class discussions and who believed that students had a right to express their opinions in class also liked their social issues classes. These students frequently felt that their teacher was one of the best teachers they ever had. On the other hand, those who gave little credence to student expression and who did not like to participate in class discussions were more negative in their evaluation. Apparently, students who do not like to voice their opinions in class were not as happy with these social issues classes as those who do.

Sugrue concluded that teachers need not be hesitant about including social issues discussion in their instruction. Not only did students return a positive evaluation of social issues teachers in general, but most students believed strongly in student expression. Sugrue also found some evidence that the social issues teacher should make sure that discussions of social issues are integrated into ongoing learning in the class and that students be aware of the purposes of the discussions.

STUDENT ATTITUDES TOWARD EXPOSITORY, OPINING, AND INQUIRY SOCIAL ISSUES INSTRUCTION

We have found that students generally have positive attitudes toward social issues instruction, but what are students' attitudes toward teachers who teach social issues through inquiry? Most advocates of inquiry instruction have stressed the importance of an "open classroom climate" in promoting and sustaining reflective inquiry. Massialas and Cox, for example, state that "the climate of the reflective classroom is psychologically open and permissive. All points of view and statements are solicited and accepted as propositions which merit examination." [6]

As we have noted previously in this book, in the open classroom

[6] Byron G. Massialas and C. Benjamin Cox, *Inquiry in Social Studies* (New York: McGraw-Hill Book Co., 1966), p. 112.
[7] Byron G. Massialas and Jack Zevin, *Creative Encounters in the Classroom* (New York: John Wiley & Sons, 1967), p. 25.

students participate directly in formulating and testing their ideas.[7] All members of the class have an opportunity to offer their opinions and influence the direction of the discussion. The teacher communicates an open climate by encouraging a range of contributions and by using and responding thoughtfully to students' comments.[8] Both questions and divergent comments are accepted and examined. The teacher never responds to a student idea with ridicule or sarcasm. Creative expression is legitimized and the teacher encourages students to "play their hunches and to conjecture." [9] Crabtree points out that an open climate is important for reflective inquiry because it encourages students to deal with problems in their own terms and allows an open search for alternatives:

> Perhaps most critical of the classroom arrangements which support hypothetical thinking are the opportunities the teacher provides for an open search for alternatives. Recognizing and resolving an indeterminate situation, a value-conflict, or an intellectual inquiry requires that students feel free to examine the situation, to take positions regarding it, to engage in a search for hypotheses. . . . Students need to know that an examination of alternatives. . . . is welcome, and that severe sanctions will not follow expression of a minority view, an early misreading of the data, or a commitment made which, on the basis of further evidence, the student may wish to revise.[10]

An open climate of discussion does not mean, of course, that the discussion is undirected. Indeed, Massialas and Cox point out that one of the unique characteristics of a reflective classroom is its sustained focus. This focus distinguishes reflective discussions from undirected discussions in which participants are free to say what they want but where the dialogue is apt to ramble without a clear point of direction.[11] Although in some classes students themselves will maintain the focus of the discussion and extend hypotheses to their logical conclusions, generally, according to Hunt and Metcalf, Crabtree, and Suchman, it is up to the teacher to insure that the discussion exhibits a sense of purpose and direction.

The key, then, to a successful open climate is for the teacher to maintain focus *without* monopolizing the discussion or stifling reflection on the part of students. The teacher achieves this kind of classroom arrangement by asking questions that instigate and push forward components of the reflective process. Massialas and Zevin have offered some

---

[8] Charlotte Crabtree, "Supporting Reflective Thinking" in *Effective Thinking in the Social Studies,* ed. Jean Fair and Fannie R. Shaftel, 37th Yearbook of the National Council for the Social Studies (Washington, D.C.: National Council, 1967), p. 101.

[9] Massialas and Zevin, *Creative Encounters,* p. 26.

[10] Crabtree, "Supporting Reflective Thinking," p. 101.

[11] Massialas and Cox, *Inquiry in Social Studies,* p. 113.

specific suggestions. In their opinion, reflective teachers avoid lecturing. Instead, they ask for hypotheses and then continually challenge and probe students to explore, clarify, and test alternatives. The reflective teacher "summarizes, recapitulates, and asks for clarification of points made by the students. During times of impasse he may raise additional questions regarding the problem at hand. These questions may help the class to see alternative ways of solving a problem." [12] Throughout the classroom discussion, the teacher builds upon students' ideas and reinforces logical operations that advance the steps of reflective thought. Only when students feel free to offer and examine alternatives and only when they perceive that the teacher responds thoughtfully to their comments and ideas will genuine reflection take place.

Because proponents of inquiry instruction stress the importance of an open classroom climate and the existence of mutual respect between the teacher and students in promoting and sustaining reflective inquiry, one would expect students in inquiry classes to have positive attitudes toward their teacher and class. In the last decade Flanders has been a major leader in investigating the relationship between classroom verbal interaction and student attitudinal outcomes. In four separate extensive studies between 1957 and 1962, Flanders found that pupils have positive attitudes toward teachers who encourage them to participate and who make use of and reinforce their ideas and opinions. High teacher I/D ratios were positively related to student attitudinal measures of teacher attractiveness, student motivation, and class climate.[13] Several other studies since 1965 also support Flanders' conclusion that pupils exposed to a teacher who makes use of and reinforces their ideas and opinions have positive attitudes toward their teacher and class. In two separate studies of classroom interaction in Pennsylvania and Michigan, William LaShier [14] and Betty Mae Morrison [15] found significant, positive relationships between a teacher's I/D ratio and positive student attitudes. Joseph Johns, studying six high-school English classes in Detroit, found that teacher behavior that reinforces and uses student ideas is related to positive student attitudes.[16] Roger Pankratz, in a study of ten physics

[12] Massialas and Zevin, *Creative Encounters,* pp. 25-26.

[13] Flanders, *Teacher Influence.* For a discussion of teacher I/D ratios, see the previous chapter.

[14] William S. LaShier, Jr., "An Analysis of Certain Aspects of the Verbal Behavior of Student Teachers of Eighth-grade Students Participating in a BSCS Laboratory Block" (Ph.D. diss., University of Texas, 1965), Ann Arbor: University of Michigan Microfilms, No. 66-1938.

[15] Betty Mae Morrison, "The Reactions of Internal and External Children to Patterns of Teaching Behavior" (Ph.D. diss., University of Michigan, 1966), Ann Arbor: University of Michigan Microfilms, No. 66-14560.

[16] Joseph P. Johns, "The Relationship Between Teacher Behaviors and the Incidence of Thought-provoking Questions by Students in Secondary Schools" (Ph.D. diss., University of Michigan, 1966), Ann Arbor: University of Michigan Microfilms, No. 67-1758.

classes, concluded that teachers who had records of high class averages on pupil-attitude inventories used more indirect influence in the classroom.[17] Paul Lauren, who used an I/D ratio similar to the one developed by Flanders, studied interaction in eight high-school earth science classes and found in his pupil survey of classroom climate a significant relationship between the percentage of teacher indirectness and positive responses.[18]

What are the students' attitudes toward the teacher and class in expository, opining, and inquiry social issues classes? Do students' evaluation of their teacher and class vary, depending on the discussion style present in the class? Our research at Michigan attempted to answer these questions.

Student responses to questions on the Minnesota Student Attitude Inventory were used to assess students' attitudes. Three scales were developed from selected items: (1) the appreciation scale, also used by Sugrue; (2) the sense of order and purpose present in the class; and (3) the students' perception of the teacher's style of maintenance and support. Many of the items on the Minnesota Student Attitude Inventory were designed to tap these three dimensions.

TABLE 10:1

Appreciation of the Teacher and Class

Type of Class	Number of Students	Mean
Expository	98	33.25
Opining	123	29.65
Inquiry	138	32.40

Appreciation of Teacher and Class

The extent to which the students in the expository, opining, and inquiry social issues classes liked their teacher and class are summarized in Table 10:1. Examining the class means in this table, we find, somewhat surprisingly, that students in the expository classes had a higher overall evaluation of their teacher and class than did students in the opining or

[17] Roger Pankratz, "Verbal Interaction Patterns in the Classrooms of Selected Physics Teachers," in *Interaction Analysis: Theory, Research, and Application,* ed. Edmund J. Amidon and John B. Hough (Reading, Mass.: Addison-Wesley Publishing Co., 1967), pp. 189-209.

[18] Paul M. Lauren, "Teacher Behavior, Classroom Climate, and Achievement: An Investigation of Pupil Perception of Classroom Interaction and Its Relationship to Achievement Within Experimentally Controlled Learning Environments" (Ph.D. diss., New York University, 1968), Ann Arbor: University of Michigan Microfilms, No. 69-21193.

inquiry classes. In the last chapter we found that teachers in the opining classes had the highest I/D ratios, and the teachers in the expository classes had the lowest. One would have expected, therefore, that on the basis of the teacher's I/D ratios that students in the opining group would like their teacher and class at least as much, if not more than, students in the expository classes. Also, the findings in Chapter 9 indicate that students participate significantly more in opining discussions than in expository discussions; one would think that students would have a higher evaluation of classes where they were able to participate more frequently. Why, then, were these expectations not borne out by the data in our study?

Students' prior experience with classroom discussions may be a factor in the higher evaluation of expository style. Many educators have pointed out that the prevailing mode of discourse in most classes is exposition. According to one educator, cognitive-memory is the most dominant thought process for both teachers and pupils in social studies.[19] Also, several studies of classroom interaction have reported that teachers tend to ask questions that require primarily knowledge or recall responses.[20] According to O. L. Davis and Drew Tinsley, "the accumulating evidence indicates persuasively that the major objectives guiding secondary school social studies classes are those emphasizing memory and comprehension."[21] Perhaps students are conditioned to expect expository discussions in the classroom. They expect teachers to emphasize knowledge and recall and to reinforce them when they give the "right" answer. On the other hand, students may feel ill at ease with opining discussions. Opining discussions frequently do not result in closure and students may be uncomfortable not knowing what the "right" answer is. They may feel that they are "not learning anything" and thus evaluate these classes lower than expository classes.

It is interesting that students in inquiry classes evaluated their teacher and class almost as highly as students in expository classes. Certainly, the literature would seem to suggest that inquiry discussions are not the norm in the classroom, so why do students exposed to these discussions evaluate their teacher and class almost as highly as students in expository classes? Massialas and Zevin have argued that the process of exploring and confirming propositions is a highly motivating activity.

[19] James J. Gallagher, "Expressive Thought by Gifted Children in the Classroom," *Elementary English* 42 (May, 1965): 559-568.

[20] See, for example, Thomas H. Adams, "The Development of a Method for Analysis of Questions Asked by Teachers in Classroom Discourse" (Ph.D. diss., Rutgers, The State University, 1964).

[21] O. L. Davis, Jr., and Drew C. Tinsley, "Cognitive Objectives Revealed by Classroom Questions Asked by Social Studies Student Teachers," in *Teaching: Vantage Points for Study*, ed. Ronald T. Hyman (Philadelphia: J. B. Lippincott Co., 1968), p. 144.

The quest for knowledge is viewed by these educators as intrinsically rewarding.[22] Although students do not expect inquiry discussions, perhaps when they are exposed to them, they find them meaningful and interesting. Inquiry discussions, in contrast to opining discussions, do tend to have a clear sense of direction; some closure is achieved in that, during the inquiry process of testing and probing hypotheses, students get an idea of what is an acceptable position—the one that can be defended the best.

Order and Purpose

Classroom teachers are frequently concerned about maintaining a sense of order and purpose in their classes. They have a low estimation of classes that are noisy and where "students fool around a lot." Four of the items in the Minnesota Student Attitude Inventory were used to measure students' perception of the extent to which order and purpose is maintained in their classroom. These statements are summarized in Figure 10:2. A positive response to the item, "This teacher keeps order

Student Statements
This class is noisy and fools around a lot.
In this class we fool around a lot in spite of the teacher.
Sometimes things "get out of control" in this class.
This teacher keeps order with a fair and firm hand.

FIGURE 10:2
Order and Purpose

with a fair and firm hand," indicates that the class is under control; positive responses to the three negative statements indicate that the class tends to fool around and waste time. Students' scores on this scale could range from 0 to 16.

Table 10:2 presents information regarding the students' perception of the extent of order and purpose present in their classes. Examining this table, we find that students in the inquiry classes and expository classes ranked their classes very high on this dimension. The means for these two groups are 11.46 and 10.84 respectively. With 16.0 the highest possible average any group could attain on this scale, it is clear that a

---

[22] Massialas and Zevin, *Creative Encounters,* p. 23.

TABLE 10:2

Order and Purpose

Type of Class	Number of Students	Mean
Expository	98	10.84
Opining	123	8.71
Inquiry	138	11.46

great degree of order and purpose was present in the expository and inquiry classes. The mean for the opining group (8.71), though, is considerably lower. The opining group of students felt there was less sense of order and purpose present in their class than did students in either the expository or inquiry groups.

Why do students involved in opining discussions feel this way? It was mentioned earlier that opining discussions tend to ramble and be somewhat like "bull sessions,'" and in bull sessions the discussion can "sometimes get out of control." Participants frequently get excited and compete with one another for center stage. Take for instance the following excerpt from the dialogue in Class B. The class is in the middle of a discussion about medically changing one's sex.

S   There is something in the Bible about taking a life . . .

S.   I think it is a personal decision . . .

S.   There is nothing in the Bible about changing your sex. There are atheists in the world, too, and they don't believe in God, so that's got to kill your theory right there.

T.   O.K., Sandy.

S.   I don't think we should change our sex. If they do, you don't know if you are marrying a guy or a woman, or what you're going to marry.

S.   It's like taking a life. If you are put on earth as a woman, you're taking the life of a woman and making it into a man.

S.   It's two different lives actually.

S.   But a woman . . .

S.   You're changing the complete life.

T.   Is your body your life? That's what you're changing, isn't it?

S.   Well, without your body . . . *(confusion, laughter)*

In this excerpt, the students are continually interrupting one another and talking at cross-purposes. One gets the feeling that in several instances a speaker isn't even listening to the previous speaker. For example, at one point a student starts to say that changing one's sex is a personal affair, but before he can finish, another student interrupts and jumps back to an earlier speaker's comment. The teacher enters the discussion twice—once to call on a student and once to try to clear up a point made by a student. Given just this excerpt, one would be hard pressed to agree with the statement: "This teacher keeps order with a fair and firm hand." Though the excerpt is not representative of all the interaction that occurs in opining discussions, in examining the transcripts of class dialogue we found that interaction sequences similar to the one reproduced here occur more frequently in opining discussions than in the other two types of discusions.

Teacher's Style of Maintenance and Support

Whereas the second attitudinal dimension determined the sense of order and purpose present in the class, the third dimension in this study concentrated on the teacher's style of maintenance and support. The six items from the Minnesota Student Attitude Inventory that tapped this dimension are found in Figure 10:3. Maintenance refers to the methods by which the teacher keeps order in the classroom. A supportive teacher maintains class order not by yelling at pupils but by establishing an atmosphere of mutual respect. The teacher communicates a supportive climate by reacting thoughtfully to students' comments and by helping them when they have problems with their work. Educational writers have stressed the importance of a supportive classroom climate in promoting open inquiry. Do the students perceive the teacher as supportive and helpful or do they feel the teacher is unfair and authoritarian? Responses to the statements in Figure 10:3 probably come closest to answering this question. On one end of the dimension one envisions an

Student Statements
This teacher helps students when they have problems with their work.
This teacher always takes time to find out your side of a difficulty.
This teacher punishes me for things I don't do.
Frankly, we just don't obey the teacher in this class.
This teacher never pushes us or shakes us in anger.
We behave well in this class even when the teacher is out of the room.

FIGURE 10:3
Style of Maintenance and Support

impatient, punitive teacher barely enforcing order, and at the other end
of the dimension one envisions a helpful, nonpunitive teacher who takes
time to work out students' problems and has established an atmosphere
of mutual respect in the class. Students' scores on this variable could
range from 0-24; the higher a student's score, the greater his perception
of a supportive teacher.

The data summarized in Table 10:3 indicate that students in the
inquiry classes react very positively to their teacher's style of class maintenance and support. The mean of this group is 18.24, considerably

TABLE 10:3

Style of Maintenance and Support

Type of Class	Number of Students	Mean
Expository	98	16.85
Opining	123	16.14
Inquiry	138	18.24

above that for the expository and opining groups. Evidently, teachers
in the inquiry classes are especially helpful and nonpunitive; students
consider them sensitive to their ideas and problems. These are teachers
who have successfully established an atmosphere of mutual respect in
their classes—an atmosphere many educators deem essential for promoting and sustaining reflective student inquiry.

Summary of Student Attitudinal Outcomes

The students in this study who were involved in expository discussions had a relatively high evaluation of their teacher and class. They
feel this type of discourse exhibits a high degree of order and purpose,
and they also feel secure in the knowledge that they are giving the right
answer. On the other hand, it is clear that students do not like opining
discussions. These classes received the lowest evaluation relative to the
other two groups on all three student attitudinal dimensions. Students see
opining classes as lacking order and purpose and react negatively to the
rambling nature of the discussion.

The students who participated in the inquiry discussions liked their
teacher and class almost as much as the students in the expository classes.
They feel these discussions have a sense or order and purpose, and they
react very positively to their teacher's style of maintenance and control.
The teachers in these classes successfully established a supportive climate in the classroom.

STUDENT CRITICAL THINKING SKILLS

Even though considerable research in recent years has investigated classroom behavior and student achievement and attitudes, our review of the literature uncovered only two studies that explicitly examined the relationship between classroom interaction and the critical thinking skills of students, as measured by paper-and-pencil instruments.

Gagnon examined the impact of teacher clarifying questions on students' critical thinking skills. His study compared the interaction in two groups of fifth- and sixth-grade classes. In one group the teacher concentrated on asking students to clarify their opinions and ideas. In the other, the teacher asked few clarifying questions. The results indicate that students exposed to a high incidence of clarifying questions not only participated significantly more in discussions, but also performed somewhat better on a written critical thinking test.[23]

The Indiana Experiments in Inquiry studied the impact of inquiry instruction on the development of students' critical thinking skills. The Indiana investigators explicitly specified the kinds of teacher and student behaviors that characterize inquiry in the classroom. Although they did not categorize the classroom interaction, they did analyze tapes of dialogue in order to verify that the inquiry method was, in fact, applied in the classroom. A review of their results reveals that in comparison with students instructed in the traditional mode, the students exposed to inquiry instruction made statistically significant gains on a critical thinking test.[24]

How do students involved in expository, opining, and inquiry class discussions perform on a written critical thinking test? In the Michigan social issues project, the instrument used to appraise their abilities to analyze social issues critically was the Harvard Social Issues Analysis Test Number 2 developed by the Harvard University Social Studies Project.[25] This test is a paper-and-pencil instrument designed to assess a student's ability to: (1) identify the substance of an argumentative dialogue, (2) judge which side of the argument would be supported by new information, and (3) select the best rebuttals to statements made in

[23] A. Lawrence Gagnon, "An Analysis of an Experimental Methodology for Teaching Thinking and Clarifying Values" (Ph.D. diss., Wayne State University, 1965), Ann Arbor: University of Michigan Microfilms, No. 66-10104.

[24] Byron G. Massialas, C. Benjamin Cox, Jack E. Cousins, and Robert T. Elsmere, *The Indiana Experiments in Inquiry: Social Studies* (Bloomington: School of Education, Indiana University, 1963).

[25] Donald W. Oliver and James P. Shaver, *Teaching Public Issues in the High School* (Boston: Houghton Mifflin Co., 1966), Chapter 10.

the dialogue. The instrument contains twenty-two prestructured responses. The students' total score on this test was interpreted as a measure of their ability to think critically about social issues.

The strength of the Harvard test is that instead of measuring various fragments of a critical thinking process, the test assesses the student's ability to follow a sequence of operations within a dialectical framework. The instrument is particularly appropriate for measuring the ability to think critically about social issues. It includes items concerned with competence in dealing with values as well as with factual and definitional disputes. The test is based on a model of reflective thinking delineated in terms of the analysis of public controversy.

Is it possible to predict from an analysis of the classroom discussions how well students in the expository, opining, and inquiry classes will perform on a written critical thinking test? Let's look first at the inquiry discussions. In these classes the teacher used his influence to encourage students to examine social issues reflectively. The students responded by identifying and clarifying problems, taking positions, and in many cases spontaneously defending their ideas and opinions on the basis of available evidence. In those instances where the students did not naturally support or clarify their positions, the teacher intervened and encouraged them to do so. Thus, discussions in the inquiry classes incorporated all aspects of the critical thinking process measured by the Harvard test—identifying and clarifying conflicts, taking positions, and deciding what evidence supports a given position. In class, at least, these students demonstrated the ability to deal reflectively with social controversy; therefore, there was reason to believe that they would score relatively well on the Harvard test.

On the other hand, after analyzing the discussions that took place in the opining classes, one would have to conclude that students in these classes would score relatively low on the Harvard test. The opining teachers also provided an opportunity for students to inquire into social issues, but the students responded only by stating their positions, ideas, and opinions, *not* by defending them. Granted, the teachers in these classes did not ask students to clarify or support their opinions, but the fact that the students almost never probed hypotheses on their own indicates that they had not internalized the cognitive skills involved in evaluating evidence and supporting positions.

It is impossible to predict from an analysis of the expository discussions how well students in these classes would perform on the Harvard test. Students in these classes did not have an opportunity to inquire into social issues; instead, they concentrated on exposition. Thus, we have no idea from the discussion what cognitive skills, beyond knowledge and recall, the students possessed. Certainly, though, these students were not encouraged to demonstrate or develop their critical thinking skills during the class discussion, and one would tend to think that they would not do as well on the Harvard test as the students in the inquiry classes.

Did the students in the inquiry group perform better on the Harvard Social Issues Analysis Test 2 than the students in the expository and opining groups? Examining Table 10:4, we find that the students in the

TABLE 10:4

Harvard Social Issues Analysis Test

Type of Class	Number of Students	Mean
Expository	94	10.51
Opining	123	9.38
Inquiry	129	11.24

inquiry classes did score higher on the Harvard test than did students in the other two groups. Because the Harvard test measures many of the same aspects of reflective thought present in the inquiry discussions, but not evident in the other two types of discussions, these results are not surprising. That the students in the expository classes scored better than the students in the opining classes is also not unexpected. We knew that students in the opining classes had trouble examining social issues reflectively, but the students in the expository classes were a mystery. Obviouly, some of these students do have the ability to deal reflectively with social issues.

In Chapter 9 it was pointed out that three of the inquiry class discussions evidenced considerable student spontaneous grounding (classes H, K, and N) and that students in the other three inquiry classes (Classes L, O, and P) depended upon teacher questions to evoke further probing of positions. Inasmuch as students who spontaneously defend their positions demonstrate the ability to select information that will support their arguments, one would expect these students to have a relatively easy time judging which side of an argument would be supported by new information—a skill that is emphasized by the Harvard test.

The data presented in Table 10:5 confirm the above prediction. The mean score for students in inquiry classes that evidenced high spontaneous grounding is 12.70; the mean score for the students in inquiry classes that evidenced low spontaneous grounding is 9.97. The difference between the two groups is considerable. Also, it is important to note that the students in the classes that exhibited low spontaneous grounding performed somewhat better on the Harvard test than the students in the opining classes and somewhat worse than students in the expository

TABLE 10:5

Harvard Social Issues Analysis Test: Spontaneous Grounding

Inquiry Classes	Mean
High Spontaneous Grounding	12.70
Low Spontaneous Grounding	9.97

classes. Evidently, it is not just the fact that students are involved in inquiry discussions that helps predict their performance on the Harvard test, but, more importantly, it is the degree of spontaneous grounding by students that occurs during the discussion that is the best predictor. Students who depend on the teacher to help them probe positions in class apparently have trouble analyzing social controversy when the teacher is not around to help them.

SUMMARY

Research conducted by the Social Issues Project at Michigan indicates that as a group students in classes that deal regularly with social issues have positive attitudes toward their teacher and class. Related items from the Minnesota Student Attitude Inventory were used to measure the student attitudes. Students' evaluations, however, varied depending on their individual characteristics and the teaching style used in their class.

Views of individual students were significantly related to their sex, grade-point average, parents' occupation, and their belief in student participation. Girls in the sample were significantly more positive in their evaluation of the classes than were the boys. Students with A averages gave either very positive or very negative evaluations of their classes. Students whose parents were employed in professional or semi-professional occupations had more negative attitudes than students whose parents were involved in other types of occupations. Students who believed strongly in student participation in class discussion were extremely positive in their evaluations.

The teaching style used in the classes was also related to students' evaluations. The students in this study who were involved in expository discussions had a relatively high opinion of their teacher and class—apparently having been conditioned to expect expository discussions. They feel this type of discourse exhibits a high degree of order and purpose, and are secure in the knowledge that they are giving the right answer. On the other hand, it is clear that students are not satisfied with opining discussions. These classes received the lowest evaluation relative to the other two groups on all three student attitudinal dimensions. Evidently, students see opining classes as lacking order and purpose and react negatively to the rambling nature of the discussion.

The students who participated in the inquiry discussions liked their teacher and class almost as much as the students in the expository classes. They felt these discussions had a sense of order and purpose and reacted very positively to their teacher's style of maintenance and control. The teachers in these classes successfully established a supportive climate in the classroom.

Turning to the three groups' performance on the Harvard Social Issues Analysis Test, we found that students in the inquiry classes performed significantly better on this test than students in either of the other two groups. The students in the inquiry classes that had considerable spontaneous grounding did particularly well on the critical thinking test. Apparently, they had progressed further than the other students in internalizing the value and skill of supporting and evaluating positions and hypotheses. These data would seem to indicate that if teachers are seriously interested in helping students improve their critical thinking skills, they must encourage them to ground their own positions spontaneously and challenge their fellow students to do likewise. It is imperative that students develop autonomy in the analysis of social controversy if they are to transfer this skill to other arenas.

11

the status of inquiry teaching and learning: where we are and where we need to go

Since 1957, many of us have been involved in one way or another with inquiry teaching and learning. We have taught in this field, conducted research, developed curriculum materials, and provided service. In the late fifties and early sixties, many social studies educators, including Shirley Engle and Lawrence Metcalf, began using the term "reflective thinking." To our knowledge, the first time a major attempt to introduce "inquiry" in the social studies vocabulary was made in a special issue of *Social Education* devoted to revising the social studies (April, 1963). That whole issue defined inquiry as a cognitive process that involves the testing or validation of ideas about man and his environment. At that time, of course, we had very little research to rely upon and we had virtually nothing in the way of school support—in the teaching act, in the curriculum, in the textbooks, in evaluation, and in classroom climate. One can say with a certain degree of confidence that in the early sixties the process of schooling in all of its manifestations was antithetical to inquiry teaching and learning. But then, gradually, we began to break the tradition and the idea of teaching and learning as inquiry started to gain momentum in the United States and abroad. Since the late sixties, inquiry teaching has become popular in Japan, Korea, Germany, and other countries, both developed and developing.

Let us consider the principal areas in which we have made progress over the past decade or so:

1. We have broadened the concept of inquiry in three significant ways: *(a)* We began to understand that inquiry is not simply a *teaching technique* but a whole way of looking at the world. A person who accepts

and internalizes this outlook develops specific world perceptions, ideas about the individual's role in society, and a theory of learning and of what constitutes knowledge. This inquiry *can* be translated into classroom practice. In an educational context inquiry is understood to be the process of discovering, expressing clearly, and validating or confirming ideas and positions about people as they interact with their environment. Inquiry implies an open classroom climate that encourages wide student participation and the expression and grounding of divergent points of views. As we said before, a truly inquiry-centered class is a social system whose members not only utilize the concepts and skills of the arts and the sciences, but draw upon their own personal experiences as they try to deal judiciously with important human problems, especially problems confronting them as individuals. The point that is important to remember here is that inquiry is not simply a teaching gimmick but, in its true sense, a style of life and a way of thinking. (*b*) We began to place greater emphasis on the affective-value aspects of classroom interaction. Though inquiry started as a strictly cognitive process, we gradually came to realize that cognition and affect are inseparable, that affect—attitudes, appreciations, and values of individuals—needs to be considered in a systematic way. We simply could not leave this aspect to chance. We thus moved away from a rather naïve notion that we are training young sociologists or historians to the notion that the classroom, as a microcosm of society, has to reflect and deal honestly with real problems and issues —issues in which the participants have a stake and about which they should form judgments through reflection. (*c*) In line with the above, we have moved to incorporate in our classrooms not only the histories and the sociologies of the new programs, but we have incorporated and legitimized as part of the curriculum the rich repertoire of the experiences of the individuals. For the first time we began to realize that in solving an intellectual or value problem the individual experience is as good as or better than any available text. This premise has been a salient feature of what we have called "discovery episodes," where the experiential is the legitimate key to the entire process of reflection. In this process each participant brings his own facts based on personal experience which bear on the case.

2. We have begun to make some progress in clarifying what inquiry teaching is. We have been able to draw behaviorally based distinctions among teaching styles—for example, expository, opining, and inquiry, which we have discussed here in detail in Chapter 2.

In the *expository style* the teacher has investigated the topic or the issue and decided ahead of time what aspects of the issue or topic are important for the class to know and remember. In this type of environment students are not really involved in exploring the dimensions of the problem; instead, the teacher presents the information he considers important. The teacher guides the class and reinforces a climate of right or wrong answers.

In the *opining style* the teacher usually presents a springboard or problematic situation to the class and asks students to give their opinions on the issue. Students are exploring on their own, they offer many hypotheses and positions, but they are not equipped in reflective inquiry and the whole process of clarification and validation of ideas. (This style of teaching is similar, perhaps, to those advocated by progressive educationists who assume that as long as the child talks, learning is taking place.)

In *inquiry teaching* the classroom climate is psychologically open. There is a definite sense of purpose to the discussion. Ideas and positions are put forth by the students and they are followed by efforts to clarify these ideas and positions and to provide explicit grounds for holding one and rejecting another. In the past these distinctions, being blurred by inadequate research, did not confirm our hypotheses about optimum conditions for learning. When these distinctions were made operationally, however, we had some solid research to indicate that inquiry-probing teaching may facilitate the functioning of the higher mental processes, that it may maximize autonomy, and that it may increase the individual's sense of political efficacy. By political efficacy we mean that one understands how the political system operates and feels competent in changing it. Certainly much more research is needed here to substantiate these claims.

3. We have made some progress in getting more schools and teachers to consider using a wide variety of springboards rather than to continue relying on the traditional hardbound textbooks. Springboards, and we have used a number of them throughout this book, are thought-provoking materials that have a high stimulating effect in the generation of hypotheses and positions in the classroom. The movement away from the textbook to multiple sources of media and audiovisuals is evident when we analyze investment figures in this area. According to John Egerton, who did a study for the Southern Regional Council, schools, "in addition to the half-billion dollars spent on textbooks last year . . . spent an undetermined amount—perhaps as much as another half-billion—on library books and the whole range of supplementary instructional materials." [1] These included materials dealing with controversial issues, global problems, discovery exercises, experiences of minority groups, and population and environmental problems. To the extent that these materials are used by the teachers in such a way as to open rather than close discussion, progress toward inquiry teaching is being made. The

[1] John Egerton, "Draft Paper on Textbooks," mimeo., (1972), p. 1. Prepared for the Southern Regional Council's Task Force on Education.

safe textbook that for years reinforced traditional teachers—their igno rance, biases, and stereotypes—is now giving way to new teachers who do not look upon themselves as the absolute authority, who do not hide behind the text, but who contribute their share to the creation, clarification, and testing of significant ideas and issues.

4. Finally, we have made progress in the evaluation of instruction. Ten years ago we relied almost exclusively on paper-and-pencil instruments to measure recall of information; today, the field of evaluation has changed in many significant respects. First of all, we have moved away from using the concepts of evaluation and grading interchangeably to accepting more and more the notion that teachers need to use evaluation as a means of improving their performance. Thus, we started using the concept of formative or feedback evaluation and to distinguish it from summative or terminal evaluation. In this context, we have made significant headway. We began to develop and apply tables of specifications, performance objectives, and criterion-referenced instruments; these types of materials were used, for example, in Michigan, Florida, and in the National Assessment Projects. As we have explained in Chapter 7, these instruments are not tests of recall but attempts to measure growth in the cognitive, affective, and evaluative domains. Though we have no exact way of knowing how many teachers and schools are using these materials, we do know that these measures of evaluation and their underlying philosophy are attaining wider acceptance.

Another movement that has gained some momentum as an evaluation instrument is the verbal-interaction analysis. By now there must be at least 100 interaction-analysis systems that attempt in their own way to provide a meaningful set of operational categories by which the teacher may study the pattern of communication in the classroom. Perhaps the best-known system is Flander's Interaction Analysis, which focuses on classroom climates. There are other observation systems, some focusing on social studies instruction (Harvard, Columbia, Michigan), that are more or less sophisticated than Flander's, stressing different aspects of teaching and learning. If we can get more and more teachers to use these tools, we will have a better perspective of not only *what* we are doing in the classroom, but also *why*—which is something the traditional paper-and-pencil tests in and by themselves cannot offer. Through the use of these materials we are able to determine interaction sequences in the classroom.

Let us now turn to some areas of inquiry teaching and learning in which we have not seen visible signs of progress:

1. Very little effort has been expended in acquainting school administrators and parents with the philosophy and the methods of inquiry teaching and learning. As a result, administrators, who have prime con-

trol of most of the environmental conditions in the school, have failed
to provide appropriate support for inquiry-centered activities. Classes
still meet in fifty-minute blocks of time, subjects are still taught by individual teachers without team or interdisciplinary work, six-week grading
periods still exist, and bells are still ringing. We know from studies of
the subject that without a reinforcing psychological climate and powerful school and family milieus, inquiry behavior—or any other type of
behavior for that matter—does not become internalized. If the chief socialization agents do not complement one another, the result is confusion
and ambiguity. One agency negates the other. School administrators, and
to a greater extent parents, have not tuned in adequately to the theory
and practice of inquiry. As long as this state of affairs prevails, our suc-
cesses will be minimal. Parents need to be informed about inquiry methods and materials and not be persuaded by certain groups that these
approaches are subversive and antithetical to the American character, as
indeed has happened in some regions.

2. Many commercial publishers, in spite of pronouncements to the
contrary, are not genuinely interested in inquiry learning. It might be
that inquiry teaching and learning is inconsistent with some of the basic
principles of the publishing industry, one of which is that if cost of production and distribution of books is in direct conflict with opportunities
to learn then the latter will have to give way to the former; learning
must be sacrificed for reduced costs. Take for example multimedia kits.
Most publishers do not want to produce them because the cost of production as compared with a hardbound text increases considerably. Another publishing principle is that controversial matters of society should
be excluded if they reduce the chances for wide adoptions; the results,
as we all know, are that many antiseptic and flat books are used in our
schools.[2] The heart of inquiry teaching is a controversial issue. Our basic
contention is that the textbook industry and a few administrators in key
decision-making positions have controlled the flow of innovation in the
schools and have and continue to have an adverse effect in promoting
inquiry learning. Efforts to counteract this control by the national government and national foundations, as well as by school districts such as
Greater Cleveland and Dade County that can afford their own materials-
development departments, have not been notably successful. If the status
quo continues, we will continue to have many publishers function for us
as gatekeepers and decision-makers. We know that as long as the primary
objective of producing educational material is the making of a profit and
not the learning of our children, classrooms will remain subject to the

[2] See, for example, William Joyce's reports in the March, 1973, issue of *Social
Education* (Vol. 37) on the treatment of minorities in elementary social studies texts,
pp. 218-233.

promotion of special interests of small groups. A healthy departure, admittedly radical, would be to take publishing out of the hands of the conglomerates and to give it to nonprofit educational organizations at the federal, state, or local levels, like the Far West Educational Laboratory, the Population Reference Bureau, the universities, or the county or school districts. If we combine the tremendous technological capabilities we have in producing educational materials of all kinds with a genuine, not forced, interest in learning, then we are bound to improve them. Perhaps we ought to think of the possibilities of making public, in the best sense of the word, part of the textbook industry, as we have begun to do with some of our health services. Other nations of the world have had a great deal of practice in doing so. Of course, if we should decide that commercial publishers and nonprofit organizations should share in the production of educational materials, we would need to guard against national centralization, as has indeed happened in many countries abroad. When that occurs, the results of educational reform can easily be negated.

3. We as teachers are also guilty of putting substantial obstacles in the way of teaching and learning. First of all, we have been exceedingly myopic in looking at the inquiry process; we have emphasized classroom behavior and neglected the world outside the class. We rarely raise the question, Does an inquiry classroom environment have any effect on how a child will behave with his or her peers or with parents or in the many decisions that are being made every day? We think that responsibility begins and ends with the class period. But does it or should it? We maintain that as educators our responsibility goes beyond the classroom—to the entire school, to the community, to our political and social systems. We believe that educators have a special responsibility to function as leaders for the creative reconstruction of our culture. To meet this responsibility, we need to know how the classroom relates to all other behaviors we and our students display. We also need to know what happens in the long run. Unfortunately, we have few studies that supply us with clues here, and as teachers we are unaccustomed to taking a look at inquiry behavior in a broader context. Though we always claim inquiry instruction makes better citizens, we have as yet little evidence to link instruction with pre-adult or adult political behavior. What we need in this regard is a two-pronged approach: a self-awareness that the results of instruction go beyond the confines of the classroom, and a systematic effort to establish the links, both immediate and long term.

4. We have also found out that important discrepancies exist between what teachers say they do in the classroom and what they actually do. When individual teachers are asked if they are inquiry teachers, as we have done on numerous occasions either through questionnaires or structured interviews, invariably they will say that, indeed, they are. But

are they? Even on a questionnaire that contains technical inquiry questions, we have found few teachers who have the capability to exhibit truly inquiry behavior. In a study we conducted in Michigan in 1970, we found that high-school teachers are often unable to determine whether a statement is based on fact or on opinion.[3] Their responses to one statement in particular stood out. Forty-two percent of the teachers in the sample indicated that the following statement was a fact: "The American form of government may not be perfect, but it is the best type of government yet devised by man." Harmon Zeigler had a similar finding in an earlier study in Oregon.[4]

When we have observed teachers in their own classroom, at their own invitation, we find that in many instances important ingredients of the inquiry process are missing—they talk too much, they encourage exposition, many hypotheses and positions are presented without probing or grounding, and there is virtually no attempt to clarify meaning. We have also followed up our observations with a presentation to the teachers of the facts—their profile as a teacher. In all cases, teachers are surprised to find out all these things about themselves. Yet despite some sporadic attempts to change their classroom behavior, their basic posture remains the same.

The implication of all this is that teachers-in-training need to be involved systematically in inquiry-type activities throughout their college program. These activities should not be limited to education courses only, but courses in all of the subjects taken, whether sociology, history, math, or whatever. Also, the teachers who are out in the field need to be involved with their colleagues in regularly scheduled programs either in their school district or at a nearby university. Intervisitations, microteaching, and materials seminars could be some of the ways in which genuine inquiry behavior can be promoted.

5. Finally, we have seen few visible signs of progress in regard to teachers of teachers, both in colleges of education, as well as in colleges of liberal arts. They have not done their job either in many respects. Many have not stepped into a public-school classroom for years. A number of their theories are obsolete because they are based on classroom conditions that no longer exist. No wonder so-called methods courses are often characterized as the worst by teachers in training. The teaching style of some of these college instructors is also highly didactic. They talk about inquiry, but never practice it. The model they present to the novice teacher to emulate is traditional. Yet this is the model

---

[3] See Byron Massialas, Nancy F. Sprague, and Jo Ann Sweeney, "Traditional Teachers, Parochial Pedagogy," *School Review* 79 (August, 1971): 561-578.

[4] Harmon Zeigler, *The Political Life of American Teachers* (Englewood Cliffs, N.J.: Prentice-Hall, Inc., 1967).

teachers will use as a beginning. And once new teachers use the traditional model to teach, they will continue to lean on it.

The other deficiency of teachers of teachers is that many of them rarely engage in research. Cox, Shaver, and others who studied and critically analyzed social studies research have found that for the vast majority of these teachers research began and ended with the dissertation. Over the years our profession, unlike for example, science education, has not gained a strong tradition of research. In the *Handbook of Research on Teaching,* in research encyclopedias, and in journals we find embarrassed reviewers reporting that no significant research and development is being done in social studies education. No wonder we know so little about ourselves and how our teaching affects children both in short terms and in the long run.

As with the teachers, these educators need to get involved more directly with research and development activity. Large grants are not always necessary to do this. The formation of core discussion groups, exchanges of visits as guest professors, continuous visits to public schools to observe live classrooms, and regular reading of journals and new materials in the field are some of the ways to keep abreast.

In spite of all these shortcomings, however, we are optimistic about the future. We believe that teaching and learning as inquiry does have a chance because it is a truly valid way of coping in an age of crises. It will be our responsibility to see that inquiry is used in its true context—to create new ideas, to challenge established institutions, and to seek fresh alternatives for the society in which we live.

index

DATE DUE

DEC - 3 1984		

GAYLORD   PRINTED IN U.S.A.